OLD THINKING,
NEW THINKING

THE SUFI PRISM

Fazal Inayat-Khan

OLD THINKING, NEW THINKING

THE SUFI PRISM

Published in San Francisco by

HARPER & ROW, PUBLISHERS

New York   Hagerstown   San Francisco   London

FIRST EDITION

Designed by Jim Mennick

Library of Congress Cataloging in Publication Data

Inayat-Khan, Fazal.
  OLD THINKING, NEW THINKING.

  1. Sufism—Addresses, essays, lectures. I. Title.
BP189.6.I55 1978   297'.4   77-7831
ISBN 0-06-064086-3

---

79 80 81 82 10 9 8 7 6 5 4 3 2 1

For Ullah

CONTENTS

INTRODUCTION

This book really came about through the encouragement of many and the perseverance of a few. It is basically an edited selection of the many lectures I gave at the Sufi Cultural Centre in London on Monday evenings between 1973 and 1975, other talks at Khankah Abadan Abad in Dockenfield, Farnham between 1973 and 1977, and a few original writings. Several of what one may call my followers asked for transcripts of these lectures and some, among them Sitara Brutnell, Amina Evans and my wife, began the laborious task of transcribing them from tape.

In the beginning I was entirely against the idea of transcribing them or even recording them because I felt that all words are lies, the truth is one, inexpressible, and especially because so many people, great thinkers and leaders and also charlatans, always goad their devotees with lots of good inspiring words which over time echo away; for no one can ever claim to know, really, anything for certain, and that holds true more about life than about anything else. But my friends and wellwishers started to exchange copies of my talks and eventually Mariusz Tchorek began sending them around to publishers—against my expressed wishes.

I still have my doubts, despite being a publisher myself, over whether anything anyone ever says should find its way into print to influence in any way the minds of its readers. And I certainly hope that presenting this material does not cause anyone to think that this is what I really think now and still will think later, for we are all changing, growing beings, and my entire outlook on reality is a constantly reappraising search in which these words represent only a picture in time and consciousness. But to introduce you, the reader, to this material I must say that the fountain of my inspiration lies in the life and teachings of my grandfather, Inayat Khan, who lived before I was born. In seeking to find out who he was and what he taught, attempting to achieve my own independent realization, free from the establishment of the movement which he left and the imperfections of the writings which were the publications of his highly edited talks, I tried and shall always try to be an actualizer of his message. In this endeavor I follow the example of my teacher and initiator, Musharaff Khan, who was for me the living symbol of Inayat Khan's personality and thought. Without this example of love and faith which he expressed by his being, I would probably have continued on another path in life.

Of course, these chapters are about Sufism, about spirituality, about identity, about reality, about life, but they are also about my own interpretation and in a sense my teachings to my friends and dissidents, my disciples and myself. I tried to live by these ideas, as all those who know me shall bear witness; and I shall discover that these ideas are imperfect and that there are others beyond them, and that we may eventually come full circle.

In these lectures, which were given to small groups of people, a tone of careful seriousness often alternates with punch and humor. Unfortunately a lot of this had to be edited away for publication because the fun related to the physical setting and the people present. Also, in re-reading them, I noticed often a particular kind of superficial quoting of facts and expression of knowledge which were either incorrect or illogical or even unnecessary to the main argument. I tried to leave most of that in to give the impression that these are really lectures spoken to people, and especially because I would like to show not only my ideas but also my prejudices or lack of knowledge; it will give a more balanced picture. The only chapter which is fully written, unedited, and was not in any way a lecture is "The Concept of Avoidance." I chose to include this from a lot of original writings because of its more mystical aspects. Basically it is about a reality that one cannot know because its operating principle avoids all.

I have expressed the names of the few who persevered to make this manuscript into a book, but I must also express my gratitude to the many who contributed in so many ways to this work, if not the least through listening, questioning and inspiring.

If I have now accepted a justification for this publication it is a signal of a change in.myself. Probably I have outgrown the emotional content of their meaning and so forth, but the main change as I see it is that I feel the spiritual search of mankind in this postwar period coming to a stalemate because spiritual travel guides appear like tourist guides and meditative techniques appear as cookbooks and, as you will read later, Jalalu'ddin Rumi's dervish dance is technisized as a do-it-yourself kit for enlightenment.

Only life as you live it now, emulating no one, following no technique or teacher, is the tao, the way.

I have dedicated this publication to this realization.

PROLOGUE: OLD THINKING, NEW THINKING

First of all, what needs to be very clear is that the terms old thinking and new thinking do not necessarily relate to old and new, or to young and old, or even to old people and young people. The terms old thinking and new thinking relate to a qualitative approach in which a particular thought pattern brings into focus a potential description or idea. It is also very important to understand that old thinking and new thinking each create a definite, different result at the end of their pattern, but may in fact have begun with the same basic idea/feeling. In a sense, then, these terms are useful to characterize how, given any basic conceptual possibility to start with, the thought about it can end up very often in quite different contradictory answers; and when you look at these different answers, of and by themselves, they are both valid, and yet they are not the same.

Often we are faced with the multiplicity of resolutions that different interpretations make of a particular problem or idea, and sometimes we cannot possibly square the two. We know very well, in different cultural set-ups, that faced with the same initial issue, one group of people will take one specific approach, another will take another, and they can never be reconciled. This is because the old thinking pattern and the new thinking pattern lead quite clearly to a different quality, a different qualitative result.

In order to come to some harmony, both in ourselves and with our own thinking—because sometimes we think along old thinking lines, sometimes we think along new thinking lines, and often we are caught in the dichotomy of indecision between them—it is important to understand what these two basic qualitative approaches are, so that the thought patterns themselves can be understood more as a pathway leading in one direction or in another. You must try to see, therefore, that the quality of old thinking leads to a manifest expression best described by the word display. In other words, the potential unformed thought, when masticated by the consciousness along the patterns of old thinking, gives a resolution which has a displaying quality. New thinking, on the other hand, gives a resolution which can best be described by the word portray; in other words, the same potential feeling, when masticated by the consciousness according to the thought patterns of new thinking, produces a manifested, observable, cogent quality which you can call portray. Here you can begin to see the difference between display and portray: display is something that is direct, lucid, concise, clear, finite and is observed in form, in structure; portray produces a luminous, much more suggestive implication which opens unformed relationships, which is not succinct and has no exclusive property in form, but rather gives the suggestion of the essence or the spirit. While old thinking allows you to observe the form at the outcome of the thought pattern, the essential spirit has been refined into oblivion; new thinking on the other hand creates a portrayal which is not really analyzable and remains basically unformed, unveiling by the avoiding of the form something of the spirit, something of the essence.

There are advantages and disadvantages, there are positives and negatives to each thought pattern, and these can be weighed in terms of the original thought pattern's need for resolution to begin with. Display obviously creates cognizance, it creates stability; through the observance of the display we can begin to recognize the form and therefore draw dependable basic conclusions. You can therefore see that, while the essence is lost, the display of form is at least as valid as the unveiling of the spirit, because it creates the kind of building block upon which the security of the mind and the personality in the manifested world is based. Of course, one can come to question and doubt seriously whether a thought pattern which destroys the essence and therefore displays the form does not necessarily lead to imprisonment therein, and I would affirm that, without a proper balance and harmony between these two thought patterns in the working of any conscious mind, there is that danger which we observe in those cultures that base themselves upon old thinking to the exclusion of new thinking. On the other hand, new thinking, which has subjected the form to dissolution so that the essence can be captured, causes the problem of the limitless non-dependable—bringing about chaotic apperception from which, while some freedom is experienced, no real accumulation of knowledge is possible.

What is important in any particular individual's growth towards the expansion of consciousness, is a harmonization of these two thought patterns. There are two ways to look at harmony: one way is to see harmony as a static situate, which means that there are two ways to think of everything, and both are valid or invalid, but that situate does not foster the freedom of the absoluteness of either. We give equal validity to each side of a coin before we toss it; but after we have tossed it we give all the validity to one, the side which came up. The other way to look at harmony is to consider it as a cyclic situate. Everyone experiences (up to a point) the progression of his thought patterns swinging quite naturally to one issue and then some awareness may come which may alter the process and influence the thought to balance naturally over to the other side. There is a natural progression towards old thinking, which must in some way be related to the need to accumulate knowledge and re-establish a new ceiling of stability upon which to proceed forward again—to take stock, to make an inventory of awareness. Then there must come a period in the cycle of swinging over the other way, when you begin to see that you want to get out of form and out of structure and reach the thing itself, whatever it is; when you begin to see that while you have plenty of meaning and clarity in life, there is no experience of being in the trance, in the ecstasy of any particular thought. The duality of

I and what I think about becomes so obliteratingly strong that there seems to be no contact. What you see is there, and you see it, and you are there, but you do not really seem to touch or exchange energy with each other; that is when the pendulum begins to swing towards new thinking.

When a need for security arises and a feeling of uncertainty and inability to adapt to all the fleeting change is working in the mind, the mind will then grope more and more towards old thinking, to come back to what can be depended upon, to what is really clear, what is showing, what is expected and expectable and predictable, thus moving away from the immeasurable unclear independence of things beyond facts, which often upsets everything which you previously had depended on. And so you can see that young people who feel embedded in the old thinking patterns of their parents counterbalance that by an excessive journey into new thinking which, while it does lead to liberation from the old display, does not bring (in the norms of the manifested) measurable enrichment. I did not say that it does not bring immeasurable enrichment, for what is immeasurable enrichment? It is like an unlimited amount of money in your bank account—you do not know how much it is, so what can you do with it? You can do nothing with it because it is not limited to a real quantity, a real, tangible asset. If you own an oil field which is twenty-five miles below the surface of the earth, unless you tap it you cannot do anything with it.

These norms of portray and display can help you to understand the criticism and counter-attacks of each way of thinking upon the other. To new thinking, old thinking touches only the form, and all that may be really real is lost; while to old thinking, new thinking touches the emptiness, and though that may be something real, it is . . . where is it? It is unfindable and therefore valueless.

The need to harmonize and allow one's thought and frame of mind to flow as freely as possible to the furthest extremes of either old thinking or new thinking is important and bring a harmonic base of real conceptual power and unreal, immeasurable penetration.

All these things may make sense to you up to a point, but there must come a time for the question in your mind: how do

I know which situation wants resolution by the patterns of old thinking, and which wants resolution by the patterns of new thinking? I can give an answer, but first you will have to try to accept the possibility of real mystic abstraction of the entire thought process itself and all values derived from it. Now, if the resolution called for requires a particular standard of manifestation, then by understanding that standard, you can choose which pathway to take. All standards of manifestation that we know of are characterized in the end by two absolutes, and these two absolutes are *real* and *false*. If the standard of the resolution asked for is real, then you should use the pattern of old thinking, and come to display; whereas if the standard of resolution requires false, then you should use new thinking and come to portray. The real creates value and, as we all know, the false creates the lack of value. The real creates a display of form which, if sufficiently attuned to the possibility of expressing in form the highest development of form itself, will in any case return you to the induction by the form of the spirit that could be embedded within it. The other way round, in that situation where the portrayal evolves to the highest attenuation and refinement possible, certainly it will create in its implication a universal formation in which the essence will find its purest expression.

Maybe this is what is described by the spin of the dervishes: as one allows the cycles of new thinking and old thinking to progress ever more totally, in the most perfect rendering of the resolution of each possible, one ends up with revolution, at which time the dual consciousness of both form and essence may be united. That may be the freedom of the captive, or the dance of the stationary, or the repetition of the fleeting, or the return of the turn.

It is very important that you understand that the end of real is false, while the greatest of false is real. Perhaps this statement of definition will help to relieve the value judgment of real and false. Here comes the kind of more mystic harmony which I have been trying to describe. We find it expressed in our life's endeavor, and it is that the old thinking is the thing which will bring us to achievement, notwithstanding that without new thinking we will have achieved nothing;

in other words, the new thinking will only lead us into the trail of the false, and so we need to pursue the old thinking so that the false can give the real its value.

There are certain more logical applications of this kind of rule which, if you do not get lost in the flood of nomenclature, can help in thought approaches to life in all its aspects. One can say that suggestive power is only as strong as expressive power is stable; or, that reality is only real as you unveil its falseness. Old thinking is our base, the unified field upon which we alight; and new thinking is our butterfly wings which carry us useless nowhere on a journey that can only lead to return. Thus, when we are in an actual, practical situation, such as trying to install a door on hinges, up to the point that the resolution which is required needs to be real, we should follow old thinking's approach to that achievement. But to the degree that we want the door to be an entrance or an exit, we need to decide the spiritual liberating or captivating purpose of the door itself, so we need to follow the patterns of new thinking to decide which way it should open, which way it should close, whether it should lock from the inside or the outside, and whether it is a door to come in or go out, whether it is a door to bring us to old thinking security or to new thinking liberation. All old thinking in its displaying characteristic is valid in the application of knowledge, but never in the superlative purpose for which that knowledge is applied; for that you need new thinking; so, both are necessary.

Very often, even in analyzing our own problems, I find that we miss the need, the timing, the specific point of contact at which we ought to depart into old thinking or new thinking. Up to the point that we are still trying to get away from our grandparents for example, we may be too much into the new thinking, which has as yet brought us nowhere, except away from our grandparents; but sometimes we need their money. . . . Or, up to the point that we have found being away from our grandparents unsatisfactory, we may have reduced ourselves to such a narrow focus that what we see is very clear and yet we feel no inner encompassing satisfaction with the sighted.

I should like to end by mentioning that you sometimes find an apparent exclusive use of old thinking in a particular culture, and you begin to wonder, how could that culture have successfully maintained and regenerated itself through time without an adequate counterbalance in new thinking? Tradition is a typical example of old thinking. And it is difficult to see, in the Jewish culture, the Chinese culture or the Vedic culture—which are so display and darshan-conscious, in which even the mode of expression is judged more by its form than by its quality, more by its preciseness than by its sincerity—how these cultures have remained intact, resisted the changes of time, the virility of the environment and successfully transmitted a cohesive security base to the population generation after generation. But here you can begin to see, for instance in the Jewish culture, where tradition and old thinking appear, on the surface, to be very strong, that over the history of that culture—not in short changes (we, who are so impatient, think that changes can happen fast; the faster they happen, the less they are changes. Falls are fast, climbs are slow and steady)—the ultimate authority, which propounded cultural cohesiveness, achieved some mystical realization, so that in the end any one specific display of tradition was false, no matter how real and absolute and dogmatically necessary it was. Thus many of the Rabbis or Mandarins or Brahmins, when they realized that any particular display pattern was not absolute, therefore valueless— only valuable in what it did and not in itself—they were able to change it, sometimes overnight, because of the freedom somewhere in their capacity for new thinking patterns. Therefore, while any particular system or culture or cohesion of thought is transmitted through the stability of the old thinking pattern, obviously it is only the new thinking pattern, in balance with it, which has been able to maintain a continual line and flow of its existence through man's mind.

I do not know to what degree I have confused you, but I should like to see you begin to be more consciously aware of the need you have in yourself to approach things sometimes more from the point of view of your forefathers and at other times more from the point of view of your LSD trips, to see that both approaches are necessary and valid, and that without learning to engage in either successfully, you are not properly developing your own conceptual power or your ability to gather vague experience into a system of knowledge upon which you can proceed further in the unknown endeavor of everyday living a little bit more—to death. . . .

Old thinking is a sorting process and new thinking is a melting process
Old thinking generates and new thinking destroys
Old thinking causes conditions and new thinking causes glimmers
When you follow a pattern of old thinking you must come to an answer
When you follow a pattern of new thinking you must come to no answer
When you follow the patterns of old thinking you are pushing before you the known
When you follow the patterns of new thinking you are pushing behind you the known
Old thinking is backward forwarding and new thinking is forward backwarding
Old thinking is sterile creation and new thinking is virile absconding
Old thinking is ordered congestion and new thinking is chaotic impression
Old thinking is a claim and new thinking is an aim
Old thinking is an unveiling and new thinking is a veiling
The most perfect display brings a portrayal

PART 1
REALITY & ILLUSION

SUFISM

There are many people who have devoted their lives to something that is called Sufism: perhaps that they have devoted their lives to Sufism is not clear even in their own minds—maybe in their minds they were simply not satisfied with the world, with their lives, with their jobs, and were just searching for an answer to the meaninglessness of their lives—but basically, directly or indirectly, that which has called them is Sufism. Therefore it serves to know, if it is to be known, what Sufism is. One could try to equate Sufism with many religious, spiritual or esoteric sects which lately abound in the Western world, and obviously it is very easy to compare Sufism with philosophies or religious groupings which share similarities. But those similarities in reality are not similarities because they are the same, because Western man of the twentieth century has, due to the cultural environment in which he lives, the same holes to fill, the same emptinesses, the same longings, and he will search to fulfill those longings in the ways his culture and his value systems can understand and appreciate. This is an extremely important point if we want to understand Sufism.

Hundreds of years ago the world was wild, unruly, dangerous, barbarous. Physical violence was the order of the land: there were no rules to live by, no values with which to appreciate life. At that time, man needed to answer, to fulfill, to satisfy a certain emptiness, and so there were extremely strong religious and spiritual movements which were quite similar in that they were all very ritualistic, formulistic, giving rules and dogmas. There was no reason at that time to be good; if you were stronger than your fellow man, why couldn't you kill him if you wanted? The abstract conceptualizations of man were different from what they are now; life was threatening, and so man had to be threatened. Who threatened him? He threatened himself, saying, "God will burn you in hell if you do not do this, or if you do not follow that rule." And so there was, for instance within the larger groupings of Christianity, Islam and Judaism, an extremely strong expression and realization of the need for an enforcing form, a coercive formula, a structure of control of behavior.

Sufism at that time was also extremely formulistic and ritualistic; it had plenty of rules which most people now would reject. It is precisely this point which begins to explain the message of Sufism, for Sufism has always tried to be an answer to humanity in the time of its need, realizing full well that as the need of humanity changes, the answer has to change. If someone is hungry you can bring him water, but it will not satisfy the hunger. If someone is thirsty you can bring him food, but he might not be able to digest it through lack of water. As one delves deeper and deeper into Sufism, one will find that on its surface it is culturally colored to give the immediate answer to man at a particular time in his humanity; however, as it leads you along further and further, it tries to bring you to a more balanced approach to life; not strictly water to the hungry or food to the thirsty or vice versa, but maybe water to the thirsty to begin with and then food afterwards, maybe food to the hungry to begin with and then water. It tries to be an answer which leads man to a greater, a more balanced understanding, and thereby an acceptance of his humanity, his real self.

Just as a few hundred years ago there was a need for law and order because that was the logical result of man's culture, so today there is another culture, and despite the fact that it is interesting to us to read the life of Muhammad and what he taught, enlightening to us to see Christianity in all its different sects and groups developing historically, answering the different needs of Western man through the Middle Ages, yet we can see that the need of mankind today is totally different.

The mystical language cannot be a language of the past. By that I mean that perhaps the ancient Vedic scripts gave a code for life and an explanation for reality, an approach to reason and meaning, and maybe because all these are wonderful and romantic ancient Vedic scripts we, with our strange spiritual hunger, will have a blown-up, sudden interest in what the old texts had to say, but what they said referred to *that* civilization, *that* period in man's level of abstraction, that time, that culture, that sense of values. One can try to shave one's hair or put on yellow robes, or don clothes without seams, but we will find that the mystical language of the search, the answer to the mystical dilemma of the man of two thousand years ago is meaningless today. If a spiritual answer is to come in this hunger, in this thirst, it must come in this life—the twentieth century, the age of astronauts, the atomic bomb, ecological disaster, the sexual revolution, mind-expanding drugs, total industrial capacity, in the ever-increasing knowledge of our external world. This is why, if we are to understand Sufism in our own hearts, we have to start by understanding that Sufism has always changed, and that is why it has always remained the same. If ever in its group-flow through time it had not changed, it would not have remained the same. What I mean is that as soon as man is no longer willing to grow in his mind, no longer willing or able to assimilate in his consciousness the new dimensions, the new perspectives which he has discovered, then age, alienation, fear of the new and unknown sets in. This is so strong today that we recognize the problem of the generation gap, of the shift in values, and we see that some people, just as human, just as good, with just as much heart and well-meaning, continue to play a little doll's game which is not understood by another group of people who play another doll's game.

Sufism is something which must help you to see life as a permanent transition. It is something which must bring you to a realization of dynamic peace: peace, not with what is, but with what will be. It is not, of course, possible to explain exactly what is meant by these terms. It is not possible because first, every general statement is in part invalid, and that part of it which is valid begins to lose its validity as soon as it has been expressed; and second, because we must be aware that to each and every one of us everything means something different.

There are people living in New York, in London and in Calcutta who have never been out of the city; they are a special breed of humans. We know that there are different races in the world: black, white, brown, yellow and whatever other colors there might be—green. But we have now bred a new race, the race of the city dweller, a person who is at home in the concrete jungle, a person who sees nature as a park, who sees a farm as a zoo, who sees animals as strange, foreign, wild objects. Although we city dwellers use the same words when we talk about a horse, a cow, a goat, an elephant, a lion, the subtle inner value of the word within our mind is totally different from that within the mind of a person who has had another experience with these same creatures. There is nothing to which you can put a label or a name which is understood by two people in the same way. In fact if there was something which we could understand, evaluate, experience, consciously and unconsciously in exactly the same way, it would not need to have a name, because we would all know. It is because we do not know something that appears to us in this way and to you in another way that we have to have nomenclature, a way to communicate.

If we think of this on a little larger scale, without fear— thought without fear is a thousand times more powerful than thought with fear—we must surely begin to see that there is nothing we know that we can be sure about, because all that we know is unique, exclusive to our own little consciousness. This may, in fact, be man's greatest basic insecurity, the fear of having to face the fact that we know, for sure, nothing.

Think of it in another way: many people in the world are sure of what they know, yet there is nothing that can be known which is not subject to change, and impermanent. Very few people are sure of what they know not, and yet all those things which are not to be known are, in the end, the only things we can be sure of, the only things of which we are certain. Sufism begins by giving man that security, which could also be labeled freedom, to approach the experience of what appears as life without hesitation, without prejudice, without fear, especially without this incredible plague of our mind which conceives that things ought to be in a particular way. This may seem to be a complicated concept, but really it is not.

As the story goes, at one time there was a dinner party in the court of Portugal, and there, after enough bread and Portuguese wine had been served (obviously the right psychological setting), a man suggested that the earth was round. But the people said, "The earth round? That is impossible." Yet since the acuity of their senses had been dulled a little and they could feel that things were floating around they asked, "How could it be round? You would fall off." They were unable to comprehend the idea, so that kind man who freed the world from one little prison into another, took an egg, which is relatively round, and said, "It looks like this, and wherever you stand on it your feet are on the ground and your head points into the sky." But the people still said that it would fall over, so he took the egg and pushed it down hard on the table, and it stood. He destroyed what people were then sure of, and he was able to destroy it only because they had arrived at that point in their ability to conceive where they could accept that the earth was not flat. Because of their intellectual endeavor, their higher abstract thinking, they had begun to conceive that the earth was bigger than Lisbon, that there were more villages than the two or three they knew, open for exploits and discoveries. The historical veracity of this story may be questioned, but that would not in any way reduce its universal truth. Like little children in a play-pen, people had simply begun to realize that you could travel by boat for weeks without falling off the edge of the earth. Life itself had begun to prepare man to accept this revolutionary change, and they accepted it. It did not make it true then, it was never less true before that the earth was round, and the fact that so many millions of people today accept that the earth is round does not make it any more true now. Whatever fact is in its illusion, it has to be a fact because it *is*, independent of the veracity which we see in it.

The question which arises today is, how many flat earths are there in our own conception of reality? Naturally it is a nice example to use, the earth round or flat, because it is a physical phenomenon; but how many flat earths are there in our whole psychological make-up?

Approximately eight thousand years ago, man began to think that after he died he did not just rot away, but continued to exist. He could not understand how or why, because he was not yet able to conceive abstractly, so gradually ancestor worship evolved, and out of that evolved the concept of the soul. Maybe the soul exists, maybe it does not exist. None of us would perform ancestor worship now, it would seem to us elementary, childish, and yet it might very well be that a few hundred years from now, people will look upon our attachment to the existence of the soul as another form of ancestor worship, another elementary concept to which we were hooked. And so it will be that whatever they think then will also pass away, as man ever increases his capacity for wider conceptualization. Just now we are incredibly attached to what we believe. If you have never seen ancestor worship, it would be healthy to see it—you would see the total belief, attachment, passionate acceptance and faith with which people pray to, worship and communicate with the spirits of their ancestors. Certainly you would feel that there may be some truth to it, but at the same time it would seem to be an old-fashioned trip. Yet, are you ready to see and understand how people in the future with their own level of conceptualization will look upon your little attachments, your little thing which you believe to be right or wrong or good or bad? Sufism brings a freedom to function in the known without fear, to function in the unknown without certainty, and to approach the apparent reality of life with a mystical insight into its unreality.

You may begin to see how so many of the hundreds of things which we do and like, as much as the hundreds of things which we do not do and reject and dislike, are part of a cultural evolution of the practices, habits and changes which attach you in life to the entire past of mankind. You could ask, "If we are all so primitively involved in blind faith, then what is the meaning of what we do?" If you could flip back an instant into the eternity of your mind and see the ancestor worship, the worship of the martyred Christ, the worship of gods of stone or whatever worship or rejection of worship with which you are involved now, you could, or you should, see a higher transcendent reality, not in the thing which is happening, but in the experience of it.

Imagine there is a rose before you. You have not smelled that rose and yet you have a certain understanding, a knowledge of that rose which transcends the sight of it because of previous experiences you have had in which its scent came to your consciousness. That fragrance has impressed on you an experience which you cannot define—it is not a reality which you can measure, it is not a fact which you can predict, it is not a value which you can weigh, it is an experience in consciousness, the experience of the fragrance of a rose. Someone can bring you rose incense, rose water, rose snuff, rose-scented writing paper, a picture of a rose, someone can even talk about the word "rose," and in all the hundreds of things which are absolutely not that rose, in that unfathomable consciousness the experience of that fragrance continues to live in a transcendent way, not attached to this red rose which we smelled, or to that yellow rose which we saw, but to the principle, the universal—it begins to have an independent life.

This is the meaning, the value, the worth, the reason of life, not in what we do, nor even in how or why we do it, since all these are forever changing—but in becoming the experience.

Some may say, this is not clear, how can it be understood? Others may grasp the concept but feel that it is not sufficiently stable, how can one build one's life? How does it help me to live? Here the third important aspect of Sufism must be brought out, an aspect which may be as shocking as, if not more shocking than, the previous ones. That is that if one really begins to live, consciously, one can never live in the same way again. You can still ride your bicycle, you can still play your doll's game, but in terms of the reasons for doing what you do, you can never accept the set of values which previously guided your life. You can never be the same pension-hunter, you can never be the same ostrich burying your head in the security of blindness, vegetating, doing what is supposed to be done because that is the thing to do. Although you will still function as a human being, you will still be able to calculate, add and divide, you will still be able to laugh and to cry, to break and to destroy, to create, to wonder, to hurt, to love, to disdain, to reject, to accept, you will be able to do all these things like any other human being, yet the coloring of their meanings, the reasons for why you will do, how you will do, what you will experience of what you will do, all will have changed, because the driving power behind your consciousness will have changed. This is the transformation of the personality, of the character, the real transformation, separating—and this may be cynically put, but it is still valid—the human sheep from the human beings.

Sufism is not something which one can define in form, it is not a grouping which one can understand in structure, it is not a teaching which one can communicate in words. It is an approach to life, a way of life, helping you at the speed at which you are able to unload the weight, the gravity of fear and attachment, bringing you to a transcendent freedom, the freedom of experience.

All these are big words, and maybe in their size you have become lost, but they are also very simple words and one usually becomes lost in their simplicity. In the spiritual search, in the cultural search, in whatever search for meaning that mankind is engaged in, we usually look for something magical, something sensational, something fantastic; an airplane which will fly without an engine, a super-fast elevator to god, something great, marvellous, wonderful, holy. And yet, when Sufism is presented to your mind, you are totally estranged from it because it is not at all the kind of answer you are looking for. It is not something to sell, it is not another gimmick to help you, another wine to dull the senses into believing that everything is all right.

It is a way to awaken. Sufism is a call, a cry to awaken, to the minds who are ready, to the human beings who have slept enough, but to those who still want to sleep it is merely a lullaby along in their dream. It is a cry to awake to life, to integration, to meaning, to honesty, to honesty with ourselves. It is a cry to drop all sorts of holy trips, flat earths, ancestor worships, sentimental attachments to souls and spirits and other trickery which exist or not, neither their existence nor their non-existence being that meaningful in the end. It is a cry to the genes of your consciousness, to the chromosomal activity of your mind, of your being, to awake, and live. . . .

June 4, 1973

THE CONTRADICTION
OF REALITY

To introduce this chapter I shall repeat that Sufism does not pretend to be a specific, unchanging, predefined form of teaching about anything, principally because we must certainly realize that mankind can function only within that which he can see, that which he can comprehend. He functions within his value-structure, his cultural system; and this environment which creates an apparent reality for him is always changing. Thus it is that man's point of view, religiously speaking, has always changed.

Man looks for some security. He knows in himself that there is nothing on which he can depend, so his first reaction is one of fear, out of which he builds up heavy security systems, prisons of thought, structures of value—and these systems, sooner or later, will all be overthrown because as our knowledge expands, as our horizon expands, as our outlook expands (or contracts), things change. Things which had meaning at one time have no meaning at another.

If you want to begin to understand Sufism, you must understand that it is not to be compared with an easy teaching which says, "Do this, follow the right path, live in this way, follow these little rules, believe in these things and everything will be all right." Sufism does not teach anything from that point of view at all. A teaching should be something that always changes as man changes, as his need changes, as his culture makes new demands upon his urge for meaning and value. Rather than find something secure in Sufism, you should be able to find in it an approach to help think yourself more free about life and reality, about meaning and purpose. This was discussed in greater detail in the previous chapter, and in the chapters to follow we will begin to talk about reality. As we build up a beginning approach to life, to whatever else we want to talk about, whatever else we want to address ourselves to, we must establish a basis of reality from which to talk, from which to communicate, out of which to build.

Man is continually trying to build for himself a stable reality out of his tremendous insecurity. In his fearful psychological make-up he has always to face the questions, what is really true? What really is right? What really is good? What is really in existence? What actually, really matters? And every time he thinks about it, regardless of where he is in his own evolutionary level of abstract conceptualization, he is incredibly afraid of coming to the realization that nothing really matters, we do not really matter, life does not really matter, my existence is not all that important. When we are faced with that thought for the first time, it gives us such a fright that we have the standard crab-reaction, quickly dig a hole and bury ourselves, or else we feel so alienated and lost that we end life. We do not want to see the total dynamic pattern of abstract existence.

The mystic has a consciousness which enables him to take for granted the fact that reality is a fleeting concept, that there is only what we see and that what we see is a function of what we can see—that reality gains its quality of realness from our observation of it. Its dependability then, which we must attach as a quality to the idea of reality, is immediately corresponding to 'I.' This is the first mystic point of view of reality. There may be another reality, but it is not real to us because we do not see it, we do not know it, we cannot conceive of it. Since reality is only what we can see, it cannot be separated from the one who is involved in it, from the observer. There is, therefore, no objective reality; there is only the subjective reality which is continuously being constructed, at least in part by a consciousness attempting to envelop, to control, to capture something of which it can conceive; and it is continuously being destroyed by its very nature, which is inconceivable, uncapturing, non-manifesting. Reality is completely abstract, it does not exist as reality separate from the observer. Inasmuch as the observer is trying to make it, create it, function in it, the tighter the noose of consciousness ties its knot around this abstractness, the closer it comes to discovering that what it was trying to contain is nothing.

The mystic tries to understand that, and instead of being afraid, instead of having a rush of panic and saying, "Oh, my god, I'm no longer important and all these enormous emotions and feelings and experiences, everything that is happening to the world, everything that is happening to me, oh my god, that is no longer real?" Instead of having this shock, this self-protective reaction, the mystic says, "What an incredible weight has fallen off!" It is no longer necessary to own something, to own reality, to own some dependable security. It is no longer necessary to live a life of flight, running behind things which always disappear. That freedom is a freedom which changes everything in life, and yet it changes nothing. Can anything be changed? Is there anything but change?

Obviously a sceptical mind—and one should have a sceptical mind—would say that it is very easy to throw objective reality out of the window, but you cannot throw away the laws of an objective material world which we see operate. You cannot discard these laws and say that they do not exist. You cannot suddenly wipe out the predictable behavior of so-called non-existent matter. We have to agree with this point of view. We can definitely say—and this is the second approach that the mystic has in his reality perception as a working hypothesis—that we are where we are because the "where" is simply a behavior-pattern which seems to have some consistency. The apparent reality, therefore, begins to appear through the repetition of consistently similar-behaving abstraction. Matter does not exist; we have finally come to that point. What does exist we do not know—

probably nothing—but in the illusionary state in which it seems to us to exist, its existence is proven because its behavior follows certain patterns. Interestingly, we call these patterns "laws," and we used to think that they were absolute. The absoluteness of these laws is a function of the limitation of our observation, because it is easy to observe two similar phenomena with a gross tool and conclude that they are the same pattern. Yet when one becomes more deeply, more refinedly able to observe, one finds that they were two entirely different patterns. There are many examples of this in simple mechanics, electronics and other aspects of material life. The mystic allows himself to approach the apparent reality with this conceptual compromise. All life is in a way the compromise that we see what we see, we observe what we observe, we make conclusions, and as a working approach we can try to function within these conclusions, but without attaching this fear, this absolute dogmatism, that what I have seen is what was, what I know is what is.

Less than six hundred years ago, barbers used to singe the hair as they cut it. As they went along with the scissors they followed with a candle, and as they cut the hair they would burn the ends of it. This was not a practice lasting only a short time, it happened for quite a while throughout Western civilization. Why were they burning the ends of the hair? Because they thought that hair bled. We know very well that hair does not bleed and in thinking back we must wonder how they could have thought that it did. What could make them, six hundred years ago, think that hair bled? What we see now as nonsense was for them a reality, and man functioned in that reality, compensated for that reality and created a whole behavior-pattern. The conclusion we make is that the barber six hundred years ago was performing nonsense when he singed the hair; but part of what we do now is also nonsense, and people six hundred years ahead will look upon things that we do now and say, "Oh, those simple people, they were not observing right." And six hundred years from then, people will again look back, and again have a different point of view of reality. We can say that in reality hair does not bleed, but reality is only a function of what one can see, of what one is able to see—we could even say, of what one wishes to see. If the barber six hundred years ago was using a candle to singe the hair, it was real; and if you claim that it was not, it is because you feel that your reality is permanent, and you are not yet ready to see the mystic approach, to make a simple, peaceful, working hypothesis which the mystic does with life, that one will do what one can do as long as it appears in some way to fit in a reality, while being always ready, ever willing to expand, to change, and to find that something that previously was thought, something which previously we did in that way, now is such, and now we will think of it in this way. That freedom to assimilate totally all the experiences which come to us, that sensitivity, brings peace.

Many people speak of peace. Some of us are beginning to think, because of the romantic Eastern sales-job that is happening, that peace can be attained by sitting under a tree in the Himalayas and meditating. This was probably true for a few people at one time, in one reality, in one culture, but Sufism's approach is that nobody can say that peace should be pursued in this way, or peace should be attained in that way; this is the formula, that is the secret, this is the ritual, that is the thing to do to achieve peace. No, peace can be attained when finally you allow reality to be less heavy, less real, less certain, less absolute, when finally you allow life and all that comes to you in life to be an appearance, when you allow good and all that appears to you as good to be beautiful, when you allow evil and all that appears to you as evil to be part of the same pattern, when you allow this anguish for reality, of trying to capture something to hang on to, something to believe, when you allow that need in your psyche to fall away, to disappear as a useless weight, as something you don't need to protect, something you don't need to own.

Maybe if you look at it from this point of view, you will see that the guy who went to sit under a tree in the Himalayas did not find peace and become holy because he sat under that tree, but because of the psychological process involved in his finding out that all these things which he was supposed to do were not so important, that all these things which he was supposed to believe were not so important. He reduced his life, reduced his ambitions, and eventually found that the thing he really wanted to do was to live a quiet life, to see the sun come up and go down, and take it easy. That was the peace. It was not the trip of sitting under a divine tree—every tree is divine. It was not the trip of doing some mantram' or meditation—every word is a mantram, every action a meditation. It was simply the psychological readiness in him to let reality be less important, less heavy, less real.

If we look with a mystical lightness into life and reality, and we ask ourselves what is real, the conclusion is that reality is a symbol. The only thing which really exists is a symbol. This is the third concept of mysticism. I hope you will deepen yourself in this approach and not simply understand it superficially. Do not think only sceptically, but let this conclusion, which is a realization from depth and experience, penetrate your consciousness. Make your deductions, but allow time for them to grow. Reality is a symbol, a form, a symbolic abstract form, and on whatever level of manifestation something exists, the level of manifestation is determined simply by the kind of symbolic form/structure which is possible there.

If we look, for example, at matter, its material entity disappears very quickly upon examination. Beyond the threshold of its material entity, all we have left is a symbol, a symbolic arrangement in form, abstraction or energy. People say, "There is energy, so there is something." But if you look at energy you find that it is simply potential. What we know as energy, the closest we can come to describing it—as we see things now, which will change tomorrow—the closest we can come now is to say that energy is a potential that longs to entreat. Potential is what we begin to divine beyond the fleeting nebulous area of energy. The first manifestation of this energy is an arrangement, it immolates towards a form, and when that form integrates itself in a particularity, it has suddenly moved onto the barrier between the non-manifested potential and the manifested portent.

The first, most abstract level of existence in this manifested world is a symbol. What is there more un-manifested, what is there closer to the abstract than a symbol? A symbol is a form because it takes its identity on this level, the particular level of material planetarization; but of course, in no way does that mean that there cannot be other entreating levels at which there are other planetarization possibilities to bring potential to portention.

Consider, for instance, thought. Where is thought? What is the space in which it is contained? Are thoughts words? As soon as thoughts become words, they become symbols. Words are sounds and sounds are simply wave-patterns with an exact frequency. If the symbol of a sound repeats its wave-pattern once, we cannot hear that sound; its wave-pattern is only a form along an energy flow, nothing else. If it repeats its wave-pattern a precise number of times we recognize that exact number of repeated forms as a precise sound. "C" on the piano; two hundred and sixty-two exact little forms per second; four hundred and thirty-five wave-patterns make "A" on the piano. What does it mean? It means that a symbol repeats itself by a numerological principle, and that numerological principle determines exactly the coloration of the apparent reality of the symbol.

You can see this also in the example of gasses. If you take a gas called hydrogen, it contains something which we call a nucleus, which, when we look at it, disappears into energy, positively charged—which again means nothing; positive charge does not maintain its existence separately, it has to exist in relation to something else. Second, hydrogen has an electron, negatively charged. This is precisely a centered arounding (some call it a circle). That is the symbol, the symbolic existence of the electron making a circle around the nucleus. If the pattern of the repetition of orbits is at a certain state, the hydrogen atom is, in a certain precise quality of identity and a precise temperature, gas. If it is sped up or slowed down, the form/symbol/manifestation receives a different coloration, a different hue, a different temperature, a different intensity and it can change from gas to liquid or to solid. That is what we know now. It does not mean that it is real, it simply means that you are able to think about it. It may all be a lot of nonsense; it probably is. But you can see the same thing in all parts of physical existence. Look at DNA and RNA—again there you have a form, a helical form. The helical form repeats itself in a certain twisting bond. It is sequenced in a certain precise way, and the numeric pattern of the way in which these helical structures sequentially repeat themselves determines the genetic code of all life.

The helical form can be found in everything that grows. This helical form came to be called the mystical twist, by mystics hundreds of years ago. Trees turn in an exact helical pattern, flowers turn, even a child emerging from its mother's womb describes a complete helical egressive turn. The mystics began to see that existence itself is a twist, there is a need to twist and to turn and to dance, following a very balanced pattern. This is the dance of the essence, a dance giving to the essence its delight of being, the dance of emanations of emptiness, expanding forever. This could be called the dance of the soul. Many examples could be given, hours could be spent, and I am sure that we could go along and step by step analyze all of nature that we know, and show you the symbols and the corresponding numerological principles of repetition of these symbols which, when planetarized, give to the apparent reality its different hues and qualities.

Symbols which operate in this repetition create the reality appearance in all its diversity, color, weight, temperature, speed. The question arises, what is the operating principle that makes reality available to the observer? So far we have talked about reality as if there were no observer, but earlier the point was made that reality is totally subjective. It does not exist unless and until it is observed. The reality is subjective as an observation created by the observer from the objective which, by being observed, elicits an attempt to make an approximate recreation of it, limited by the observer's own peculiar observing capacity and intrinsic focal associative resolution. The objective in the absolute, being entirely unrelated and independent of observation and observer, remains forever veiled, unknown, not recognized. The reality is thus an illusion, a suggestive construction which more and more preadjusts the observer's recognizant and resolving setting in future observation.

If the objective could ever actually be observed so as to be seen as it is, which is the observer's expectation, what would be observed would dissipate under the strain of the apperceptive process, for if its granulation is seen as it is, the space between the granules would be beyond focal concentration. So if we are going to describe reality as a symbol which follows a pattern, then what is the required principle of the way in which the observer interacts with that non-existing reality so that it becomes the apparent real world which we feel, see, understand, comprehend, and think is so incredibly important? The only principle that allows the observer to enter into and give it by his presence its observing existence, its reality as a property, is the law of contradiction. Reality is a function of contradiction. The point of reality which can become real in our subjective experience can gain that property of contradiction only when it is contradicted. In other words, nothing can be observed which has no opposite. It appears to us that there is light, it appears to us that someone loves us, it appears to us that the earth is hard; it appears to us that we think, it appears to us that someone else is speaking. But there is light only because we are able to observe darkness, there is a hard earth because we are able to observe softness. In other words, we observe light as a function of darkness, darkness as a function of light, and if there were no darkness, there really would be no light. If the sun always shone there would be no night in our reality.

This function of contradiction is not necessarily true, it is simply the contradiction which the observer creates in his observation because it is always light, it is always dark. The day and the night are not opposites to one another at all—it is a great big lie. The sun shines always, our seeing these two as opposites is our contradiction created in order to make reality function. It could very well be that darkness is a contradiction of liquid, it could very well be that love is a contradiction of music, but that makes no sense to us because we think that light is a contradiction of darkness. We have created these, we have lined up these separate symbols and given them a functionality in our observing consciousness, a relationship to one another. That relationship is determined by the gradation of contradiction which we can create, but whether it is really a contradiction we do not know. If we were to examine it, we would know that the Bible, of all incredible books, says, "God created light, and the light shone in the darkness but the darkness comprehended it not...." Light and darkness are there, they are totally independent, they have nothing to do with each other. The fact that we think that light is the absence of darkness, or a gradation in between, or the other way around, is our little mind creating, imprisoning, capturing for our consciousness a particular, functional relationship which appears to us to be real.

There is no attempt here to claim that the absolute and holy truth can be expressed in words by one or another individual; the rationalization for that which has been expressed is not at all that it is truth, but that it may have helped you to be nearer to that which you conceive as probable. Even if you do not agree with anything I have presented—and minds are not made to agree but to express beauty—I think that in beginning to think about these things, and essentially thereby, to think about yourself, you will see that things which maybe mattered a lot do not really matter so much; things which you knew, or thought you knew, will only temporarily appear to be so until you discover that they are not. Whatever your point of view as a result of experience, as long as you approach life with this lack of gravitation, you have begun the mystical life.

Sufism never takes someone out of life. Sufism never says, "We are going to make a holy master out of you, put a nice yellow robe on you, put beautiful flowers on your car...." Sufism just puts you back in your own life, but it seems not to weigh so much, so you can go a little lighter, a little faster, a little easier, a little higher, but in the same place and in the same illusion and in the same truth.

June 11, 1973

THE CAPTURE OF REALITY

We ended with the point that contradiction, which is a quality of reality, is totally subjective. We all know that light and darkness are not opposites at all, that the day is ever and the night is ever, and as it says in the Bible, god made the light to shine in the darkness and the darkness did not understand it. Before going further, I must emphasize that this idea is not more or less true by the fact that it is out of the Bible. These juxtapositions which seem to us so incredibly real, full/ empty, good/bad, pain/pleasure (forgetting that pain is the greatest pleasure and the only experience), are totally a fiction of our own creation. When the mystic's viewpoint reaches this level, we obviously come to see that maybe love is not opposite to hate, maybe black is not opposite to white, cool is not opposite to hot maybe.... Hundreds of symbols exist, and those which exist to us are those which we are able in our present mind-structure-pattern to contradict to one another; there might be just as many millions of others which, because we have not yet connected them, are inconceivable. In eternity always everything is.

By experience it has become clear that it takes some time sometimes, no time other times, to see this liberating escape from the bonds of our mind. If then reality is an apparition which gains its realness only through the functionality of contradiction in the subjectivity of our mind, which then classifies it "objectively," meaning that it prevents it from changing, there must be the possibility of a whole new way to experience this reality, a whole new way to travel in the void, a whole new way not to exist—and that is the point of presentation in this chapter.

How is it that this incredible fear-syndrome, in which man continuously has to defend himself from asking what is real, comes into being? Man continuously blindfolds himself, to function in an over-protected park with plastic flowers, artificial smells, evergreens with leaves that do not fade, and the cry of all of us in our hearts is why? Why do we do this to ourselves?

There was once a composer who was called Tyagaraja; that was not his name, it was the title given to him because everyone felt that his music was the greatest. Tyagaraja composed for thirty or forty years and almost all of his compositions were written down by his pupils. One scribe would take down the melody, one the rhythm, one the texture, another the words, all written on palm leaves or mango planks. Thus an enormous and lasting influence was made on Carnatic music. All of this we know, but what we may not know is why it is that millions of people, living today in a different culture, who do not necessarily understand the music or the words, the sounds or the meter, the poetry, the rhythm, the song, and certainly not the culture in which this music was written, think that this music is the greatest? Basically Tyagaraja wrote one song, in my view, which he and others repeated a few thousand times. Thus a stamp, a form, a shape was forged into the mind of every Carnatic musician after him, so that instead of developing, instead of having the freedom of thought and emotion and expansion, they could not compose anything except second-rate Tyagaraja music.

Why did this happen? Why has it happened with scientific knowledge, with medical science, with theology, with religion, why is it happening today with the whole meditation trip? Man seems to be born or bred with the desire to be something, to know something, to keep something, to do something, to express something. A little child immediately receives the indoctrination of how to be, though it is born simply with the unformed, unconscious, un-symbolic stream of life, to become. A child learns to be a baby, a good child, a sweet child, learns to read and write and play music and think like this, act like that, behave like this, do like that and procreate like this, because that is the way it should be. So already, from the instant of our descent upon this planet, the desire to become—wherever that comes from, which is something we will talk about later—becomes altered in the accumulation of how to be. As the weight of being increases with the taking of cognizance, the driving force of becoming is loaded down, weighed down, strangled and eventually stopped. This is a completely natural process which probably has to happen. As the force of becoming, the rising force which makes the flower open, becomes fulfilled by the weight of being, which says, "You become just like that, this flower, this form, this fragrance, this color, this thing, this shape . . ."—when it reaches that, it is dead.

We all know that a few years ago they began to try to figure out how to send pictures from satellites to earth. They took a picture up there with a camera, put the picture under a strong light and placed it above a mesh. Under the mesh was an electric cell which was programmed to move at a particular speed under each little division. Think of this incredible symbol of our civilization today. The light cell was under this little hole and there was light, so it sent out code 1; it moved to the next hole and there was light, code 1 — and so on until eventually after three hundred holes which had light it came to a hole which was a little less light, or almost dark, so it could not send out code 1 because it did not receive an electrical impulse. As the pulses were translated into radio waves, we on earth knew that it was light here and dark there, without physically (which is meaningless anyhow) bringing that little picture, a marvellous little Kodachrome print, without bringing that capture of death which we call reality, down to earth, and so we could make a replica here of what that picture apparently looked like to the electric eye. It is interesting to think about what we can do, and what it implies to the way our thinking goes.

In this way the grid of education, fear, heredity, environment, and we should not forget the mesh of love, whatever that means, has become impressed upon the mind of man, upon his consciousness. What we actually captured was not the way that picture looked, but the way they had divided it up, and the way we had reconstructed that division. If we look tonight or any night into the sky, we can sometimes see stars. They are also there when we cannot see them, but when we can see them they are not there. Why are they not there? Because all that we are seeing is an extremely subjective, geocosmic time-sequenced, personalized, individualized reconstruction of a universe which is definitely not the way it appears. Some of the light is two million years old, some five thousand years old, some five billion years old, and all that light is coming down, yet what we see is not its reality, but the way it appears to us. What we see is entirely different, from your mind to my mind, to his mind, to her mind, depending upon where we are geographically and where we are in time. Some of our eyes observe more, some of our eyes observe less; but whatever we see, there is one thing which we could, in a limited way, say about it, and that is that it is something that is always changing. Not one star is still where it was. Most of them might be gone; for all we know new ones have come, old ones disappear. All we see is a false capture of being; a time grid.

We are saying in our observation of reality, "That star is there," yet all we know is that it is there subjectively, in the illusion of our mind. Even if it were there, the instant we said it, we killed it, because we captured that thing, we took a picture of it. Any picture of a thing is something we have captured, to treasure, to hide. (People who take pictures, especially camera-freaks, are, from a psychological point of view, basically desiring to shoot a bullet. Theirs is a desire to kill, to capture. The camera to us today is the gun, with which we can perform the same psychological process as we do when neurotic or perverse forces bring us to blows—"Smile," click—and the power conquest which adds to the whole surrealistic scene . . . a color print. But that is only an interlude.)

We do not know where those stars are, we do not know what they are, all we know is that there is something there which is becoming. We do not know what we are; the instant you think about who you are, why you are, if you really think about it—apart from the answers that your mothers or grandmothers had to give, "You are here because god made you," then you ask, "Why did he make me? How did he make me?"—all the answers are meaningless escapes. You can only know that what you are is what you are becoming, where you are is where you are going, what is real is what is changing. The very instant that we, unable to have that freedom, that liberation, that chance to let go—that very instant we try to say, "Oh my god, I want to be like that . . ." we lose the chance.

In the very act of reaching a state, we have sealed the commencement of its destruction. Nothing can maintain itself. Everything degenerates or regenerates. Everything is continually evolving or decaying, whatever our point of view, and man needs to reach the point where he really is all the things he is supposed to be. Like the old tale, I suppose, of the nice young lad or debutante who went to the right school, wore all the right clothes, did all the right things, followed all the right people, rules, laws, regulations, married the right person, only to find that as soon as he or she was as he or she was supposed to be, it began to wither.

That is the point which the mystic discovers about his or her apperception of reality. All of us are born, bred, forced, grid-patterned, branded, to see what is. There is nothing. What is is what is functioning, what is changing, what is becoming, the inter-relationship of abstract symbols, on a dance, a path, the mystical twist, the dance of the soul, a path of expansion, a curved path continuing in an ever-changing direction. It is not that there is something here on the path, or there; it is that there is a movement which gives it reality.

The conclusion is that being is death, becoming is the beginning of eternity, and that if becoming ever becomes, it is finished. This is a philosophy which might be strange to you. Obviously you can have many objections to it, and some are right, but we do not know whether what we think now is really so; all we know is that it is as it appears now. This is our present working hypothesis in our journey of inner devolvement, that it is an attitude which gives hope, not emptiness. It is an approach to life which gives direction, not limitation. It is the search for reality which gives expansion, deepening, widening, not definition. So the mystic has stopped understanding and begun to flow in the sequence of becoming and unbecoming.

This is the essence of what Sufism concludes, when mystically we look upon reality and our relationship to it, our fear of letting it fly away like a carpet under our feet.

It is the flight-plan nowhere which momentarily any-where alights and there captures the experiential nectar which infused that trance of having been really.

June 18, 1973

BEING & BECOMING

We have addressed ourselves together to the general subject of reality, what really is, with the aim of finding relative reasons for our own existence. Without explaining everything again, we know that we can look around a room full of musical instruments and see that each one is like a person: some are very rough and simple, some are very complicated and evolved, yet they are all different. But those instruments are all useless, they are just hanging there, they have no purpose, their existence is only in potential. The true relative meaning of their existence comes to life only when they are being played, yet when they are being played they suffer, they have pain. Every time a string is pulled, it is a strain. Music is the cry of the soul, the cry of the individual, "Do not hurt me, you awakened me." So in the lives of people—we are instruments and we all long to be played and yet we long not to have pain, and these seem to be mutually exclusive desires. It is only through harmonizing this exclusion that one can arrive at acceptance of life, based not on a lot of dogmas, but on a pragmatic formula, a pragmatic resignation that things are the way they ought to be, and pain is there as the greatest of pleasure, to give meaning in the meaninglessness, to give purpose in the entropy, to give enlivement to the death of existence (the enlivening kill).

What happens is that mankind, each and every individual, sees himself or herself as the center of the universe. You have all seen pictures taken with a fish-eye lens, in which, the lens being convex, all lines curve towards the center, and in a way our view of reality, of life, is very self-centered. We interpret everything across our pain-pleasure interest, we evaluate most things as they relate, to add value to our own valuelessness. There is no one reading this, nor anyone in the world who does not in his heart admit that there is really no value to an individual. We all know that even if the whole earth blew up it would make substantially little difference to the universe. We are all groping to be important, to have value, and yet life comes and goes, generations are born and disappear, fads come and go; at any one time everything seems so incredibly important only because it is not important. It is with our need to be important, to have a value—we do not want to see this emptiness, this valuelessness, this meaninglessness, we want to shut ourselves off from it—that we interpret the value of all the things that come through our intelligence.

Sufism is not a teaching. If anyone said that Sufism teaches this and that, it would be to me as if he had seen through a window into a house and from that glimpse had decided what the house was like. In a way it is true, maybe intuitively speaking we can, and yet it is not true; we do not know what is in the house. Sufism is not a teaching, it is an approach, an approach to life which brings first of all detachment, relativation, perspective. Relieve yourself of this overweening weight of reality which is pressing down on the top of your head; reality is but a symbol. It is an approach to life that helps you to see that there is no meaning in life outside of living.

The purpose of this whole exercise in life lies in developing the potential that one has. It is like the description of a direction. If there is movement in a particular direction you can say that the movement has direction, and the purpose of the movement lies in its extension in that direction. As soon as the movement ceases, the directionality ceases and there is no more life.

The reality, therefore, is not that which is, but that which is becoming, and we as individuals are not what we are but what we could be.

In all this which, granted, does give some peace and some

freedom, less weight, in the day-to-day exercise of trying to accept the things we do not want to accept, one question must come to every mind, and that is the basic question, why? Why are some flowers yellow? Why is there suffering? Why is pain the greatest of pleasures? Why do we search for meaning? Why are we afraid? Why is there a universe? Why is there a why? Why do we wonder? Why am I? Why are there fads and cultures? Why is there illusion? Why are we born without knowing what we want to know? What started this whole game? Why is this trip? A very easy answer would be, "Because god made it so." In some part of the Bible it says, "I the Lord thy God am a jealous God," but why is god jealous? Why did he make it so? Why does god exist?

I think you would be disappointed if an answer to this "why" could be given. Any answer to it is going to be temporary, an answer which our mind can grasp, within the framework of our value system, our culture, our point of view and what we are willing to accept. Frankly there is some sort of answer to "why," a partial answer that Sufism brings, and this is that things are because you see them that way. Far be it from me to suggest that things are the way they are because god made them so, but if someone accepted the existence of god and accepted that god made things the way they are because it pleased him, then that is the way he would see the thing, that would be the answer to "why."

Why is there suffering? Maybe because we see it. Why do things not go easy and well? Why does everybody not live happily? Why is there life? Why is there death? First, because that is how we see them.

Not only is reality a symbol, but within our creative minds we seem continually to play with these symbols. The symbols have no separate quality of reality except in their being played with in our consciousness, and in the very fact that they need that quality of reality, they create, in their symbolic repetition, the need to be played with. Each and every woman and man, in her or his consciousness, is continually playing, toying with symbols, observing them and measuring them in certain sequences. Things are the way they are, therefore, because we observe them that way.

It is extremely difficult to admit this to yourself. It is extremely difficult to come to the point of freedom of functioning within our intelligence and our consciousness—seeing pragmatically that this is a rug, this is a chair, this is food, this is painful, this is good, this is not so good, this is what I like, this is what I do not like, this is what I desire—functioning within that framework and at the same time realizing, which is probably the first beginning of illumination (whatever that means) that all these things, this pragmatic framework of our consciousness, are primarily made by ourselves. It is we who thread principles, symbolic principles together in a chain of apparent reality which we hang around our neck, and ever thereafter walk in bondage to that mojo. But suddenly—and this happens always in a flash, and it has happened to everyone in his life sometime, especially when we are bogged down by a problem which we cannot solve—suddenly we come to the point where we throw off this necklace and we see—we are free, we are free to move, to live, to go on, to see things in a different way. Causality, which cannot really be explained on the level of planetarization, is in two parts: ourself, and our attempt in relativity to see things the way we still see them; and things themselves, which we should attempt to see knowing that they are what they are because we see them that way.

It is interesting to see how thoroughly unconscious behavior patterns and value systems are transmitted through parents, through society, through schools, through the system in which we live, through our own fears. Very few of us really have freedom, maybe no one. Imagine what life would be like if we had the freedom to see things the way they really are—what would we see? I think we would see unrelated symbolic principles, their relationship being gained only by the way our mind grasped them in related sequence.

DNA and RNA, the genetic codes of our make-up, are long sequential chains of amino acids—complicated molecular structures which are very, very subtly put together. These chains, these sequences of molecules, forming longer chains and helices, eventually become a pattern, a mold, and that pattern, that mold naturally carries with it the continuity of that particular shape, form and structure. In the same way, as our intelligence grows, what comes into our consciousness through observation begins to be sequentially organized by the way our mind works, by the way our intelligence orders, and eventually we come to this point: things are the way we see them.

Sufism, then, is an attempt to bring us to the point at which we have the freedom, the courage, to look at things as a baby does, without foreknowledge; to let whatever new reality apperception comes, let it come in and experience it fully and totally, without understanding it. For understanding is only classifying something by previously established patterns of thought.

What about the other part of causality? What about the things themselves that we see? Frankly speaking, the question, why is there a "why" about things cannot be answered; or, it could be answered in the negative. If there were no "why," what would there be to seek? What would there be to develop? What direction would there be in which to travel? As soon as man no longer wants to look at that question "why," life has come to an end. As soon as he accepts any one particular answer as permanent and established, the real evolution of that being has come to an end. There is no one who has the final answer to anything, and if there were a final answer, the entire tension of the illusion of reality, which creates the apparency in which we function, would come to an end.

Why is there illusion? Why is there a why? There are certain answers which are not really answers, but which can help us to approach the longing, the desire in the heart to unveil. This is what Sufism calls the unveiling of the belovéd: the dissolving of the illusion. It seems—and this goes back to numerological patterns—that there must be some original first cause. It seems that way to us, because that is the way we think; there might be two original first causes, but we are really unable to conceive of these. How could you have two original causes? How could you have an unstoppable force and an immovable object at one and the same moment? Think of that—how could you have an unstoppable force and an immovable object together in one universe? Yet you have these two things now in your mind, although the one, because of the way we think, the structure of our thought patterns, absolutely precludes the existence of the other. You can have either an unstoppable force or an immovable object, but you cannot have them both. Yet you have thought of them, you have conceived them. How could there be two original causes? We cannot think of it, but at the same time, or for an emotional or sentimental reason, we could not possibly conceive that all of the universal truth, even if that be an illusion, could exist without a first cause. There must be a cause, there must be something which made the first thing.

Could you conceive of a lake existing without a source of water at some time in the past or in the present?

When we look at the basis of reality, albeit an illusion, we come to void. What made the void? Even the simplest atom, such as hydrogen, consists primarily of void, yet somehow we are all emotionally, sentimentally attached to the need for a first cause—"There must be some intelligence that made this all the way it is. I do not understand why everything is this way, but something must have made it for some reason." It would be incredible for us to consider that all this conglomeration of illusion is there for no reason; we would feel so estranged from our life, our whole structure, why we do the things we do; everything would just fall in like a house of cards.

Do you mean to say that there is no original first cause, that things are there for no reason at all, just because they are? But then, inasmuch as we cannot conceive of there not being a first cause—and I repeat, this is primarily because of emotional and sentimental attachments—this is why we must begin in our approach, though that approach be totally pragmatic and free, to think of some first cause. We must have the pragmatic willingness to discard it later when we have no further need for it. We are all willing to discard wrapping paper when we no longer need it; we are all willing to use it when we need it; so we must be willing to use everything there is to be used and to discard it as soon as it becomes a weight.

That is what Sufism teaches; discard things when they become heavy, remain light.

Think of a first cause in this way. There was void, and yet, because there was only void, it was not. If there is only void and nothing else but void, how could anyone say there is void? This void, by definition, by the very definition which we are now able to conceive, within the level of abstraction that we think at now—this void had to have one inalienable quality, which is that it had to become void. It was non-existing void, and yet it could not be void, it could not be what it was until it became.

Try to follow that, do not think of it as honors in philosophy—it is very simple, it is the beginning of real mysticism. The void, which was not, had to become void, because otherwise it would not be, and yet it was.

This first quality, to become, is the major force, the major cause, the major strength, the power which has remained in, behind and throughout everything that has come of that void. If you have a brown cow, the potential of that brownness is going to remain in all the cows that come from that one cow. This supra-genetic power of becoming was so basic, so forceful, so strong that it was behind everything. The desire to become is the desire which makes a little seed, which you can hardly see, grow into a three-hundred-foot tree; which makes a bird fly three, four, five, six thousand miles for food; which makes a little infant with basically no ability to survive, grow into a fully-fledged human being. It is the creative force itself.

The desire to become can be fulfilled only in one way. If there is only void, there is not yet void because there is but void, and thus it is not. The desire to become what is, is the emanating force of its existential. This desire creates the first illusion. We are unable to conceive what it is, but we could propose that the first illusion is void asserting, "I am void." That illusion continues for ever and ever to operate. The power of entropy and disorder and disharmony, self-establishment throughout all, came from the void acquiring existence from itself.

Every potential must assert existentially what it is in order to be. The process of this assertion I call becoming, the realization being the acquisition of identity. We have to create laws and systems and societies and lord knows what else in order to prevent people from over-asserting this first illusion, which is, "I am something," because when the void is, it is something, it is void. This is the end of becoming. But since void is not, it is an overstatement or illusion, i.e., being.

How does this original cause relate to us? Why is there what there is? On a planetarization level let us not forget that most things are, at least in part, a function of how we see them. They might not be that way at all. Let us take the example of yellow flowers: I assure you that they are not yellow—they reflect the color of yellow more than any other color, they reflect all colors to some degree, but basically they are colorless. Reality is always an illusion and by greater and greater depth of perception and investigation the illusion or identity gradually disappears. However, the charm, the romance of the reality is also gone then. Suddenly a petal becomes a laboratory-examined cellular structure, it is no longer part of a flower, it loses something.

In every gain of knowledge there is loss of substance.

Second, if we want to function, if we are forced by our sentimental makeup, our emotional crisis, to accept that there is a first cause, we must see that that first cause, based on what we know now, was the incredible desire to become; and then came about, in order to satisfy that, the illusionary assertion of being.

Becoming is life, and being is death.

July 17, 1973

PURPOSE

We are arriving at the point where we are descending more and more towards a specific, less abstract address to man himself. Painting reality as a symbol, functioning by certain principles of contradiction, looking at causation and trying to see that causation is in fact the key to the illusion in which we function; now we are coming to purpose. If the previous chapters have served to free us from weights, helped us to have a less emotionally attached view of reality in ourselves, then the question which must come next to every mind is, all right, but why do I exist? What is the purpose of my life—of life?

To look at purpose we should maybe start by thinking of a little fish in the sea. To the degree that it has a consciousness, and allowing for that degree to be minimal, the fish in the sea seems to be propelled by forces of self-preservation, of survival; and the fish follows definite patterns, a feeding pattern, a swimming pattern. The little fish may—it probably does not, but it could—see its little life as incredibly important, in fact, sufficiently important that it will fight for its survival, and it will observe good things and bad things (whatever that may mean subjectively) from the point of view of self. If it finds food it is good for that little self, if it is threatened it is bad for that little self. If we were to go and tell the fish that it had no purpose, it could never accept that, it would say, "No, I have to swim, I have to eat, I have to reproduce, I have to experience what I am doing." And yet its basic purpose may be to perform a very small, incredibly precise function, a link in a very large chain which is beyond its comprehension. Despite that, to the individual consciousness of that fish, everything that is happening is happening to it. All the important things in the entire universe are happening to it. Its whole life is so incredibly, marvellously purposeful, and it never sees the function it performs in the instant of eternity in which it appears to be a little fish. It does not see itself as protein, it does not see itself as an ever-increasing cycle of awakening consciousness, consuming and being consumed, expanding and expanding; it simply sees its supremely important and perfectly complete little self, "I, this little fish." A tiny pinprick is so critical in its feelings of pain or pleasure, and yet in all probability, whatever the little fish does, its purpose is inescapable. There is a larger fish which eats our little fish and many others, and there is a still larger fish which eats that one, and so it goes on. Yet on each level there is the wondering why, and the certainty of individuality in purpose and specificity in life.

Another example, maybe far less cruel—if cruelty exists—and therefore also perhaps less just—if justice exists—is the example of a musical scale, a raga, a Greek mode or a Western scale. Imagine that you are playing a major scale on a piano or a sitar. In that moment of intertwinement with the scale, we really seem to be playing a scale, we really seem to be melodiously experiencing an aspect of it, but the mystic point of view is that the scale is playing the musician, that that particular probability, that particular existential set is simply releasing an infinitesimally small potential in a manifested form. It may be that things are reversed, that we are not fulfilling a purpose, but that the purpose is fulfilling in us, just as the little fish or plankton-animal has no real individual function, yet functionality is fulfilling it.

The little fish was eaten by a bigger one, and that one by a bigger one and so on and on until eventually we come to man. It is becoming more and more true every day that as we multiply we become more like the little fish. I read recently that the entire population of the earth over the past two hundred thousand years does not equal the number of people being born in the world every twenty years at the present time. Regardless of numbers, there is not so much difference between the little fish and its feelings of identity and importance, the centralization in its little consciousness and in ours. We also do not want to be purposeless, we feel that we are really doing something of importance in our lives, but if we really look at ourselves, the majority of us are doing very little which is original, constructive, purposive—we are being lived rather than living. Can we not come to a point of realization that the purpose of our life lies, very much as the purpose of the little fish, not in what we achieve, but in what we sacrifice, not in what we build, but in what we surrender, what we give? Just as the little fish is unable to conceive of the various cycles in which it fits, and the larger whole of which it is a part, can we truthfully say that we can see the larger cycles? We can see the cycles of the fish, some of them, but are we not, in universal consciousness, far smaller than the little fish in the ocean?

Some people may feel that this is eliminating the last grain of worth that an individual has, and possibly it is; but there is another way to look at it which gives tremendous security, certainty, safety, and that is that whatever the little fish does, inescapably it will fulfill its purpose. In the same way, whatever we do, in whatever way we try to escape, we also will fulfill our purpose. Man's purpose is born with his birth, even if his death follows soon after. What one can do to conceive of one's life is to begin to comprehend that what we see can either be an incredible weight, the weight that what we can see is all there is; or, it can be a door, many doors, doors leading to the unknown.

Usually, when we begin to have a certain idea about meaning, purpose, we quickly build a wall around it, a wall without a door. We all know the mysticism of the horizon: the horizon is the limit of observation, the limit of the wavelength of light, the limit of the height from which we observe; it is the built-in limit of this planet, and beyond the horizon there is more than we can see. We all know that the horizon can never be reached, it always remains; could it not be that it is the same with our minds? Just as there is a limit to what we can see at any particular time, there is a limit to what we conceive at any particular time. When man is limited by his horizon he goes on a journey to see what is there where the earth and the sky meet, yet when he comes to the horizon of his mind, all too often he reacts by saying, "Now I have seen all there is to see." The horizon has then become a wall, a great impenetrable wall, the Berlin wall, the Great Wall of China, the barbed-wire wall of a concentration camp. Then we begin to ask ourselves, what can be the purpose of our living in this concentration camp? Certainly there must be some reason to be here, trapped in this wonderful Brave New World.

It is at this point that there begins what we call the inner life, a journey within, a search for truth, spiritual development, whatever you want to call it; the beginning of trying to go towards and beyond the horizons of our mind, trying to see further than the purposes which we set for ourselves, trying to experience more than we already know. It is at this point that we can begin to say that there is a definite elementary purpose that man has, after procreation and all of the other natural purposes, which we can call unconscious purposes. The first conscious purpose that we have is not to save the world, but to search for a purpose to save it for. As we begin to see, to unload this and so many other emotionally-laden, protective purposes which we have used to sentimentalize our lives, as we begin to push back, to go further and further into the horizon of our mind, past the limit of conceptualization, we go to search for the next link with which we will unmistakably, undeniably, just as the little fish did, conjoin.

I have a feeling that most people in the world feel purposeless. They do not honestly know why they are alive; they often need a drug to kill the question. They go through all sorts of contortions to congratulate themselves and others that they are on the right path, because basically they know inside themselves that they are not. My feelings could be wrong, but they become more strong for me every day. People vegetate all over the world; some in Ghana, some in India, some in England, some in America, some in Russia and, just like growing string beans, they climb up because there is a force to climb within them, but they do not know why, and that is the thing which they try hardest to forget. We can forget it for a while; you can forget it by the interest in learning, by the ambition for power, by the desire for pleasure, yet this question will remain to the end of our lives. The more superficial people are (if I can make such a judgment) the more they have been able to turn off this signal from within. Why?

Some people may say at this point that, if they understand what has been presented, man has no purpose. The answer is yes and no; man has no purpose who does not search for it. He who searches for it will never find it; he will go across a thousand purposes, a thousand passes of the ever-expanding horizon, and never come to an end. It is precisely this which justifies all the philosophy, search for meaning, religion, devotion, churches, gurus, yoga, because there are so many people who are searching, each in his own way, at his level or her degree of conceptualization, from his or her cultural point of view. It is this agonizing search for a purpose, for an answer—for purpose gives meaning and wholeness, it gives security—which has caused the whole religious trip that man has been on. Now we can begin to understand these religions a little more, we can begin to classify them into those which help to put the question to sleep, which are the opium philosophies, and those which help to break the question open, deeper and deeper into ourselves. You can begin to see that the majority of people have always gone and will always go to that easy path of putting the question to sleep. What is my purpose? Put it to sleep. We cannot face that we are purposeless, that when we satisfy our physical and psychological needs we end up by being incredibly complicated things. But why? For what? For mutual congratulation?

Purpose lies in its search, not in its protection or its justification. This is the difference between the little fish and the little man: the little fish cannot search for its purpose, and man can. I do not know whether you sense the wonderful courage and hope of that statement, the positive power of that point of view. The difference between what makes us human and what makes us animal is that we can search in the void and purposeless creation of illusion for a purpose.

Some people may become lost in this approach or will begin to wonder how to search. It may not be simple—no one can truthfully say how—but there are some things which we can learn about it. First, we must free ourselves, discard, as much as possible, sentimental attachments to right and wrong, good and evil, to our own importance. These things make sense, they are simple; it does not take a whole book of proof for each of us to see clearly that in the universe we are not important. Our own importance is to ourselves, and the attachment to it is sentimental.

Second, the purpose cannot be found in denying life. If one is looking for the purpose of life it must be found in being alive to the fullest, in the very essence of that experience. This is an important deviation from many different teachings which look for the purpose of life outside life; or after death, which is simply an unwillingness to face the fact that we will all die; or, in some artificial application of it such as denying natural emotions, natural functions, normal life-energies and directions. The first and foremost purpose of the little fish, for instance, is procreation, and as there are different levels of purposes, so one of the purposes of man and woman is procreation—a normal, natural, healthy experience through which we must go. That is one place where the purpose may be sought, not in being a monk or an ascetic.

Sufism does not look for fulfillment of the purpose of life in any artificial application, but in life itself, which is why, symbolically, we say that our bible, our holy book, is nature, the book of nature. It is the only scripture that can really enlighten, can help us to free ourselves from over-emphasis on our own importance. It shows what peace really is: not the peace of sitting on a soft carpet between four walls, but the peace of nature, which includes tension, thereby making the peace real. Not the peace of a park where all the weeds are nicely pulled out, the roses neatly cut, the verges of the lawns kept straight and the fallen branches are gathered in—that is not nature, it is an artificial application of it.

Third, the purpose lies in the search which leads us to become lighter. What does that mean? I do not know, it is a subjective statement. If one moves in one direction to search

for a purpose, and finds it makes one feel much heavier—
"Oh my goodness, there is a crisis and I have to do something!"—then it is that purpose which individualizes, which
tends towards a fearful, messianic justification of our life.
The search for our purpose lies in a path which becomes
lighter and freer. As we rise from the earth we lose gravity,
we can jump and with one bound rise forever, losing the
resistance which brings us back to the heaviness of imperfection, to the density of manifestation—because, in any case,
we all know that we are destined to go there, whether or not
we believe in life after death. At that point of separation
there is a loss of weight—bodily weight, mental weight,
emotional weight, all kinds of weight. If while alive in life we
search for a purpose, our purpose, a meaningful purpose that
is pursuable, balanced and consistent, it must be one which
leads to lightness, however we want to conceive of that
subjectively.

What a marvellous feeling if one could dance in life with
the joy and peace of saying, "There is not necessarily a cause
for my dance which is absolute; there is not necessarily a
purpose for my dance which limits its moving; there is only
the joy of the dance." If one begins to dance and says, "Now I
am going to dance because I am required to do the dance
because it is a good thing to do, because it will bring me
towards holiness," then the dance is meaningless, it becomes
a performance.

The conglomeration of modern life, of thoughts and
structures, science and philosophy and the marvellous details
of economic and social organization which we have built up
could be likened to an opera: a wonderful stage, a make-
believe thought out in the infinitesimal detail that an ant can
experience. The opera seems to be a legend, something
which was true at one time, but became a legend because we
forgot what it was really all about; we forgot what really
happened and so we re-enact it, we act it and re-enact it. So
we all go, the stagehands, the singers, the violinists, the
conductors, and we perform this fantastic opera. Yet deep
within our subconscious, all of us know that the legend was
true, but we wonder, what really happened?

Eventually one or two rebels leave the opera scene, ponder, return, remove themselves from the noise and the beauty, the drama and the marvellous stage which weighs incredibly in the power of its entertainment, in its hypnotic trance. As one walks out of the door, out into the forest, one can experience the legend of the opera, but new subtleties also come. The whole weight of what happened in the opera lightens, and then we will suddenly have a vision of what really did happen. This is the mystic path. Purpose he searches for, resigned that it shall never be found.

July 23, 1973

AGGRESSION

We are trying to cover the whole realm of existence, life, reality, and to assemble that into the meaningful whole we can use to approach the relation of ourself with whatever is not ourself. The previous chapters on reality, causation, purpose, are the philosophical base for any other contemplation, and in the next few chapters we will begin to look at the individual, with the questions in mind, what can I do? Can I live? Can I develop? How can I approach, individually, this universe? Approach it as an illusion in which, from a more mystical point of view, you try to approach meaning from void, from the point at which all things resolve themselves into nothing. That voidness gives the greatest base, a base not of attachment and fear, but of freedom and insight, with which our mind can understand more deeply why things appear the way they do, and yet are not. The first few chapters may have been a negation of reality, of truth, of purpose, of cause, of absolute values, even a negation of meaning. Now we come to the individual, and naturally the first question which comes to mind is: if I live in an illusion, if my very identity is an illusion, if the things in which I believe are only temporary and find their existence primarily in my fears, in my faiths, how can I live? What can I do? How, in the illusion, can a worthwhile function for my life be found?

I am not going to try to prove the existence of our individuality—I rather doubt it—but there is some kind of life-force energy which unites the various parts of our being in a certain purposive function or direction. To look at it from a physical point of view: we have bodies, we have eyes, we have ears, and something co-ordinates their functions. Although what we see and hear are illusions, within those illusions there seems to operate a certain purposive continuity. Part of our individuality is this self-perpetuating, continuous energy which integrates all the loose parts of our being—our emotions, our desires, our hopes, our fears—into an apparently united and directed entity. This energy, this force which pushes us forward, is aggression. The aggressive force of man is the main thing working behind our identity, our self. It is very difficult to accept that it is almost impossible to take an action in thought or in matter without aggression. We attach to the word "aggression" connotations of bad, destructive, and completely reject the idea that our every thought and action is an imposition on the peace which reigns.

There are ways to prove that aggression is the driving-force of man, proofs not of fact but which should be considered and then subjectively evaluated. If we look at evolution, we cannot escape from observing that it is always the most aggressive that survives: the strongest buck, the best hunting lioness, the fastest shark, the smartest fox, but on an even more original level, the strongest plants, the drone with the greatest driving-force to reach the queen bee ahead of the ten thousand other drones. We ourselves are the products of the fastest sperm. The most aggressive force is the one which over eons of time has perpetuated itself. It is the aggression within us to be, to know, to think, to feel, to act, to understand, to give, to pray, to love . . . with every new act in our existence there is another rape of the peace of the universe.

Hopefully you will now come to see the word "aggression" not exclusively with the connotation of destruction, but with the connotation of self. What was the force behind the first crawling kind of fish to inch up and up and eventually, despite itself, despite the very functions of its organism, to leave the water and go onto the land? It was an incredible driving-force to have more territory, more food, more light, and it is exactly the same force that brought the cockroach into evolution which has brought man to bury himself in his cities. There is always a force to know more, to do better, to simplify, to achieve, to correct, to progress, to expand territory, to expand power, to express more, to own more. What is the difference between a rhinoceros defecating in a little territory, a dog urinating on a fire hydrant, and the real-estate ownership that man lives with today? There is no difference at all; it is still the same aggressive territorial behavior, to possess, to have.

Imagine a meadow somewhere on earth, beautiful, undisturbed, with a little pond mirroring the sky, a little frog croaking by the pond; the shadows, darkness and light, various shades and hues of green; totally peaceful, silently existing. Now comes man, and the first thing he does is to say, "Oh, what a beautiful meadow." And he steps into it and takes possession of it. Now the meadow has been destroyed, because the beauty of its non-existence, of its not having been observed, of its existing without consciousness, has been violated. It has now become part of the known card-deck of what I own in my mind, what I have experienced, what I have conquered, what I have observed. The better and more detachedly you begin to think about your own existence, the more you will see that behind your every act and thought, be it to do good or to do evil, be it to give or to take, to love or to hate, there is the same force that made the little creepy-crawly mud-bug of three billion years ago become a cockroach, the same force that has unleashed wars, the same force which makes us ever desire more peace, more knowledge, more realization, more spirituality. Why should we be spiritual? Why did the trilobite crawl into the light and become a cockroach? Why are we looking for more light? What is the difference? Only consciousness. As our consciousness, our ability to conceptualize ever increases, the level of our aggression becomes more and more powerful, and also more and more refined. Some day we will wage wars, not with weapons but with thoughts. Some day we will no longer search for knowledge that is permanent, we will search for knowledge that is temporary.

The first thing that a man or a woman must do is to accept his or her aggression, to make peace with it, understand it, be honest about it, at least to the self, and to begin to understand that development has always been a process, conscious or unconscious, of guiding the aggressive force to increase consciousness. Whether the trilobite became a cockroach, or the ape an ape-man, whatever biological and chemical changes take place as the aggressive force has evolved, progressed, expanded, it has always been an expansion of consciousness, an increase of awareness. Here, now, we complicated human beings have got to come to terms with our aggression. It is possible that we have reached the turning-point of the aggressive force: whereas previously it has always been the aggressive force which expanded consciousness, it may be that now in man, consciousness has reached the point where it can guide the aggression. That is really the first thing that all development is about. It is not about becoming holy or reaching illumination, going into samadhi, finding peace; those are concepts which are cultural and temporary, not really existing. It is simply about arriving at the point at which we are in control of our self, our nafs; the word "nafs" means our aggressive self, there is no other self. The self at peace is nothing, it is disintegrated, it has unbecome, it has transcended.

As soon as you find that the most important thing to do in life is to arrive at the point where your consciousness can begin to guide your aggression the question comes up, how? Before beginning to find out how it can be done, it must be clear that it is a process of psychological self-development. It brings us back to the old words, "to thine own self be true." It is a process in which we can begin to see the real reasons why we say what we say, why we do what we do, why we hide what we hide, why we reach for what we reach for; it is very difficult to be honest with oneself. It is difficult enough to see that most of the things which we accept in our value-structure, in our way of thinking, in the formation of our knowledge, are flat earths, concepts inherited from the dreams of the past, from the romance of the future, without integrity.

Now to investigate: why do we travel? Or should we say, what are we running away from? What commitments are we afraid to make to the world? What are we trying to hide in permanent flight? Or we could ask, why do we always like good food? Why are so many of us food-conscious? Why are we so bent on self-love? Why do we try to feed, to pity? With what love are we trying to substitute the love that we really desire? They say people who eat a lot of sweets, and this is an age of sweetness, miss affection in their lives. These are simple examples, and there are many more subtle ones which will show that much of our functioning is sublimation, many of our thoughts are rationalizations, and the primary motivating force behind our actions is somewhere between justifying our own existence and denying the existence of others. We will indeed come to discover that we are far more aggressive than we would be willing to admit. Why am I shy? Shyness is often seated in finding oneself so much better than another that one withdraws. Why am I afraid or embarrassed? Very often these feelings are seated in not wanting to be known, because people will then find out how weak, humble, simple, how human we really are. The first answer to the question of what approach to take in the illusion of life is on a primarily psychological basis. Why do I perform spiritual exercises or meditations? Is it perhaps that you will then feel that you are better than others, or is it because you are trying to justify yourself?

The next question is, what tool can I use to understand my aggression psychologically and guide it better? There are definite answers to that, answers on a level which people sometimes reject as being part of reality. The first answer is: to be interested in everything. It is only by knowing what is outside us that we can come to know what is within us. Half or more than half of all the people in the world have, at a certain point, ceased to wonder. When we cease to wonder we have in a way ceased to live, we have come to an end. Another thing that can happen, and this is a very dangerous development of late, is that we remain interested, but only in our speciality; if we are car mechanics we will be interested in cars, if we are spiritual we will reject being interested in money or business.

The moment we begin to close ourselves off from the

whole, total, dynamic becoming process of life, we begin to close ourselves off in certain areas which we do not want to know within.

We can learn a lot from criminals about our own criminality. Is criminality an act only of commission, or also an act of omission? Is criminality an act only in matter, or is it also an act in thought? We can learn a lot from touching the earth: the wholesome influence of weeds or raccoons, the presence of the innocent, the sinless, the pure, the unconscious, in which the aggressive force is still so simplified and the consciousness so dormant. Nature can teach us justice, natural law can teach us relativity. The whole ecological interchange can teach us our own interdependence, something about our own role to harmonize in a great circular chain of life and death, in which we are very small links. The wind can teach us music, the seas can teach us everything. . . . Yet we continue in an erudite way to live in jungles of concrete with concretized minds, unable to unite with the outside and, by the same inability, with the inside. We all know that love is not obtained in the love we receive but in the love we give, but we often do not understand that recognition does not come in what we expect others to give us but in the recognition which we can give to others. So it goes, on and on, and we could continue to discuss for hours the subtle psychological process of becoming aware, of remaining interested in the world, thereby remaining ever searching in ourselves. No man has ever understood himself, no woman has ever come to know her real being, without having lived.

The first point then, is remain interested in everything, shut yourself off from nothing, neither from the good nor from the evil, as neither is permanently existing. And the second point is, live. We all long to live, and we go out and travel and hide. You can hide in a tomb and you can hide in flight, you can hide in protecting what you have. To live means to develop your potentials. Every person is born a musician, an artist, a scientist, a mathematician, a writer, a reader, every person is born to preach and to worship, every person is full of talents and abilities, but a bitter few of these ever develop. We talk about great people—Galileo for instance; we know him as a painter, a writer, a scientist, a philosopher, a thinker, a statesman, a military strategist. The difference between him and ourselves is that we are buried in our mediocrity and he was alive in his potentials. Every man and woman has these same potentials, but for many reasons we close them off. The primary reason is laziness, which is basically an unwillingness to suffer. Think of the value of money; money is always and everywhere. Think of two people with the same intelligence quotient, the same potentials, the same heritage, having gone to the same university, with the same diplomas, the same background and the same abilities: one inherits a million dollars, the other earns it—a tremendous difference. The one who earned the money probably suffered and worked for it, so that the intrinsic value of the money for him will be quite different than for the other. One developed his potentials and the other did not. You may ask, why does one earn money, why does one earn anything? When you die it is of no use to have earned possessions that you cannot take with you. The only thing you can take along is that which is carried in consciousness.

What is carried in consciousness?

Experience.

In our consciousness we know the smell of a rose; it is not a physical nor even a mental knowledge, it is a completely abstract concept which has come through experience. The whole subjective realm of the conditions when we smelled it, what happened to us, our thoughts and our awareness, both consciously and unconsciously—that is the reality, those are the things which we earn. That is why we must develop our potentials, because it is through developing every potential that one can earn the wide variety of experience which is the richness, the real richness of the illusion of life.

As for the question of what one can do about this imponderableness of life, it is valuable to compare man with machine. A computer has a limited memory; does anyone know the maximum amount of things, experiences, memories, thoughts, feelings, emotions that the human mind can conceive of? It may be limited also; try to reach that limit. Try to reach the point in the real maturity of having lived that you can say, "To the innermost core of my being, I have lived. I am satisfied. I have experienced everything there is for me to experience. I have learned everything I really can learn. I have done everything that with this body, mind and spirit I could do." What an incredible, peaceful, mellowing strength that thought would be. Think of approaching death, which we all will reach, luckily, knowing that we have really lived.

Whereas the first two things which you can do were aggressive, becoming things, the third is to try to detach, to unwind, to let go and become indifferent, lose weight, unload. Let things happen, try not to express anything, not to be anything—be empty. Realize that while it is true that everything matters, at the same time nothing matters; everything is important, and yet everything is nothing. Every thought you have is passionately filled with the quality, the vibration, of meaning, purpose, cause and effect, and at the same time that thought is completely inconsequential. There is not anything that one man, nor one million men, could do that would be of any consequence in the universe, not even in the universe we know, let alone the universe which we do not know.

Man, be free, let go, be indifferent. Learn to laugh at your own impotency, learn to realize that we are like tops, spinning and spinning, and eventually the spinning comes to an end. How marvellous, finally the top can flop over and be still. It is in temporariness that eternity is experienced. Woman, let go, be an independent beauty queen at freedom's emancipation. Man engenders through woman's womb the conic animation of rapture; that lives on. The decadence of love denies only its possession and never touches your life. What one lets go can live on.

It may seem to be contradictory to say, develop your potentials, become, do this, do that, and at the same time say, drop it all, throw the whole thing in the garbage, do nothing, let go—yet that is mysticism. The mystic who fights without anger, the dervish who travels and yet thinks he is always at home, the thinker who thinks and thinks and then comes to the thought that not one of his thoughts was worthwhile thinking, and therefore continues to think—they have the freedom which allowed them to begin to live a different kind of life, not a life of tombstones, still or moving, in which we bury ourselves, but a life wherein we accept the eternal reality of our temporary nature, where we find peace and harmony with the inconsequentiality of logic, where we even come to see the meaning of nihilism.

Gradually, in the progression of this line of thought, we will look at the disciplines of mind needed to remain continuously interested, the methods by which we can discover and develop our potentials, and some ways in which we can unload all that our aggression has brought us—until eventually we will come to the point at which a certain new man or woman can integrate itself out of our confused state, a person whom we could call human. To find our own human quality is the final remaining life value. This in its purest form is aggression.

July 30, 1973

INTEREST IN EVERYTHING

In going a little deeper into the discipline of the mind in being continuously interested in everything, we should not lose sight of the fact that in this illusionary existence in which purpose is not really separate from life, everything man does is done either in vain or in vanity. The mystic chooses, rather than to do things in vanity, to act in vain, chooses rather than to find that nothing is interesting, to be interested in everything, while knowing that there is nothing to be known. This is a very important and powerful point: that life, existence, purpose, meaning, reality, logic, progress, evolution, all these and many other things, exist only subjectively in our mind, in our life experience, in our value structure. Although there is nothing to be known, although the greatest purity is in not knowing, the mystic attempts to know everything. This may seem contradictory, but it is the first concrete, meaningful key to our attitude in life.

Living in vain is a new kind of attitude; it has to do with what we realize out of the experiences that life has brought us, or what we have made out of them. When a candle burns, it emanates heat and light, it gives of itself. Its very existence is transmitted as it burns, and after the candle has gone it is soon forgotten. We might say that in its burning it is accomplishing a purpose, but if the sun was shining or the light was on, the candle would be burning in vain. It would bring us light, but the light is always there, just as the darkness is always there, and we burn the candle to counter the darkness, to enable us to see. But should we see? Should there really be light when there already is light? Should there be light when we ask it to counter the darkness? If you think in a subtle way, accepting that everything happens which is supposed to happen, you begin to wonder whether you should light the candle, take this action, live your life.

To all these questions there are as many answers as there are minds and people. There are as many answers in every person as there are moods and attitudes, yet the person who has sufficient interest to look at everything, to look at the inter-relationship of himself with all that is around, will find and uncover continually more and more meaning and meaninglessness.

The average farmer, about to sow some seeds, will not be thinking strenuously of anything, or if he is he will be wondering whether the seeds will grow properly, if the weather will be favorable and whether the market will offer the right price. Most of us do not think very far ahead in the things that we do, and very few of us think far behind. What farmer will be interested in whether or not the seeds should be sown at all, or in the meaning behind his sowing the seeds? The present and the future inter-relate. The seeds he sows will grow into a plant which will take up an empty peaceful space. Few will think that this plant will give different insects the chance to come to it and to suffer by being trapped or captured by others. Few will think of the incredible suffering, life and survival beyond the little plant that they sow. Few will be interested in whether the people who eat the grain will receive healing from it. Few will think that it might be better not to grow food, so that the earth could return to peace and the long drawn-out emptiness of the lives of millions of people might be altered in another way. Very few people are interested in what they are actually doing, therefore they live a very superficial life. Generally we do what is easiest, what we like to do, which means that we confine ourselves to what we know and do not open ourselves to new things, which we might like far more. It means that we often do not open ourselves to the experience, the satisfaction, the crucifixion of having done what we do not like doing. Because we are not really interested in the interrelationship, in the meaning, in the function of our existence in the universe, it has no meaning. Meaning comes into the consciousness which is aware, which can see; meaning comes to the heart that has bled, that has given; meaning comes to the mind that has thought, that has questioned, and to most of us it comes very little.

One could ask in which way the increase of our interest in everything would help us to develop greater knowledge, greater wisdom. It is important to understand the meaning of the word, "development." Grass was developed, through man's interest, into wheat, and the only way to see that wheat was developed is by comparing it, not to wheat, but to grass. Thus you can understand that development has no meaning in an isolated cell; it has meaning only in a scale of existence, albeit illusionary.

I once knew an old lady, a wise but average American. She had met and worked for many saints and sages who came to America, people who, in their way of thinking, were masters. All of them had lived in monasteries and followed rigorous practices and disciplines and had developed strong magnetism and influence. When they visited America, however, all of them fell sooner or later—either through sudden wealth, sudden sexual freedom, the incredible power they had over people, or by leaving again, never having understood the real need of a search, never having seen what American culture was all about. The conclusion this lady reached was that it was easy to be a saint in the Himalayas. To a certain degree these people had developed because they were extremely interested, they focused their whole mind, thought, concentration, life energy on one or two points, in total disregard of and isolation from the real illusionary world. When they transplanted themselves from Kashmir or Rishikesh to Los Angeles or New York City, they were faced with people with thoughts, emotions and ideas which they had never met, never been tested with, and never developed within themselves. In the end she saw that a good person living in the world is more developed and has more meaning and depth than all those "masters."

It is true that up to a point you can develop by isolating

yourself and meditating, but that is living without any comparison, it is not developing to that height, that level of thought, that ability to conceive which, as a worldwide evolution, is becoming possible. Many people are interested in meditation, but not so many are interested in computer programming. Yet computer programming is so similar that you could call it meditation. Most people would think that it would seem artificial, few would understand the incredible wonder that we have been able to capture consciousness, at least in part, functioning separately from ourselves. We are all interested in mantrams, but few of us realize that the words with extremely powerful logarithmic and other functional effects used by programmers are exactly the same as mantrams. We are all interested in yoga, but few of us realize that the simple exercises of the Canadian Air Force perform the same physiological and psychological tuning on the mechanism of our psyche. Very few of us have realized that as we move on from culture to culture, from specialization to specialization, gradually more and more normal functions of our life need to be replaced by artificial things. Few of us see that although we may know more, although we can conceive to a higher scale of abstract thinking, at the same time the interest, the passion, the experience of being at one with things with which we need to be at one, is being diminished.

We do not know how most of the things in our life work. We flick on the radio or the television and they work, we turn on the tap and it works. A typical example is the birth-control pill. Less than half of the people using the pill know how it works. Thousands of people in the world are searching for somebody to give them meaning in their life, while all that really needs to happen is for them to take an interest in all that comes to them. When a car passes you, do you ever look at the licence plate and wonder why it has that number? If someone cuts in on you on the road, do you wonder why? Do you look at him? There are three kinds of people who cut in: those who cut in hard and look the other way, those who look and look away, look and then look away again, and there are those who cut in and look straight at you. What is the difference? When you cut in on them, which category do you fall into?

The whole crux of development is that no one can do it for you; you have to do it yourself; but there are certain rules which will help you to be more able to function with interest in life. The first rule is that everything is equally meaningless, therefore you can be interested in everything. If there was one thing which in and of itself was absolutely meaningful, then that is the only thing in which you should be interested, but if everything is meaningless you can easily and with complete indifference be interested in everything. If you are so interested in something that you can no longer be interested in something else, the beginning of conservatism sets in, the beginning of closing the mind to the only permanency, which is change.

Everything is like a cloud of thousands of butterflies flying along your path; look at it, dance with it and let it go on its way. Otherwise you will become a butterfly collector.

The second rule is that in the experience of being interested, there must be passion. If you are going to hate someone, hate him passionately, because the meaninglessness meaning which you will experience will be far greater. If you are going to love someone, let your heart break, bleed to death—because the totality of that experience, in the end, is going to give a far greater value than if you give yourself conditionally.

The third rule is that everyone has a sleep cycle. Life is a dance and every person has a particular rhythm in which he or she fits best. Every day we go through cycles of activity and passivity, we go through cycles in which we should be reading a book or discussing philosophy, and other cycles in which we should be playing soccer or digging graves. We go through cycles of strong expression and strong impression. There seem to be four basic cycles: one is to rise at about five-thirty and go to bed at about eight-thirty; one is to rise at about seven and go to bed at about ten; one is to get up at between eight-thirty and ten o'clock and go to bed at about midnight; and then there are many who are at their most strong after midnight, about two o'clock. In fact, it is a tradition, whatever teacher you follow, that the best time for meditation is two o'clock in the morning. If you can learn to be more in harmony with these cycles as they flow in yourself, all sorts of things will suddenly become soft and transparent, new beauty and subtlety will appear. We all want to feel high and good. We can take drugs or meditate, but one of the best ways to feel high is to be tired, a certain satisfied tiredness, when there is not too much food in the stomach and not too much activity left to do—a physical rather than a mental tiredness. You must be able to have enough chemical action in your life cycle, so that twice a week you have been really, wonderfully tired; not overworked or depressed, just satisfied, feeling in your bones that you have lived.

The fourth rule is that there is nothing that cannot be learned. When we stop learning we are no longer children; there is not really any period between being a child and being an old man or woman. A child learns language, muscle coordination, psychology, how to get his way, how to do things, how to behave, and he learned these things practically, not theoretically. Suddenly we reach a point when we can no longer learn, primarily because we have no interest and do not make an effort, but also because the methods of education through which we have gone have forced us to learn with the mind active and the body still. The body should sit still when it is tired, so there is a dissociation in our education, an alienation, and eventually learning stops. Being interested really means wondering, being ready to learn, and life is the greatest teacher. We can learn to a certain extent from books, depending upon how we read and how we learn, but the real learning is in doing it, in the direct contact with it. There is nothing which cannot be learned. There is not one normal person who could not learn and understand anything. All of life is a game of learning and unlearning, there has to be learning in order for there to be unlearning. Learning is establishing knots of relationships, and unlearning is unravelling these knots and seeing what they have bound together. Learning and unlearning are both spiritual development; the more you can develop, the more you must have to unlearn; the more you must have to unlearn, the more you must have to learn.

The last rule is to be interested in the things you see that interrelate with you. You cannot be interested in absolutely everything at the same time, but if you follow the rule to have a questioning attitude, why you are here, what your relationship is to what you do, this continuous researching and evaluating will always bring some answer. It is when you become interested in things which do not relate to you that there is no answer, simply because there is not yet any relevant interaction to you. The answer is what you can see, and therefore, for every person the answer is different.

These are all simple but important points. Accept the freedom to see that nothing matters, approach everything that does not matter with passion. The matter becomes the passion that you give to it, but this can only work when you remember that nothing matters, otherwise it is not passion but possession. Examine your rhythm, your life cycle. Most people sleep too much because they sleep at the wrong time; if you could sleep exactly when you should sleep, you would not have to sleep for so long. If you cannot do enough to be healthily tired, then your life is unhealthy at its very base. People with no vitality, which comes from lack of exercise, are not alive, they are hanging around, and they are the ones who are searching for something fantastic outside—but where? Interest in everything that living brings before the screen of consciousness, with passion and indifference engenders meaning in the meaninglessness of the passing illusion. That meaning I call independence.

August 6, 1973

POTENTIAL

Before going into the subject of developing one's potential, it is important to make clear that these chapters cannot be viewed separately: each one must be seen in the light of the previous weave of thought, and as we weave on, a pattern will emerge. In making the pattern one needs to understand the perfection and imperfection of each thread; nevertheless, one should try to grasp everything in the totality of what is being presented and the purpose for it, so that it will be as meaningful as it can be.

The question of how we can develop our potential can be looked at from the point of view of each of us as an individual, or it can be looked at from the point of view of humanity in history. Let us not forget that we are a race of the fauna of this planet and as near as we can tell—although we may each be as different as the leaves on a tree or the needles on a pine, as each design in nature is unique unto itself—we are also very much the same. We are all of one race, and every individual within that race in the past and in the present represents some of all of the capacities that any one member of that race has, to a greater or lesser degree. In using the word "race," I do not mean the black race, white race, yellow, green or orange races, I mean Homo sapiens, the erect man. There are people who can climb palm trees many many feet into the air without any aid, and if any of us were to try to do that we could not. Yet if you were to bring that person down from the tree and sit beside him, you would find that you are brothers of the same race, and that his particular capability is also in you. Athletic games are held regularly and great champions are found who can out-jump, out-swim, out-run, out-throw any of us, yet the very fact that they can out-run us means that we also have that same capability of life.

These examples are rather simple, but when we look at the other side of the coin and think of our own potentials, we are generally blinded by the extremely limited environment and culture in which we have grown up or in which we live, and we think only of the potentials that we know. If we live in a world of offices and we are young and starting as office hands, we will see in our universal potential that we could also become a clerk, or that we could become a managerial secretary. On the other hand, if we lived in another society, then we would see our potential within the framework of that environment. The first step to take in trying to see how to develop one's potentials, then, is to see the total potential of the human race. Everything that man has ever done up to now we can do, each one of us. We may not be able to jump as far as the longest jump that has ever been made, we may not be able to type as fast as the fastest typist, we may not be able to reach a level of abstraction and conceptualization as expansive and encompassing as that of our best scientists and philosophers, but all that they can do is done by that tool called a human being, and that human tool is what we are also.

Rajasthan is a province in India, a dry sandy land without a single large river; therefore wells have to be drilled, which is no easy task, but for the people of Rajasthan it means digging wells. First comes the question of where to dig, where is there water? Then, how to get through the sand which collapses inwards, how deep to dig; and finally, how to bring the water up? A little boy here asked his mother for water, and she asked him how the water gets into the tap, but he did not know. Yet every little boy in Rajasthan knows how water comes to his hut. Most little boys in Rajasthan have never heard of the words "intuition" or "dowsing," yet every boy knows that some day he too will go to look for the place to dig a well on his own land. He will never think of it as a special gift, an exotic ability, an occult power—he will do it and die in the eternity of the passing of generations performing an act of faith, knowledge, bringing into reality a potential which we also have, which every human being has, and yet to which, by the very nature of the specialization in which we live today, we are completely blind. Water comes when you turn on the tap, light comes when you switch on the switch, and therefore the real contact with life is not made.

Once when I was driving round Rajasthan I needed water, and since I was a little used to judging a proper well I eventually found a very large, very deep well, where you could almost, subjectively speaking, see the water flowing as if the well were over an underground river. I stood there with my bucket on a rope, and as I let it down I found that the rope was too short, so I took some more rope from the car, made a knot and lowered the bucket. As I drew the bucket up, full of water, the rope broke, exactly at the knot. Why did it break at the knot? Because I did not know how to make a knot. Then along came a peasant, a simple man who did not know how to read or write, who had probably never left a fifteen- or twenty-square-mile area, who could not possibly begin to imagine all that exists in the world; there was the man with no education at all, and there was I with whatever my university degree means, and yet this man could bring my bucket out and, on top of that, do me the favor of untwisting my rope and splicing the two ends together over a much larger distance, so that at that spot it was in fact stronger.

I began to realize then that my intelligence, my knowledge was useful only in a society where water comes out of the tap, where the light goes on when you switch it on, where you learn by reading a book, where someone teaches you, where there is no real self-development in terms of survival, and where we continue to develop only in terms of the specialization of the city. This may not seem so real to you, as you did not go through the experience and the subtlety of thought and the contact with the reality of that moment. I also began to see, as you must try to see, that whereas we learn music, no African tribesman ever learns it; he does it, he grows into it. We learn counting, we learn thinking, we learn analysis, we learn logic and yet potentially we do not need to learn anything. The biggest block to unlocking potential, to developing potential, is thinking and accepting that one needs to learn, one needs to acquire theoretic, abstract knowledge. All of man's development has been into that which he was developing, out of which he derived the theoretical knowledge.

It may be difficult for you to conceive, but basically there is nothing that you cannot do; the block is that you think that you need to learn it. If you began to do it, you would learn three, four, five times as fast as you would at school. It does not mean that going to school is wrong, it means that there is something wrong with the methods of education. A child learns a language from nothing, without books, without grammar, just by doing it. Sixteen hundred years ago in the time of Muhammad and still, until only forty or fifty years ago, there used to be meetings of villagers when, for whole weekends long, every person freely improvised poetry. Now we like to read poetry, but if any of us had to sit down and write a poem we could not, or it would not be a good poem, or it would be difficult to make it flow. I do not know whether you realize that; think of those uncivilized, illiterate, wild Arabs, living in the time of Muhammad without grammarians, without writing, without anyone who could do the things that we can do, and not only remembering thousands and thousands of words of poetry developed in their little villages in the past, but going on and having competitions and agreeing amongst themselves as to who was the best poet. Gypsies never learn music formally, there is nobody who tells them to practise from four to eight, they do not read a book or have notation, although they invented the binary notation system we use in computers today, but in the same way that a little child learns its language from its mother, the gypsy continues to learn music.

By being alive in life, keeping an interest open, you can develop whatever you put your mind to.

This is an extremely important point about spirituality as well; we see more and more books about yoga, about metaphysics, about meditation, more and more explanations of how to do it. The first thing that happens when someone wants to meditate is that he finds a book on how to do it, but the people who were originally involved in these things, from whom did they learn? They learned from themselves, from simply developing the potential within themselves, from having an interest and putting their minds actively, passionately, into that process. Did they ever have so strongly the man/woman idea that we have? We seem to think that a man can repair a car and a woman cannot. Why not—is a woman's brain different from that of a man? We all see intellectually that this man/woman idea is a block, simply a specialization-block of society, but in the same way there are blocks with which every one of us prevents potentials that we have from coming out.

If we analyze within ourselves the things that go into developing some ability, some potential, we find that of course we require practice because there is a gap between the thought and its execution. Chopin might have reached the point at which he could play what he heard, what he thought and felt; on the other hand, it might be that having developed as far as he had, he heard so much more that he still could not play it, because the gap between the thought and its execution must always exist. So we need to practice.

If you are looking for a particular development, the answer lies strictly with thought power which, if you look at it, has two aspects. The first aspect is, within the thought power, an act of faith; there is no faith but in oneself. Never mind how intelligent a person is or how strong his or her concentration, if he cannot make the mental act of faith, which cannot be described or defined—it is more a thought-form, an action of thought—he will not develop, or will develop with much greater difficulty. If you cannot make this act of faith, that second aspect—which is to concentrate, to contemplate, to exercise mentally upon something of yourself which you want to develop—though that aspect of thought power goes on, it has no effect. You can easily divide the people whom you know between those who are able abstractly to make an act of faith, which is a thought action, and those who cannot.

A typical example to explain the act of faith can be seen in the first effort to walk. A little baby a few months old cannot stand, it has no balance, it is not strong, it cannot support its weight well, it is not coordinated, its muscles do not work well, every possible mechanical explanation would prove that it could not do what it wanted to do, and yet it wants to reach something. That is development, wanting to reach something. We can only reach what we can see, we can only develop that which we are able to conceive within ourselves. Some of us want to be doctors, but only because we know that there is such a thing as a doctor. In the same way, a little child sees its mother, or it sees a rock, or a flower, a pattern on the rug, or a color which interests it. It sees something, and without really cogent, coherent, rational thought, it makes an act of faith that it can reach it; maybe it is sitt ing, maybe it is lying; from whatever position it is in, it begins to worm its way towards where it is going.

The first trauma could also start at this point if the child is not growing up in an environment of security, because while it wants to reach something, it cannot have that same unqualified confidence, it is afraid and does not understand its fear. It may be the tension of the mother, it may be something else. . . . I use the example of a baby because its thoughts are not rational, clear-cut, definable thoughts that we can look at, like $1 + 1 = 2$. These thoughts are on the threshold between being a thought and not being a thought, and yet they are at the most instinctive, most intuitive level of our existence. You can become a painter, a musician, a racing-car driver, an elephant-tamer, it does not matter what, if you can make that act of faith out of which the thought can be executed.

This is very often where mental illness, fears in life, shyness and all sorts of other things come into play, because as the thought begins to execute itself, begins to take form, something comes in to stop it, to prevent it from finding the foundation from which the other aspects of thought power can come. That other aspect, which was referred to as concentration, contemplation, is simply a coordination of hierarchical commands. Go back to the example of the baby—it needs to worm its way to where it is going, so some command has to come for an arm to move, for a leg to go forward, for the motor muscles to begin to function, and those commands have to happen in the right order. If the leg moves before the arm, it will topple over, or it will stand upside down. Here is another area where we are often enemies of ourselves because so often we attempt the things we want to do, the things we want to develop, without due consideration for harmony. Harmony and hierarchy are the same thing: harmony is just another way to look at hierarchy; harmony is pleasing hierarchy, functioning hierarchy. Without that harmony we become frustrated and impatient. We find that the distance between our abstract thought or desire and our physical execution of it is too great, so a feed-back system sets in and we say, "I thought that I could do that, but I can't." If this happens enough, we lose once again the ability to make a thought act of faith. This is why the mystics always say that the person who has success will have success, because every success will be an impression and a further re-impression of the ability to succeed, the ability to bridge the desire and the execution; whereas a person who has failures continues to be impressed with this inability to make a bridge, and therefore he is blocked.

If this chapter is to have meaning, it cannot be about success, for in wanting to explain success, one fails it. For those of us who have faith in hierarchical patience to translate our thought into action, the only limit to our development is the number of hours there are in a day. But most of us are somewhere in another situation where we cannot quite step over this threshold, we feel that we want to develop but we cannot—why? First of all, no one can develop without the foundation of having accepted himself. Why are we the children of these parents? Why were we born in that astrological period? Why have we inherited a certain form, a certain interpretation of the unlimited heredity which is available? It is of no use to analyze why you are a Scorpio, a Leo or an Aries—you are what you are, and that is where you must begin. Most people make the mistake of wanting to be different from what they are, of wanting to be like someone else. You cannot develop someone else's mind: it is your mind, your body, your soul, your totality of being. Accept that, make peace with it. You and I, we, are each a particular imperfect drawing of an idea. Why want to be like another imperfect drawing? Although that other drawing perfects some of our imperfections, it also has mistakes which we do not have. Be what you are.

Once we accept what we are, there must be some guide-lines as to what our potential is, and basically these can be determined by every person intuitively. You do not need psychology or astrology to explain to you what you are, but because we are so afraid to accept ourselves, to understand what we are, how we tick, how we work, maybe we need some help, and of course there is help. There is astrology, there is psychology, there are other people giving you feedback about yourself in different guises, but no help can be taken as absolute. If you read an astrological book which says (to give an example which is not valid) you are forever condemned to be afraid of goats because you are a fish, then that is not a book to help you, it is a book to hinder you, to limit you, not to uplift you but to classify. If there is a teacher who tells you what horrible things you were in your previous life, and therefore you will forever suffer in this life, this again is what the power trip of mankind is all about: trying to limit, to control, classify and condemn everybody in little cubbyholes. These are part of the whole range of limitations which make man an inanimate object. I can tell you what you are forever condemned to be, every one of you: you are condemned to be a philosopher, a scientist, a lover, a painter, a musician, a hunter, a parent, a child, a friend, so try to leave aside those things which do not give you freedom.

At this point another problem arises. A pigeon is one of the fastest flying birds in the world, its navigational system is marvellous, but it has one flaw which we use to great advantage. If you take a pigeon and put it in a little cage and lock the cage and keep it there for a certain period, it will slowly forget that it was once free. You make it used to the fact that it gets its food from you, you make it used to the security of its cage. You only need to keep it in that cage long enough for the memory of what it really is, a free bird, to wane. When that has happened you can open the cage and let the bird fly, knowing for certain that it will always return. You can take the bird to Africa, let it free there and it will come back. We are very much like pigeons; we always home in to a certain security which is all that we can remember. We may have been free before, we have some vague longing, some unclear recollection of it, but we always home back in. Even if the food we get there is not quite right, even if the cage is too small, even if all sorts of other things are not right, even if due to over-population we begin to fight, we home back in.

When man suddenly finds himself free, he has the same reaction as the pigeon—he is afraid, he does not know where he is, he wants to know that he is somewhere, he wants to have a center. We can fly around, some of us twenty miles, some of us two hundred miles, but then what if we lose the center?

There is definitely a trap which we long for, the cave of the early erect man, a place to hide, to feel safe and be at home. As you look at the sociology of religious, spiritual, moral and governmental development, from whichever angle you want to approach it, you will see that man has always tended to reconstruct his cave. He always tends to have a more comfortable cave, a nicer cave, a better-lit cave; we now have burglar alarms instead of look-outs, but we still hide in a cave. On the mental level you can understand it in the same way. The early cave-man facing the unknown—thunder, death, destiny, frustration; he felled a tree and it fell the wrong way—why? And it seemed as if there was some power which he could not understand. He needed to understand that power, so he needed to contain it, just as he needs to understand his freedom and contain that, and therefore he lives in a cave.

One's development is very much tied in with one's security, because over time, due to the trauma of life, of existence, we have not been able to make that thought act of faith in ourself. We have had to construct a moral law, a god, a temple, a government, a school, a counsellor, a social worker, all these kinds of things on every level of our reality to help us over that threshold, and inasmuch as these things have been helps, they have become hindrances, because they are the things which continually channel our self-development, our potential, into certain pre-conceived, nicely defined specializations.

I read in the newspaper once that a man of twenty-four had committed suicide. He left a note to apologize to his parents and friends for what he was doing, but there was nothing left for him to live for. He wrote, "I have learned everything there is to learn, I know everything there is to know. Life has no taste, no meaning." The article went on to say that the man had probably the highest intelligence quotient of any living man tested. The genius of his thought-ability was greater than that of all the other five billion little ants that we are; he was doing his second or third doctorate at one of the famous California universities, and he committed suicide. He might have been the man to save mankind (whatever that means) but he could not find any meaning in life. What he did suddenly, quickly and effectively is what most of us do slowly, laboriously and ineffectively; what he did in one second, in an instant of doubt, is what we usually do in a long and dreary lifetime of slowly by slowly turning off interest, little by little losing vitality, finding meaning slipping through our fingers, and eventually living as ants. What point had this man reached? It was the point at which, somewhere in his mental security pattern, in order to continue to develop, he would have had to abandon, go out of, transcend his cave. One very often hears that real spiritual development is not learning, but unlearning. That is the same as saying that being a human being is getting out of that cave, losing all these marvellous structures, psychological, mental, social, religious structures, avenues, paths of thought, values, stepping out of all of that. As that man was faced with having known, within that which was defined, everything, there was no more taste left, there was no real contact.

Development, then, is essential to living. The end of development is the end of life, it is the grave, the cave. At first development comes within the cave, i.e., there needs to be security, safety, confidence, love, tranquility, to give to the intuition-thought, the thought which is not yet a thought and the intuition which is no longer an intuition, to give the possibility, the strength to take form, which is, "I have faith in myself." Once that faith-act, which is really the religion in which we are our own priest administering to ourselves the sacrament, can be made, we can leave the cave. When we are able to make the act of faith we must leave the cave; go north, south, east, west, up, down, all around, and learn, develop, grow, express, experience all that comes along. Without doing that we all come eventually to the same point that our young brother came to, finding that in the cave there is insufficient meaning and outside the cave we are afraid.

A few concluding thoughts must be shared in order to give light or meaning to the sense of developing at all. The first, which has already been given, is that without development there is death, just as without change there is no reality; that is probably the strongest reason for developing our potential. The second reason is that there is no purpose in living in the cave to hide in a scopeless life. As we leave the cave, as we make that act of faith, purpose, real purpose in life, real purpose in thought, in feeling, in action, in contemplation, begins to emerge, and that purpose is developing, learning.

Imagine: if we were to build a giant dam in the middle of a desert, we would find purpose because we would be building the dam. Why? Because we wanted to, because that is what we found sense in. Other people might come and say that it was senseless simply because they were not doing it. So it is with the great Egyptian pyramids. We can go and look at those marvellous structures and wonder what is their reason, and we should not overlook the fact that their reason is not in their being there, dead structures, their reason is in the experience of the builders. In life the purpose is in living, and the purpose unfolds as we develop, naturally—as we develop naturally. It will develop on and on, up to a point where we can say anew that there was no purpose. Whereas before we said that there was no purpose because we had blocked it from unfolding, now we can truly awaken to see that purpose is not necessary, which is a totally different experience.

There are these two aspects of developing, primarily by the mind: one is to think, to contemplate what we want to develop, to think of the execution of that which we want to develop; that is meditation, every thought is a meditation; that is clear to us and we can all understand it. The other thing is the aspect of thought power on the intuitive level; a thought which is not a thought, an intuition which is not an intuition; that we have faith in our thoughts, in ourself, in our development, we have faith in our purposelessness, we have faith in the purpose of our purposelessness. That act of faith, of and by itself, is a very meaningful and important thing; that is religion, that is spirituality, that is behind all other knowledges which develop.

August 13, 1973

RIGHT THINKING:

PART ONE

I am not an expert on Buddhism, or for that matter on anything, but in the message of Gautama there is one issue which he brings out very clearly and that is what he calls "right mindfulness." If we think of the idea of right mindfulness we begin to come to the problem of knowing what to think, how to think, what attitudes one should have about one's thoughts, and Buddha taught very clearly that it is right mindfulness that is required for spiritual evolution.

The best way to approach this subject, which is very vast, is to separate the process of attitude and the process of thought. I hope that in separating these the concept of right thinking, right mindfulness, will become clearer. The reason for separating them is that any fact is interpreted by different people in different ways because, although the thought process of observing, recognizing, analyzing and concluding the fact was correct, and the denotation of what was happening was correct, the attitude, the connotation of what was happening was different. In the process of developing right thinking, you must understand that the mystic tries to come to the point of seeing the denotation, seeing the connotation, and seeing himself in relation to each.

If a candle were burning in our midst it would be a burning candle, and yet the meaning of it would be different for everyone. One person might be reminded of a church or a synagogue, another might dislike it, another might wonder why it was burning, another might see it as a beautiful symbol of the consumption of the false self and the transcendence of the hard, crystallized, dense wax into energy and light. Although everyone sees the fact, the mystic tries to see how the fact affects his attitude and how his attitude affects the fact. The first concept of right thinking, then, is that it is the ability to complete a circle. We can call this a circle of harmony, a circle of thought, a creation of thought triggered abstractly inside our consciousness and then a return of energy to the point of origin. Most people find it extremely difficult to separate the pure thought from the subject connotation, and if you were to ask me, I would say that it probably cannot be done, because ultimately the thought and the thinker are one; but the cultivation of right thinking is the attempt to arrive at as clear a thought form as possible before the subjective quality begins to color it.

The first, and maybe the only discipline in arriving at a clear thought form is concentration. The person who can concentrate on a particular thought form for long enough, who can focus upon a thought-pattern clearly enough, is the person who can arrive at this thought form, who can bring it out of the fog, out of the mist of disassociation and focus on it. It is like lightning which suddenly strikes in pitch darkness: suddenly, clearly, you see the whole landscape, but just as suddenly, it is gone.

Concentration is an attempt not to have lightning which lightens thousands and thousands of square feet of space, but to focus a light, a force, a thought, energy, like a laser beam, on one point, one thing, one idea, one subject, one object.

Over hundreds of years the mystics have developed a tremendous culture of concentration. They have begun to see that if there was anything which confused them in life, in the vast expanse of feelings, emotions and desires, the bewilderment was not in the expansion, in the possibility, but in the fact that we try to look at everything at once rather than to see everything separately and clearly. There is a clear example of this, which you can all see in your life, and that is the many people you know who have hundreds of ideas, yet who achieve none of them. They start a thousand things, yet they finish none, because they did not stay, they did not beam their concentration on one thing for long enough. These people usually end up being more confused by their own ideas.

There are many methods for developing concentration through all sorts of disciplines which are very clear, very simple, very well-known; one of these is the concept of mandala. Mandala is the bringing of an idea into a symbolic representation; that image is pregnant with the depth of the idea, but the image is only one, and by concentrating on it, by visualizing the image, by looking at it, by, as it were, branding the image on one's mind, in one's consciousness, one develops a power of concentration on that image so strongly that one begins to enlighten the whole range of symbolic reality, expressed, implied, pregnant within that form. A typical example is the mandala of the Buddha. Are Buddhists idol worshippers? No; if they have become so it is by the unfortunate, but normal, expected degeneration of mysticism. The image of the Buddha, as any image, can be used as a mandala by visualizing the Buddha as a symbolic form in such a way that eventually that symbolic form is branded on our consciousness, and all the aspects of Buddha, the ideals, the principles, the universals behind it, are then slowly suffused into thought forms.

The other development of right thinking is concerned with the ability to will, by your ethical judgment, what you want in your mind. Out of the totality of our being there continuously rise into our minds thought forms, desire forms, which demand satisfaction—the sexual drive is an example. Everyone finds sexual thought form desires in his life, whether they rise from outer stimuli or inner urges. Freud, in his way of understanding the symbolic language of man, recognized how strong these thought forms are. Another example is violence. If a person comes to me, man to man, person to person, and says, "I feel no violence, no aggression," my first reaction will be that that person is abnormal. Aggression, the nafs force, is continually rising into man's consciousness, and the very idea that it does not rise, the very attempt to deny it, or to deny sexual thoughts, is simply nonsense. It goes towards complete psychological deviation; we are aggressive. It is the same with suicide; any person who claims that he has never contemplated suicide is not alive. You must have contemplated suicide if you want to arrive at the existentialist choice, the real choice to live; not the choice of the little baby who is propelled into the world, but the choice of a human being who wants to live his or her life to the extent of its potential.

There are standard thought forms continuously rising out of the totality of our being into our mind. The development of right thinking is to try to go in a steady, subtle, healthy process from lower thought forms to higher thought forms—of course, such a qualification is inaccurate and indefensible, but having defined it as such we can still use it. We must decide by will what thoughts we want to think, what we want to have in our consciousness, and after concentration has become more powerful, we are more able to overcome the continual rising of these lower thought forms, so that we can begin to choose and bring into our consciousness higher thought forms. This is achieved by living life. In other words, if you think that the way to overcome the sexual desire which always arises is to live in abstinence, to become a monk or a priest, from the mystical point of view you are seriously wrong, you are really missing the boat. If you think that you can arrive at the existentialist thought of living without having faced suicide, death, you have not really transcended facing life. The mystic concept is not to deny these things, not to attach to aggression or sex or suicide a bad or a good connotation—it is to go through them, to let life take its natural course, to learn to satisfy, to complete every impulse, within reason, within balance, which arises into your mind. This is a very important concept which I hope you will not miss about the development of right thinking.

Another way to describe it is to say that there is in our mind a gratification center, and that gratification center is desiring, it is like a hunger for certain kinds of satisfaction, reward, achievement. If we go through these things, then we have gratified that level of desire and our thought forms can begin to rise higher. If we do not go through them, then there will always be a blank, a void, a weight, a hunger, dragging us down. The gratification center is a center which begins by asking for pain, it asks for certain forms of aggression, it asks for sexual satisfaction, it asks for certain needs which very naturally develop within the human being and which we must not deny. If you watch a little child grow up and even if you think that you can shield it totally from all aggression, you will see that it will demonstrate aggression. There are many who think that children should not have aggression, but strangely enough you find that as you deny aggression on a simple level, the need for it is transferred to a more complicated level which then prevents clear thinking at that level. You will find, for example, that if the normal desire for sexual gratification is not satisfied on the simple, real, direct, natural level of life, it transcends and warps itself into a much more complicated psychological sickness, where one can no longer think clearly about oneself or anything else because there are chords of emptiness which are not tuned, which are not satisfied. This is why it says in one of the first chapters of *The Inner Life* by Pir-o-Murshid Inayat Khan that if you want to live the inner life, first you must satisfy all your desires, learn all you want to know, experience everything you wish to experience, fulfill all the things which you want and need to fulfill, so that you can live the inner life out of the freedom of having fulfilled the outer life.

Most people go to spirituality as a flight, a flight from the outer life, wherein they find that they are not satisfied or they cannot be satisfied, where they are rejected or where they cannot achieve, or where they cannot reach a healthy, satisfactory relationship. Then they say, "Oh, this life is all bad." Every life is bad, every life is good; even so, they run towards the spiritual as an escape. But in the inner life they will also not get anywhere, because these same drags on the personality of unsatisfied hunger, or searches for certain forms of gratification which have not been satisfied on the simplest level, have now been complicated at the level of character and personality, rather than at the level of natural, of almost intuitive, instinctive behavior. In this way you get people who, whatever happens, are unhappy, or those who, whatever chance they have in life, are unsatisfied, or those who will quarrel with anyone they meet, or those who are continually depressed, whatever circumstances they may be in. This is because the normal healthy needs of the intuitive human nature have been denied and then the same desire-need continued on in a much more complicated personality that has been built up on an unsatisfied foundation. The development of right thinking is to go back within your character, your personality, your life—and obviously sometimes you may need help and guidance for that—and to relive that life and to catch up in all aspects where you have failed to satisfy the normal needs upon which, had they been satisfied, you could have built and transcended into higher thought forms.

The first step for developing right thinking is the development of concentration, and we gave as one example the mandala, but there are many more methods. The second step is to gratify the thought forms arising out of our being into our consciousness, which demand satisfaction, and to satiate desires on the simple level where they are holy, where they are divine, rather than to escape from them so that you complicate your life with grating, unacknowledged dissatisfaction. Get these things out of your mind, take care of them, free yourself. The more you can free your mind from these strange deflected urges, the more your mind can open itself to new light which can come into it, to new forms which it can conceive, which it could not conceive before because it was unfulfilled to previous patterns, previous circuitry connections it could not mature. The third principle of the development of right thinking on the thought level is to learn to choose, to cultivate, to time, within the cycles of your thought, what to think about. It is very clear that certain people are evening people, others are morning people, and denying that serves no purpose at all, because if you are a morning person and you arrange your day so that you have to perform your best in the evening, you will never be in harmony. If we refine that not only in terms of eating or sleeping cycles but thinking, we begin to recognize that at a particular time it may not yet be ripe to conceive of a certain form. This may seem confusing, but really it is not; it is a very natural thing that is within you, and I have no doubt that everyone has that capacity. If something is not clear, drop it, and it will come back again, and then you can think about it clearly.

One member of my family taught for many years in a girls' school and claimed that girls do not have the same mathematical abstract capacity to conceive that boys have. Then I remembered having learned previously that on the average girls are more mature than boys; a girl of twelve is up to one and a half years more mature than a boy of the same age. So a twelve year old girl is more mature, but a twelve year old boy can learn plane geometry better.

Pursuing this further, we begin to see that cycles and stages apply not only in terms of boys and girls, but also in terms of the individual. Whether we can will these cycles or whether these cycles will us can probably never be decided—maybe both are true. There are stages in the day, there are stages in the progression of thought, there are stages in the whole life of an individual, when we grow into certain aspects of thought and out of others. It is not possible, maybe it never will be possible, to say exactly how these stages work, but there seems to be a pattern to them which is that we go either from an aggregative to an amorphous level, or from an abstract to a concrete level; or maybe we go round in a loop. You will notice that if you can, by will, by choice, begin to filter out your thought attention and that if your thinking has reached a certain level of abstraction, then if you suddenly go back to very specific practical problems, you are out of phase and you become confused because things do not relate. It is the same the other way round as well. Every person can definitely find this growth of movement in his thought during the day and during his life. Thus it becomes clear that girls develop a thought pattern which goes towards the role of motherhood, towards the role of a certain responsibility, younger in life, so that their thought energy, their life energy, develops well in that area early on. Boys however, do not go toward the thought of fatherhood so young, so the spare thought energy which is not spent in that direction can be used to develop in others.

I would like to say a little more about the concept of "spare thought energy." A young child of two or three years old has a tremendous learning energy; it can learn to read and write very quickly. You will be such a proud parent, "Look, my little child is learning to read and write, at three years old he can read the newspapers." But when that child reaches nine years old, it will be mentally depressed because there is a certain amount of thought energy that must be channelled in a way corresponding to the natural development of the thought of that being. Many studies have been done on this which correspond with what many mystical people have been writing and saying. If the thought of that being is focused upon something which is not naturally in harmony with its need, psychologically, emotionally, intellectually, physically, it is spent, it is a drain, and the thought energy is taxed. Many people suffer from a depression of thought energy in which they find that they cannot think of anything long or complicated. There are ways to rest and to regain thought energy, which have to do with focusing concentration on thoughts which give energy, rather than on thoughts which take energy. Thoughts which are complete give energy, thoughts which require a solution take energy. In the development of right thinking, then, you must begin to see within yourself how much intellectual abstraction was sped up in you, how much of it you can rest from, how much of it you can regenerate, how you can find the proper cycle of your thought development in the day, in the week, in the month, in the year. A lot of things you can put off, not bother about them, say, "Ten years from now I'll think about that," so then you can begin to beam and focus your thought energy on what is really worthwhile to think about now. If you try to conceive of too many things at once you are lost. What would be too many? For every person it is different, but you should conceive of as many things as you can, without losing track of any of them.

These three things were brought out: concentration—mandalas, visualization, a very important way to learn to beam, to learn to focus your mind; gratifying the lower thought forms—not denying your natural self by all sorts of inheritances of morality judgments or Christian ethos-type morals which deny the divinity of the natural man—so that these thoughts which want to come into life, into focus so that they can be clear, are completed; and choosing the cycle of your thought so that you think at the right time in the patterns, the forms that attend to the right things. As a part of that, you should remember that many people (especially today when as children we are already heavily taxed) have used up too much thought energy, and continue to use up too much thought energy because they continue to believe, unfortunately, that they are obliged to think about things which seem unclear to them. Then they become more and more tired, they need to sleep longer, and they are depressed.

Learn to rest your thought, to gain thought energy by choosing to think only about things that are complete, that you are able to resolve, that are clear, so that you regain energy. This is primarily the aspect of arriving at a clear thought pattern; it is only later that we will concentrate on the concept of the subjective interpretation of this thought and the return, creatively, of something to that thing which triggered the thought in the first place.

There is nothing which happens that does not go through the mind either before or after. You cannot be guilty of a crime you committed unconsciously. You cannot be innocent of an act or a thought which you should have had, but deliberately omitted. The acts of omission are far heavier than the acts of commission; and with acts I include thoughts. It is because man tends to be in error that this world portends to be imperfect. The plan of this level of creation tends towards entropy. Recognizing that the act of omission is far greater than the act of commission because it is a non-development, a non-use of potential, the mystic chooses, as a most important part of his or her life, to develop thinking, right thinking, because it is in that thing, that consciousness, that mind, that all the acts of commission are performed, and in developing thinking he can decrease the omissions, the non-development, in his life. Since there is nothing that exists which does not go through the mind before or after, the development of spirituality is not a development of magnetism, occultism, it is not an external development of any particular "-ism." It is simply the expansion of the mind in all its qualities.

I hope that you will see this chapter in relation to the first few because, from the Sufi point of view, even the development of right thinking must be done with clear goals, utter detachment, and the acceptance of a reality apperception in which everything that the mind can conceive, is not.

October 1, 1973

PART TWO

Having looked at the observing, or constructing part of thinking, we can now continue to discuss the question of what to do with the thought. We have a mind, a consciousness, the power to think—even emotions are thoughts—and if we look at it from the most elementary point of view, something must be done with it. Even if we were to deny any religious or other emotional meaning to life (and sometimes that is very useful and valid) if we simply return to the existential recognition of the fact that we are alive, then something must be done with that power; otherwise, not only does it remain meaningless, but it has no issue in that meaninglessness, as though, for instance, we bought a camera and left it on a shelf and never used it. It is very strange and symbolically meaningful that most of us have hundreds of totally useless objects, while we have also reached a period in man's development where the mind itself is often without use.

It is impossible to separate man from his evolution. Man evolves through struggles and strife; in Sufi terminology this is described by the word "jehad"; in Christianity there is a mystical indication in the Bible, which says, "The kingdom of God must be taken by force." Man reached this point of ascendence in this domain of the limited creation of which he can conceive by his mind. He employed his mind to conquer his environment, thereby, of course, building a prison round himself—but he used his mind. In practical terms, he used it in the continual striving for safety, security, food and power in life, so that we have now reached the point where there is hardly any struggle left in life. Not only have we killed nearly all the tigers there were, but we have evolved a society which is painless, therefore far more painful because there is no fulfillment, no satisfaction, no achievement. We have become slaves of a system of comfort, of escape from pain and striving; we have become softies. None of us can conceive of the nafs force, the striving force that man has used to drive his mind further and further. It is this very lack of real challenge in life that creates the hunger for meaning, the pain of emptiness, which we in our generation are experiencing and trying to sublimate. Aggression is normal, natural, human. It is made by life, by evolution; it developed in this way for eons of time before human sperm ever existed. But what can we be aggressive about? We cannot beat our heads against the walls we build; they are too strong. We have so over-populated the earth that there is no place to be free, so we try to arrive at the sublimation of our aggression by publishing every possible meaningless murder in every newspaper, by engaging in sports, games, competitions and gambling, in all forms and techniques of danger which you find in society.

This is why the development of right thinking is really necessary. When we have come to the point where, freeing ourselves from the groove of finding no real challenge and fulfillment in life, we begin to penetrate into an enormous mine, an incredible potential called meaning, its existence unfolds deep satisfaction. When a thought form arrives clearly in the consciousness, of and by itself it is useless; ultimately there is nothing in the world which is more useful than anything else, material or abstract—the use is something which develops in its relationship to other useless things. A chessboard has sixty-four squares, thirty-two black and thirty-two white, and all sorts of little wooden pieces on it. Whether you know chess or not, you can clearly see that you could look at the chessboard and find it meaningless, simply little pieces of wood dancing on little black and white squares. The chess player might agree with you, but he could also point out that one pawn is threatening another while you see no threat, no tension; he can show you that one pawn is covered by a bishop—"What do you mean, 'covered,' I see no bridge...." The only meaning in those useless pieces of wood lies in their interrelationship; in themselves they are meaningless, and so it is with anything. A light is meaningless, you are meaningless, but the fact that a light illuminates the area in which you are looking—that is meaningful. Right thinking recognizes the deepest, most sublime interrelationships between any things, aspects, existences, voluminations or absences.

Before you can do anything with a thought, you must be sure that the thought-image is clear, concise, exact. If you do not know what you are thinking about, why are you thinking about it? If you had myopia you could not play chess, because in order to see each piece you would be so close that you would knock them off the board. You have to move back far enough to see all the pieces together, in order to arrive at the interrelationship in the abstract which gives each piece its meaning; but if you had myopia, all the pieces would become so fuzzy that you could not see anything clearly. While discussing people's problems with them, I have noticed that often there was no problem but simply an unclear thought-image. This is obvious in education; when a child learns, why is it that he does not understand something? A child's mind is probably faster, freer and less encumbered by emotional contexts than an adult's mind, but sometimes, as it is watching a logical thought form travelling along the symbolic shape of the thought patterns, it loses track of where it was. For this reason we repeat the same pattern of thought a hundred times: if a train travels from A to B at 60 mph, how far did it travel in twenty minutes? And we repeat this thought pattern to the child again and again until it can arrive at the solution.

The first and most simple principle of what you can do with a thought, then, is to repeat it, reconstruct it, see if you can recall the image. This is the same as the step from a photograph to a moving picture. The camera takes a single image, you look at it—fine—but the moving picture is a series of many photographs, each, by definition, slightly different. That has to be—you can never stand in the same river twice—you can never twice repeat exactly the same thought, but as you begin to repeat a thought form, reconstruct it, think it again, it becomes a moving picture, it becomes a meaningful, evolving principle.

You may wonder, as you repeat your thought form, how you should guide it so that it moves in the right way. The answer to that is that it happens naturally; if you try to force it, you will not be able to flow into the life of your thought. The next question is: you have repeated the thought forms many times, repeated and reconstructed the image and it begins to make sense, begins to show a movement, but—and this is very difficult, subtle thinking—what to do with the movement? At this point the principle of dual consciousness comes in. You are sitting in your chair watching the movie, and while you are watching it you are also in it. When you can develop dual consciousness you have, in a sense, moved enough from the myopic view of life, retreated enough to begin to see, to construct and to interpret interrelationships between that particular thought and every other thought gathered in your memory.

Having said that as you repeat a thought form you should let it change slightly by itself and flow into its change, I now seem to be contradicting myself by saying that once you have repeated the thought form and can remove yourself from it and see it, you can begin to construct an interrelationship with it. If this seems to be paradoxical, it is—it is the paradox between relaxation and control. Uncontrolled relaxation is not relaxation, and relaxed control is not control. Controlled relaxation is the right amount of control to be relaxed. When you are uncontrollably relaxed, you are collapsed, which is what happens to the thought-life of many people.

We have brought out the idea that first and foremost you must repeat an image so that first in its repetition it becomes more clear, and second in its repetition its potential variants can evolve. Then you must move back, retard, you must watch yourself think, you must develop dual consciousness, you must think about the fact that you are thinking, so that the thought forms evolved can, by themselves, yet with your own memory control, find interrelationships, find meaning.

Think again of the chessboard. It is clear that you must

look at a particular pawn or king or queen and concentrate upon it, re-repeat, realizing that the piece is there, until you really know that it is there. If you glance at it without really branding its existence in your mind, it is lost—it has not made a deep enough impression to be useful. As you look again and again at a certain position, you will begin to see all sorts of interrelationships, you will remember that the pawn moves this way and the rook moves that way, and by looking at just one pawn, you could analyze a whole set of meaningful inter-relationships. Yet at the same time you have to be removed from your concentrated thought-pattern, so that although you are totally and completely into the very wood-fiber of the chess pieces, you are also able to watch it as a game from which you are free, in which you try to respond. When you make a move you must allow your partner (or your enemy, depending upon what you want to call him) to make his move, and so it is also in life. If you are white and you begin with a move and then make the next, and continue to move independently, there is no game. After every thought-pattern of the game you have to move back and watch to see how the reality of the universe that your mind has concentrated upon will change again. You change the universe and the universe changes you; it is the cycle of action and reaction.

When I play chess I usually decide that I will play a certain position, put this pawn here, put the queen there; I get the whole structure beautifully laid out and think, that is how it is going to be. Then I start playing with my son and after six moves, I have lost. He does not play to my position, and I am only trying to construct my position; I am not watching what he is doing. I have an absolutely impenetrable position— which is also indefensible—and suddenly, my god, I'm mate. This happens to people all the time; they think everything through, but are then unable to respond dynamically to the fact that what they have thought about has changed. It is like deciding to stop for a red light, after you are through the intersection with a big bump in your front fender. Frustration usually stems from people's unwillingness to compensate for the fact that reality is change. The tension of the chess game is not in having one particular impenetrable position. If black and white each make thirty-two moves and we stop the game, mold the chess set in plastic and hang it on the Empire State Building and the Tower of London and tell people to look at it, they will say, "How nice"—someone might even buy it for an antique collection—but the real sense of the game is not that dead position, it is the continuity, the tension, the life of the game, the continual abstract interchanging reality.

How many people enjoy watching a game of chess when somebody is sure to lose from the first move? Few people enjoy it, for there is no meaning to it. They enjoy watching a game between Fischer and Spassky because there is so much tension. This is interesting, because people usually want to go away from tension, controversy and challenge; then, all of a sudden, they look round, feeling that there is no meaning in their lives. If you suggest that they go and do something challenging, like conquering the Chinese in Tibet, they will say that they do not want to do anything hard. This is the problem with thought and feeling, with the whole meaning of life. The meaning of life is the striving, the tension in it, the action and the changing in it; it is the progress of the game you are playing with yourself. If both you and your chess partner decide that you do not want to change a particular position, the game is over; you can go and have a drink together, there is no more to play; the meaning has dissolved. The meaning is a combination of the intoxicating involvement in what is happening and the freedom to watch it happen.

There are some people who run away from tension and thus have no meaning; there are others who are so lost in the tension at a particular time that they almost die of a heart attack. If something does not go right on the board they curse and swear and smash the board to pieces. These are the people who are unable to have dual consciousness, to remove themselves from their thought and watch the play of life. They are so attached by their thoughts, emotions and feelings, which are all thoughts, that they have lost meaning because they have no perspective, no detachment.

So what do you do with your thoughts? First of all you must allow yourself to have thoughts, to think about everything and anything, think about them clearly and totally and to complete the thoughts. Every uncompleted thought you have had is like breaking a weft thread while weaving: there is a hole in consciousness, it is an uncompleted part of the weave. There are many people with that problem because they have not completed so many thoughts, that when they go back and look at the weaving, the firmament they have made is a rag, a useless rag, because nothing in it was complete, nothing in it was sufficiently interconnected with other things to make it a whole, a life, an akasha.

There are certain rules about complete thinking, and the first is that when you have a thought, you must decide whether or not you want to remember it. The development of memory is very important. If you decide that you do not want to remember that thought, that it was not really useful, it will wipe itself away. You may have noticed in your life that during certain periods you have absolutely no recollection of certain thoughts, although you may be reminded of them later. Under memory drugs or hypnosis, or by reading old letters or diaries, these thoughts may come back, but that is not important to this subject. What is important is to understand that we have an active memory, and in that memory we want to be able to file away useful, complete, meaningful data, so that any new thing that comes up can find other images of inter-relationship and therefore meaning. The way a computer works is similar to the way in which thought function works. First there is a working memory, a temporary memory which you are continually destroying. When you want to add 2 and 2, you must take one 2, put it in the memory and get another 2, then you can put them together and you have 4. To know that it is 4, you put it in the working memory and look at it—yes, it is 4. The process of $2 + 2 = 4$ is no longer important so you wipe 2 from the memory, 2 from the adding register and remember the answer. The working memory is now clear; you put the 4 in your data file so that you can refer to it again. Now you can make a new computation: $3 + 6 = 9$, file the 9. Now you want to know the sum of 9 and 4. Both numbers are sequentially filed away, so you get them out and add them.

These two memories are important, the working memory

and the real thing you computed, the data file. The third important thing is the input; a particular data file is complete with all the things you want to remember for today, but tomorrow you want to do the same analysis again, so today's data file becomes tomorrow's input, and tomorrow's data file becomes the input for the following day. Thus you have three memories, the working memory, the old data file and the new data file. The old data file is important because if by chance someone pulls the plug on your computer, all the data you are working on is lost. This happens sometimes when people lose their memory; some incredible trauma happens and they can no longer reach the old memory file, so they can no longer derive a valid new one.

In order to think properly, when you have finished with a thought, you must decide what part of it you want to remember and keep, and what part of it you want to forget and throw out. This is the vein in which Einstein said that he did not care whether he remembered anything he learned as long as he remembered how to find it again. The principle of the new mathematics is not to teach computation in the old way, but to teach them how to compute—not $2 + 2 = 4$, that is meaningless, but how to add 2 and 2. Those people who have arrived at the power of right thinking are able to complete every thought, to compute, to function so that there is not a dragging knot, a slipping connection, so that they can throw out of their memory what they do not want to remember.

It is important first of all to learn to repeat thought forms; that is the first thing you do when you have a clear image, repeat it again. Second, it is important to arrive at a stage of dual consciousness where, by removing yourself sufficiently from the mental process, your identity, you can see that mental process gaining meaning as it finds interrelating functionality with all that you can recall in your memory. Third, complete your thought, arrive at a conclusion and throw away what you do not need so that you are free to think of the next thing. Why are people confused in life, why can they not think properly? Because they try to think of too many things at once, instead of thinking of little pieces, constructing these pieces and eventually being able to see the whole. This is why we teach children to put jigsaw puzzles together. We take a puzzle with a hundred pieces: what is this little piece? I do not know, so put it somewhere temporarily, look at it again and again, and at the other little pieces which you do not know where to fit, and suddenly a fitting pattern will come. Maybe it is right and maybe not; try it, if it does not fit, put it back. Now you know a little more about it, that it does not fit there, and you will find where it does fit. Eventually the puzzle is in one piece. Forget about the image of the puzzle itself as a whole, just remember the principle of how you were able to put a puzzle together.

We have primarily addressed ourselves to thoughts as if they were mental pieces of cardboard, as if they were impersonal numerical values on a computer data tape, but they are not. We have not yet said anything about the emotional interpretation of thoughts. Thoughts have a quality of hidden potential. As a child I had to walk to school through several streets, and in one street lived a grocer whose dog barked at me every time I went past. I would get very scared and would cry; sometimes the grocer would call the dog in, but more often he was not there. I decided to walk in another street, although it took ten minutes longer; but there was a dog on that street too. So pretty soon I was thoroughly afraid of dogs. Now just a little while ago I was walking outside to get some fresh air, to organize my thoughts, and suddenly a dog barked very loudly. The thought was suddenly very clear to me: a thought barking, a dog barking, a thought barking, it is the same thing. Straight away my metabolic rate went up, my heart rate went up, my hair began to rise, my breath became irregular, my knees began to shake, I turned round and saw a great big dog barking. Suddenly the six-year-old boy was alive again, but of course I could not cry because it is not supposed to be right to be afraid of dogs. But I immediately recognized that the thought form "there is a dog barking at me" had all this emotion-laden, established, interrelative pattern of fear and anxiety. This is a rather simple example and one we all know, but so it is with many thoughts. There are thoughts with pricks or points to them, and as the thought proceeds into our consciousness it punctures something, cre-

ating a whole series of other thoughts: run, kill the dog, jump,
scream. All sorts of pricking thoughts come into your mind
which are probably not at all necessary. Rather than watching these pricks develop from a detached vantage point you
are crushed by them, buried under them and unable to
control them; therefore you are unable to let them be free.
The emotional contexts of thoughts are probably the most
important reason for not thinking clearly or arriving at a clear
image. As soon as I realized that I was afraid, which in itself
was a great victory, I looked at the dog again and I realized
that it was barking at another dog, not at me. I could breathe
more slowly and walk away.

Thus it is that all our thoughts evoke emotional contexts,
traumas, fears, reactions, pre-established patterns of interrelationships. It is like a chess book which says: if A happens,
you always do B. Those who really know chess know that that
is impossible. Those who know computer programming know
that if we were to start a chess game between the greatest
chess mind of the world and a computer, the man would
make a move while the computer would be programmed to
analyze all the possible alternatives. There is not enough
time, nor enough energy in the universe for the computer
ever to make the first move if it were to pre-analyze all the
possible ramifications. If you fed in all the electrical energy
in the universe, you would not have enough energy to supply
the wattage to run the computer to think about every thought
and every consequence of every thought for the computer to
make a move. That is how vast is this little game of a few
blocks of black and white, and how unimaginably larger is
life's imagination; can you face that? That is probably why
people look at life and quickly write down: if this, do that; if
that, do this; if dog barks, run.

The mystic is a human being, a man, a woman, who
deliberately tries to evolve in his thought-life new interrelationships, new possibilities, new consequences. This can only
be done if you program yourself wilfully, conduce yourself to
have all the thoughts, to conceive of all the things that you
can. If you cannot conceive of the tower of Babel forging a
military alliance with the chimney of Queen Elizabeth II, and

thereby melting the south pole of Mars, you cannot think well—or, you are a computer programmed by some master who says, "Sweetheart, do this, do that, take this, add that, do it this way, think this way, and by the way it costs $1500 to come on earth, and please pay up the $5600 it will cost to bury you. . . ."

Although this sounds sarcastic—and that is an enjoyable thing to be sometimes—in the issue of thought the attempt of the mystic is to unload enough pre-programmed thought-patterns, emotional contexts, enough ethical pre-judgments, moral commitments, enough choice in his or her thought so that the real and the grandest expansion of the mind, of right thinking, can happen; and that is free, total, creative imagination. No human being without imagination can claim to live.

In conclusion it should be pointed out that there are definite exercises, if you can call them that, for cultivating every one of the aspects of thought development described. There are exercises for concentration, which involve the use of mandalas for the eyes, the ears, or for every sense. There are forms-of-thought disciplines which help to develop the ability to select the thoughts which you expose to your consciousness, and these are primarily concerned with certain kinds of thoughts which you are given to think about. These exercises fall under the concept of the word "muraqaba." There are exercises to develop the potential, symbolically speaking, of the lower thought levels (and please *re*member that the word "lower" has been clearly defined as being simply a temporary measurement, and that in the end it may be higher, but it is more instinctive, more intuitive); these exercises could be characterized as a form of psychodrama, games in which the thoughts which we could not satisfy by living a full life in this artificial concrete jungle can develop and find an issue, be satisfied, be gratified. These, in a sense, are probably the most important series of exercises that we need do for real development, not for development to become holy and divine and useless, but to become human.

There are exercises to learn to hold thoughts long enough, to repeat them long enough, so that we can have and create clear thought pictures. These involve the use of wazifas or mantrams: continual repetition so that our mind learns the pattern of repeating. There are exercises to cultivate the ability to have complete thoughts: complete thinking means selective control in a relaxed, detached play of mind, and that involves the use of breath control. Breath control is mind control; mind control is breath control. To learn to breathe deeply is to learn to think wholly, consequentially; to learn to breathe completely is to learn to think completely.

There are exercises for training the memory and for clearing it. To learn to clear the memory, of course, involves learning to sleep at the right times and to sleep properly, because it is in sleep, through dreams and in all ways that the mind is able to clear useless information out of its working memory. There are also exercises for training our thought, mind, energy to have access to memory. To develop access to memory is rather subtle, maybe not as clearly an exercise as in gymnastics, do so many push-ups, but it is definitely a pattern of cultural development that we can recognize so that we see a pattern and a result.

In the whole realm of all forms of meditation, exercise, development technique, whether in psychology, psychiatry, psychoanalysis, in Vedantaism or Yogism or Hinduism or Buddhism or Zen or Sufism or whatever else, all these various so-called spiritual exercises fit very precisely into the thought-development processes; because, after all, there is nothing that occurs which does not go through your mind either before or after its manifestation. Nevertheless, it is important to point out before ending that exercises, whatever kind, whether spiritual as defined by you or anybody else or educational or psychological, are still only exercises, and not an end in themselves.

October 8, 1973

PART 2
HUMAN NEEDS

INFERIORITY

In the next few chapters we will try to look at different examples of mental illness. One thing that we all know about and probably all suffer from is inferiority. I realize that "inferiority complex" reminds one of the classic textbook definition of a particular neurosis, but we will attempt to form a much more subjective, though more free idea of what it really is and how it works.

To begin with, what it really is should only be described in terms of chemistry. It is one thing to be discussing the psychology of the mind, moods, feelings, but to be more accurate, we really are simply electro-chemical happenings of atoms, molecules, compounds. As soon as we approach the chemical definition of, for instance, the feeling of having no energy, of being tired, depressed, weak, we enter an area which is vague. Exactly, chemically, we can say it is just a lack of iron, not enough sugar or something else in the little laboratory; but how does that express itself in the mind? That has to remain vague.

Everyone knows that an inferiority feeling is really just a wanting to belong, to be respected, to be accepted, to be fulfilled in life by someone or by all: by our Mummy, by our Daddy, and by the ever-widening circle of people who enter our consciousness. The desire to overcome this feeling of inferiority is, in my view, the main reason, the main cause for human development. I am sure that in wanting to overcome, to be equal, leadership qualities are formed. I am sure that it is in wanting to belong that one tries to be better, one wants to shine, one wants to radiate. I think that if we were to talk of people in terms of herds of buffalo or flocks of sheep, I would say that the bull buffalo with the strongest will to overcome the inferiority complex will fight hardest to lead the herd. In other words, this need to belong is the very same force, built in us instinctively, which keeps the groups of buffalo and of fish, whales, doves, together. But at some point that need to belong, to be accepted, to be involved, meets with the imperfections of life. A mother has two children; just at the moment when one of the children wants to belong to the mother, she is holding the other one, and suddenly the child is aware, "Oh, I am not in that group." This awareness is not even a conclusion, intelligently speaking, but simply a jarring of that herd instinct. Many such experiences come in life as one grows up, and the sum total of these brings us a feeling, a complex, a fear, an inferiority.

You could ask why I have not called it being rejected, or insecurity, and the answer is that as long as one feels that one does not belong, in some vague way—maybe not a highly-evolved, intelligent idea but just vaguely—nothing wrong has yet happened, the mind is not yet ill. One can still say, "I shall take a step forward in the herd and then I shall be in." The key to the mental anguish comes when a feedback mechanism begins, no matter how simplistic and elemental it may be: I cannot move into the middle, I cannot sit on my mother's lap, I cannot swim as fast as the leader of the whales. It may even be much vaguer than saying I cannot; it does not need to have an intellectual identity; but when that concept begins to evolve, then that becomes an inferiority feeling. The simple mechanism of the aggressive force of wanting to enter the group, is natural; that force is right, it is not yet a mental disease.

I began by saying that we all suffer from an inferiority feeling. Why? There is only one group a sheep wants to belong to, the group of sheep; but with humans there are many groups. I want to belong to my Mummy, I want to belong to my family, my neighborhood, my class, my school, my nation. I want to belong to all those smart people who write books about science. I want to belong to the adventurers who brought the Golden Fleece. I want to belong to the warriors ... We are continually confronted by that basic drive, that we belong to a herd, a grouping: and everything that is a form of human development is, because we are human, something that we ought to belong to. Of course, we cannot perform easily on all levels of physical, intellectual, spiritual prowess or belong to all the groups with which we are confronted. A very simple way to prove this point, even objectively, is to see that in communities which are very homogeneous, as in India in the caste system, or simple agricultural systems in France or Austria, there is far less insecurity amongst the people, less stress to belong, less feeling of inferiority, therefore people are more peaceful and development is much slower and expansion of consciousness remains on the same level for centuries. In heterogeneous communities, where influences, standards, groupings, ideas, have such great variety, the feelings of insecurity, inferiority and rejection increase tremendously.

Once the feeling of not belonging develops, it can take many forms. The healthiest form is saying, "Let me fight this, that I cannot," overcoming it, falling back on the natural nafs, the natural aggression of man, putting out a little more to enter into the light. That is the basic drive which you see behind all men of leadership, valid leadership, in the herds of the human animal.

The degrees of this falling-back on natural aggressive life-desire are different, of course, and you can sometimes see that people with an inferiority complex become incredibly aggressive. As they gain more and more self-respect, inner security, their overt aggression levels off. You can see in yourself that when you are nervous and do not know if you will be accepted or respected or loved, you are closed, you are hard, you are on edge; by that you create an atmosphere around you of rejecting others and as a result of that you are rejected. I am sure all of you have noticed, some more, some less, that if people appear unkind, overly harsh, hard, very often they are hiding a basic feeling of inferiority or uncertainty. If you are wise enough to know that, there are all sorts of tricks you can use to give them a chance to come out of this cockyness. One trick is to give them a chance to come forward with the aggression.

Pir-o-Murshid Inayat Khan tells a story about a man whose fiancée wanted to become a mureed. He was a very simple, good, solid person who had never thought about spiritual things or strange concepts, and he was a little bit jealous—why is she interested in that man? So he decided to go and meet Inayat Khan. He came into the room and did not even greet him, he just came out with a sea of criticism and bad words, and he talked for an hour about how bad everything was. Inayat Khan just said, "Yes, oh yes, you are right, I agree." And when he was finished, the man took a deep breath and asked to be initiated. I am sure that if a conversation had ensued and Inayat Khan had said, "Well, that is not really true because . . . No, you are wrong . . . Why do you say that? . . ." that they would still be arguing now. Both people recalled that as a memorable experience in their lives. When the man told me the story, he finally admitted that he was still just as angry as before, when they met. He did not really know what he was angry about, all those years later, because the anger, the criticism, the rejection, in an intellectual form was all nonsense. It was simply a feeling of inferiority: this great master from the East comes along, he will know what I think, what a little man I am . . . The man became a Sufi, a devoted mureed and a leader in the movement all his life.

Inferiority is something that stays with you, but its form changes. When people are young, you can see the strong rebellion come out—they become more conscious of themselves, they try to form a self-identity and the need for rebellion comes out—they want to express their new identity anew. If you are all young puritans and these older people are so wise, so smart, so experienced, they have all the power, and you also want to be respected, you also want to be a man—you all cut your hair. Two hundred years later the new young puritans come along, but by now all the old people have short hair, so you let your hair grow long. In some societies they handle this much better, they recognize the conflict and give the young men a chance to fight the older men, like the bullocks and the rams. Maybe the older man, who could fight much better, helped them along to win; then they became buddies. You need a way to allow the release of that natural aggression which you fall back on to get through that inferiority feeling; so maybe we should build in our society more systems which can allow the aggression to come in and to be absorbed.

Gradually let us descend a little more into disease. Another form that an inferiority complex can take is to say, "All right, if I cannot belong to the herd, then the herd is bad and I am good." That generally causes a resolution in that personality, because now you have a new identity. Now that group is bad, you do not want to belong to it any more. In any case, they are no good, you are good. Now you have a new group and now we come to the more diseased part of it; you need more psychic strength, more fanaticism to use your aggressive force to go against the natural tendency to belong, when you make this new group, you yourself, you continuously have to support, by value systems, by habits, by norms, by means, by psychological reaction mechanisms, this need for your group to be really apart from the group which you could not get into. Gradually this builds up into more deviant behavior, a more specific, sharp neurosis and eventually extremism. This kind of person forms a very important part of the leadership of the world, because other people with inferiority complexes, being unable to reach their natural aggression sufficiently, seem to be attracted to this group. This is how you have such phenomena as witches. I am not going to say that witches are bad and the Church of England, for instance, is good; obviously there are many more people in the Church of England than there are in groups of witches, and there may be many who are in both; but the groups of witches are basically exactly the same: ceremonial, ritualistic religious groups, exactly the same as the Church of England, just slightly different ceremonies. The in-group/out-group situation causes it.

The witch leadership needs continually to assert more and more of its deviation—Jesus is no longer good, or god is no longer good, so god is the devil. The devil may be good, but in order to ensure that you are not among those sheep, you have to keep doing everything on all levels that you can see, to assert the fact that you are not in there.

For a whole deviant new behavior-pattern, value-judgment, everything has to be reformed; and it can only be maintained by even more inner aggression, which means that you need almost fanatic strength, satanic strength, to maintain that out-group. That very strength will then attract people with insufficient self-identity, so that in the more deviant groups you will find more and more people with feelings of inferiority, who are also terribly weak and therefore latch onto outside aggression to help them to be in somewhere, to belong somewhere. It is very important that you understand how that mechanism works; in a way it is an explanation of the fanatic leadership in the world, such as the leadership of Hitler (his name is always used; it is difficult to use another name, but there are many others). Interestingly there begins a struggle between the different kinds of leadership and of role, because although you have two groups of sheep, now there is a struggle for dominance; who will get to that pasture first? The small grouping may be able to move faster than the larger one. Leadership of the small group is more precise, more disciplined, more exact. There is always far more competition for the leadership in the larger groups. The leadership in the large group is on a fairly even level of aggressive life-force, whereas leadership in the small grouping is more fanatic, one has very great power and many have very little. You find that world leadership is very often heavily influenced by dominant extremism because, as the small group fights to get to that pasture first, the large group also has to react, everybody has to react—the group of sheep, the people, everybody.

In a way, one little coven in Sherwood Forest, with five little people around one little person, doing a ceremony tonight, is influencing the whole of England, the whole of the world, where we are all moving in our value systems, in our value structures. Sometimes these little things have much more influence. Why? It has to do with the need for gratification, the looking for sensation, the whole reporting phenomenon. No newspaper reporter would be writing about the fact that the trees in the forest have grown another one or two millimeters in thickness, because everybody knows that; so he writes instead about the five little witches and everybody reads that and their minds are immediately influenced.

The way in which society works, inferiority is always re-challenged, because now you know that you belong to one in-group, but there is a little out-group and you do not belong to that, so you must reject it; they are bad and we are good. You are continually faced with new things, your life continually meets with new challenges, things you want to belong to, to be familiar with, to be at peace with, and they are all very complicated, very subtle interrelationships.

One form of inferiority feeling rejects the group to which it cannot belong and forms its own, and this kind of group attracts people with insufficient natural aggression, weak characters. Those people, those minds which have not found their aggression at all, who have inferiority feelings and who fall out, who have not the strength to fight that inferiority complex, are what I would call chameleons rather than followers—people who really have not enough basic inner mental power, magnetic power, to deal with that inferiority complex. They always walk at the end of any group, trail along; they develop very complicated mental diseases, be-cause there is no identity that is strong, no nafs force that is floating out, no aggressive line to march along with in con-sciousness; their whole life has no meaning, everything be-comes inadequate, senseless, tasteless, purposeless—the whole life is impotent. These people become so enveloped in this lack of energy, mental energy, life energy, that they cannot be moved out of it. These are the people who usually adhere completely to form, live out of form, out of structure, and have no commitment to any content, to any sacrifice, to any worth. They can just as easily be in one form as another; they can just as easily be a soldier of fortune in the French Foreign Legion as a choirboy in Westminster Abbey, because it is only through an outer form that they find an identity, not through any particular inner-directed force.

The inferiority anxiety is a natural mental disease, the first, the foremost one we all have. It develops in different stages—a mild reaction, a fanatic reaction, no reaction. As a result of these different general stages you can find mankind dividing itself into leadership groups which are continually affecting each other, and you find that the inferiority complex is always greater the more it can be grasped and conceived in the consciousness. The higher, the more evolved the mind, the more is its threat of whether it can contain, absorb, fit into, assimilate what comes to its consciousness. Inferiority, that complex, that disease, is part of the evolution of man. Luckily it is built in, because it causes the evolution of man; it is built in right behind, right with, the leadership cycle of human development.

April 15, 1974

INADEQUACY

As I have said in the previous chapter, inferiority is something that everyone has, and has to have because it is the very force, the very symptom which is channeling the energy of human development and leadership. If you do not have a feeling of inferiority, there is nothing to challenge you to go forward to overcome it. It is the thing which channels the aggressive nafs life-force to come out of its barriers. We have spent some time describing different degrees of inferiority in groups of people, groups of minds; some groups are middle-of-the-road, others are small fanatic groups which reject the middle-of-the-road groups, and then there are groups of people without any modus operandi at all. The inferiority complex and the way in which one deals with it and overcomes it definitely sorts the minds of humanity into these three major groups.

In this chapter and the one following we will talk about the specific forms of inferiority feeling relating to the male and the female. You can call the female mental disease the "inadequacy complex"—feelings of inadequacy; you can call the male disease the "impotency complex"—feelings of being impotent.

I am not a woman, so in a way I do not have the right to speak about the feelings of inadequacy that women go through; they could accuse me rightly of not being inside that experience. On the other hand, having known some women, I can talk about it as it appears to the outside, to a man, and maybe to women to a degree. I realize my limitations.

The feelings of inadequacy which rule the female mind are very much the basic neurotic, energy-consuming feelings which cause a lack of purpose, a lack of scope in the life of women.

What is the cause?—basically it is the relationship between the mother and the daughter. As a little girl grows up, her example is the mother, or some other human being who takes that role (or several human beings who take that role, depending upon the structure of the society and the life of that particular individual). This is the beginning: when you have a model or an ideal, you have also the reality that you are not equal to it. The feeling is then ingrained much more strongly by our male-dominated society; because as soon as you widen your scope from little baby, little girl, young child, you find that the boys are more aggressive, they speak louder, fight harder, do sports better. It is not necessarily true but it appears so, and the sense of inadequacy deepens further. In adolescence the need to be beautiful, to be sexy, to be appealing, strengthens it even more because, although we are a male-dominated society, we have formed a very definite picture of how a sexy, beautiful woman should look or act; unfortunately those who look that way are very few and far between (though, to my personal taste, this is rather fortunate). And so all the feelings slowly build up; you know and understand the details very well. There are feelings of jealousy—a woman eventually comes to the point where she feels completely inadequate. The man runs the bank account, he earns the money, he is the hunter, he drives the car, he designs the buildings—he does all the things, he lives, he is free. The woman is stuck with the baby, she is stuck with the house, with the cooking, with this, with that . . . and so it goes on. Eventually a heavy neurotic pattern develops which is inescapable.

Lately, in the modern culture of which most of us are a part, some of this is tending to break down. We are beginning to see that women's metabolism is far more efficient. They can do the same amount of work with less food, the same amount of activity, even emotional activity, on less sleep. They are emotionally more resilient, they are often able to express themselves much more freely than men—these things are beginning to be recognized.

The best way to resolve inadequacy is to go back into early childhood and see that the father is the one who can make the little girl see the mother ideal, the example, better, and help her to overcome that feeling of inadequacy which grows over time. It is the father who makes a healthy woman, and it is the mother who makes a healthy man. That is a very definite problem in our society; a father is not supposed to make love to his daughter, so he cannot communicate with her easily. Somehow or other his daughter represents his wife, his woman, but without her sexuality. He is supposed to have contact with the boys and be tough and robust. Very often he continues the practice of saying "little woman, little thing, little girl." Thus, although the inadequacy complex is natural, because no little girl can compete with her mummy, it is definitely either improved by the richness and depth of the father or worsened by the lack of it.

The little girl competes with her mother for the affection of her father. When Daddy comes home, Mummy is open to Daddy, Daddy may be open to Mummy and not at all open to his daughter. Later on the girl realizes that certain other girls who are more "vulgar" seem to have this appeal—they get everything. Most girls do not, and so then a dream life begins. One of the characteristics of this inadequacy is living in dreams; these dreams are compensation for the inadequacy. This is very clear in the stories you read to little girls—very heavy, very cloying, sticky sentimental images—beautiful princes come and save you from this, glass cages where you sleep and someone comes and kisses you, you are thrown out in the forest by your mother; all these stories are part of the structure by which we force minds to become a woman or a man in an artificial way. Inadequacy therefore relates immediately to a woman's relationship with a man, in the same way impotency relates immediately to a man's relationship with a woman.

The first thing that we teach in the Sufi movement is that you must accept your basic sexual role; you must accept your gender. If you live in the world, act in it, react to it, you are a woman or a man—as long as you do not know what that is, as long as you cannot respect that within yourself, accept that within yourself, you will be inadequate, or impotent.

People will say, "Well, what is it to be a woman?" You can only talk of being a woman in terms of what you express. If you are completely, totally aware all the time of your femininity, of that gender, then you are the bearer of children, the mother, the comforter of broken hearts; but you are also the rock, you are stable, you give very much inner confidence to a man. In terms of the sexual play, it is interesting that women think it is the man who should come along and court—overtly that may be true, but covertly the truth is that the woman invites the courting. There is nothing wrong with ninety-nine per cent of the women whom nobody courts, they are fine, they just have not figured that thing out, so nobody courts them and they feel inadequate. In much higher and deeper levels of sexual contact you find that if there is a dominance at all, the dominance will tend to be that of the woman. That is tied up with the problem of the impotency complex of the man; man is a drone and woman is a queen.

As long as this is not understood—your basic sexual gender and its strong implication, which you express every moment of your life, when you are in your being, in your body—you will always have these feelings of inadequacy. So that is the first thing to resolve. Once you have accepted that and resolved that in yourself, then it becomes a much easier matter to express your essential womanhood within your culture or value system. You cannot hide your womanhood; you can hide your breasts, you can cut your hair short, you can have a low voice—there are many things that you could do, but in the end you could not hide the fact that you are a woman. It is a very beautiful thing to be a woman; it is at least half of life that we men will never know.

As I have already said, the inadequacy complex of the woman is intimately tied up with the role of the father. That means that if there is a father and later on a husband or a lover who can bring understanding, contact, communication, to encourage the expression of natural feminine feelings, who can express appreciation of them, then the inadequacy fear is overcome. Thus it is really the impotency feelings of the father, which make him closed and hard—his heart is bleeding to express itself, he lives and dies, and he never does—which cause the inadequacy feelings in his daughter, who later on will become a mother, who will cause an impotency feeling in his grandson . . . and so it goes on. Somehow we must break through that circuit.

There is nothing wrong with being a woman. The magazines say that a woman should have a body in a certain shape, she should be lusciously inviting and submissive, she should also be passionate and smell like all these exotic things, but it is just not true. The stereotype of what a woman should be kills the freedom to be expressive. Woman is very rich. Think of woman as a feline, the killer of the hunt. It is woman who has more responsibility, woman who always is ready to work towards stability. Woman is the basis of society. Woman gives the security which maintains culture. Woman is the transmitter of depth, of feeling. Woman is the negative potential out of which intelligence can rise. If, therefore, an inadequacy feeling, in whichever form it may be, is to be overcome, it has to be in terms of your relationship with your own gender. We know very well that men often marry their mothers and women often marry their fathers. That is also why a girl will very often, if she has an inept father, tend to look for contact with older men to replace that. There again, the interesting thing is that the older man probably had a dominating mother, so he was looking for a younger girl, because a woman of his own age would be more mature, and he would be unable, mentally, to meet that challenge. So these two things compensate and sometimes help each other, and sometimes weaken one another.

Somehow, whether your father is still alive or alive in your memory, you have to come to terms with what your father thought of you in your childhood, what your brother thought of you, whether or not you were as good as your mother, whether you could compete with your mother for the affection of your brothers, for the attention of your father—all these things are quite closely tied up. It is simple to go back into childhood in your memories, because the things which cause these neuroses are right on its surface. All people can know basically what went wrong with them as they grew up, if they are honest with each other and with themselves. What they do not do is to run through it again, reprogram it, change their attitude towards it, iron out the problems, accept not to run in the same groove they were running in when they were four years old. The experiences in our life which cause neurotic living are right there, very clear; they are not far away and difficult to find.

There is a lot that can be done on a physical level to overcome the feeling of inadequacy, and that is probably the strongest method of healing that I have ever experienced. If there is one thing that almost always works immediately and totally, it is breaking out of the luscious, submissive, weak-woman-without-muscle image. Because woman is emotionally so rich and wise, she can be helped on a physical level. You will find that if a woman trains her lungs as physical exercise, begins to build up her energy, enrich her blood supply, increase her heart rate, make herself stronger, get herself to breathe better, think better, be more active physically, become more "sportsmanlike," a lot of the feelings of inadequacy drop away. We want woman to be like soft little pillows which we put in bed beside us, not to threaten us. We men, who feel impotent, we want you to be a nice little balloon; we just put you there and climb on, it's not so tough. Because of that you are anemic, you do not get enough. . . . If you read *Aerobics*, by Kenneth Cooper, it will astound you to see how closely physical health and physical function are tied up with mental health. Anemia is something that women usually suffer from; they think that it is because of menstruation, which it is not; it can be resolved by eating good foods, but also by doing physical exercise, even singing.

I remember so well introducing reshastics in South Africa. Reshastics, like aerobics, is based on breathing, and there are a few exercises in which you use your arms. Most of the girls in South Africa did not want to do them, and I finally learned that they were afraid that it would build up their biceps so that they would no longer have arms like a woman.

This is what is all screwed up—maybe some men have large biceps, but there are not many men like that; men's arms may tend to be a little stronger and a little heavier. In the same way that we have this warped image that a man's biceps are incredible hand-grenades, we have this idea that a woman's arms are little sticks that cannot slap us in the face. Many years ago I lived in California, and for five or six months my wife and I got up at 6:30 in the morning and ran round the block a few times. Finally we had to stop because we got so much enmity from the neighbors, especially the women, that it became impossible, socially, to keep it up. The female role in which the women had, in a hypochondriac way, installed themselves—"I am so happy to be unhappy, I have so much to complain about. I am sitting here with these horrible kids that I can't discipline and my husband goes away in a big car and he has a big job and he drinks a lot of beer; I have to do the weeding and I'm getting sick and tired of it . . . "—and at the same time, became set in maintaining so that they could continue to complain, made it impossible for them to accept a woman running round the block and doing exercises and being happy and singing and jubilantly dancing. It just blew their minds, they could not stand it!

To be adequate is to realize that you may not be able to lift one hundred and fifty pounds, but you can have a strong, healthy, athletic body; and when blood begins to go through your brain and heart and there is good aeration, the anemia will go away, and everything will work better.

I have not yet talked about the menstrual cycle, and there again I realize fully that because I am a man and do not have a menstrual cycle, some women may get angry at me and say that I have no right to talk about it. Men also have a monthly cycle; and you can see it in their moods, they also go down regularly. They do not bleed so there is no physical show, but it is very much the same—there are similar hormonal changes as happen in a woman. Psychiatrists studying this concluded that there is no such thing as a menstrual problem, only purely a mental problem. Of course, it is a culturally indoctrinated problem, it is pushed into us; I shall try to explain where it comes from. A long time ago people did not know that when a woman menstruated she was not actually bleeding; they did not know that she had no wound inside her, that the blood was already very old and had long since been taken out of circulation and replaced. They thought that something broke open, cracked off, that she was really bleeding, and this was a difficult thing to interpret, especially because a few women did have problems. There are societies in which the menstrual blood was used as medicine, was caught in beautiful vials and became a sacred thing. This was how they tried to resolve the problem in a positive way. But slowly by slowly the impotency problem of the man intruded—"She's bleeding, I can't make love to her tonight, it stinks, it's dirty, it's no good"—and he pushed her out, and it became a negative resolution. The man can say that she is dirty, no good and impure, and to show that he is not impotent, that he has the right to have a woman, he goes and gets another one. You can see that in polygamous structures, the menstrual cycle plays a very important part in deciding which woman will sleep with the man that night.

Those women who feel most inadequate as a general rule have heavy menstrual problems. I do not want to laugh the whole menstruation thing down the drain and say that nothing happens—obviously something happens, something most natural. It happens to all mammals from whales to mice. But basically what often happens is that a woman latches onto that period of feeling dirty or impure, or down, or bad, to feed and justify this reason to feel inadequate. A woman who feels inadequate wants someone to sympathize with her—wants her Daddy to come over and say, "Oh, daughter, come and sit on my lap"—so she goes off to her bed, or she feels tired, or she feels ill, but it is really a form of saying, "Come and love me." Unfortunately, because of man's impotency problem, it does not quite work. These two problems are closely tied together. Normally, a woman who has a healthy, active, natural life has no menstrual problems. I do not know the feeling myself because I do not have any ovaries, but maybe she knows that something is coming down or breaking loose, maybe she knows she is a little bit more tired, but that also corresponds to writing down on the calendar every month when you are going to menstruate. Then you prepare yourself mentally to go down so that you will not have to cook that day and your husband will care, and all these rituals . . .

Some people may wonder what menstruation has to do with spirituality; we must not get this thing wrong, it has everything to do with it. Spirituality (which is, in a way, a meaningless word) involves life as a natural, whole human being—a woman, a man. What a terrible thing it would be for a woman not to menstruate. She probably would not be able to get pregnant; her motherhood, the main part of the gender to which she belongs, would be cut out. So it is wonderful that every month you are reminded that you are able to be a mother, that you have other ducts, other possibilities in your body which make you the woman, the queen, the fertile soil.

The inadequacy problem can be resolved very easily. Accept your femininity, accept your father and the lack of communication with him, understand the situation, understand the cultural structure, then break out of it. Accept that you may not be physically as strong or active as a man; you may not be able to lift five hundred rocks in eight hours, but you can lift five hundred rocks in ten hours, and after eight hours your old man will snore for sixteen hours and be dead tired, and the next morning you will wake him up for breakfast. Women are stronger, women live longer, last longer, women are less locked up emotionally. They are richer, they can express themselves better. They possess something very beautiful, positive, something very simple which man lacks. Man may be more analytical (though that may also be a cultural judgment) but analysis destroys everything. With the intuitive feelings that woman has, she gives beauty; woman veils, that is the mystique that gives something the unknown quality, the unknown value. The center of romanticism is the feminine mystique, not the male power trip.

We began by introducing the fact that the feelings of inadequacy that women have are universal; and that is why it is so important to talk about it, because it relates to your femininity, to whether you think you are beautiful or smart or good or loved or wanted. If we are going to break out of these traps and create whole, healthy, positive humans who can rise to their potential, we must realize that it is woman who can save the world, woman who can change. She can suddenly say to herself—and that to me is women's liberation—"We are free to be what we are, we do not have to compete with men any more. We can be what we are."

One little encouraging word of sincere appreciation can resolve so many things within the heart of a woman. . . .

April 22, 1974

IMPOTENCY

In the last chapter we talked about the problem of inferiority as it applies to the female gender in the feeling of inadequacy. The main problem of inferiority as it applies to the male gender is the feeling of impotency, the subject of this chapter.

The first thing to qualify, before any misunderstandings arise, is that there is really no such thing as sexual impotency. "Impotency" refers much more to the mental, psychological lack of vitality, lack of energy, the inability to express oneself—a cloud of subtle, mixed concepts; with the words "male impotency" we mean the incapacity to receive love or to surrender, the fear to give love yielding.

Just as a woman needs a good father and a good feeling of acceptance by the father to develop a personality which feels adequate, so in the same way a man needs a good mother. Here is the first definite contradiction to the way society sees masculinity. Old-fashioned thought in the western world holds that to be a man you need a good father, and that it is the father image to which you must aspire. In a way that is right—you need good parents—but that aspect of masculinity is the image of the aggressive, strong, self-assured, determined, dominant male. In our society we want the male to be competitive, strong, tough, and often overlook the fact that just as there is depth and feeling and warmth in a female, these same emotions, these same doubts, these same needs, are also in a male. Through a warm relationship with his mother man can learn how to bring these out. The male character is formed by looking up to the father image in whichever way it materializes before us; but we look up to that image in terms of competition. Every young man will some day have to be as good as his teacher, as good as his father, as good as his elder brother, as good as the political or religious leader who is his masculine example. The first feeling of impotency begins to form because a young boy cannot compete with his father. To make matters worse, in the same way as with a young girl, the mother's attention may be focused on the young boy, but as soon as the father comes into the picture, the mother's attention will switch to him. Thus, although you may love your father and realize a good contact with him, his image remains a threat to the development of a feeling of acceptance and identity. Every male who grows up and forms his personality is in competition with every other male in the world, and every aspect of maleness is very much hyped up towards the part which is strong, tough, dominant, aggressive, in control. We distill and pull out the female from the male and make them two opposite poles, denying thereby a warm, subtle richness which is in every character and needs to be expressed.

When a boy becomes a young man the problem deepens even more, because the natural instinct in a young boy around the end of puberty is a very strong sexual need. The trouble is that we teach girls many protective ideas, that they have to be virgins, or that they can only give themselves to a man if he is ideal and wonderful. Although it is perhaps not as important physically to be a virgin any more, we still have a very strong symbolic virginity. Thus the natural strong male urges for sexual contact are frustrated, and that immediately translates itself into forms of impotency. A boy can be familiar and warm and playful with other boys, but not with girls. Through all these subtle conflicts with his natural needs, a young man slowly by slowly ends up feeling that he cannot master himself if he lets out these natural feelings, natural desires, natural warmth; so he closes up, squashes them.

Impotency is developed in another form through compensation by overaggression, and that is a form which is very much accepted because it fits in the hyped-up male role. Another way is to channel the needs for male expression into outer forms; such things as sport, later on business, fame, become natural outlets for denying the feeling of impotency, which has subtly developed all along the line.

The third way in which the feeling of impotency is translated is through religious attitudes and social religious functions. Manhood cannot feel deeply or express but, if we take the Middle Ages, to god he can. Man cannot express his normal sexuality—neither can woman—but through a religious worship he can. So you find that pious religious directions develop which finally do give the man the right to feel deeply, but only through effeminizing parts of his gender. This is clear and strong in Brahminism, in many religions, Buddhism, Christianity. Our ideal religious leader in the West has been and still is Jesus; although we may have thrown him away and all decided to go to eastern religions, it is still the baby Jesus who is with us. What is Jesus? Beautiful, effeminized, clear-eyed, pale, pure, untouched, above sex—no children, no father, a virgin image, a man who we believe never became angry, was never upset, who was always in contact with god, the son of the divine—we are all sons and daughters of the divine. As the Christian form becomes no longer acceptable, we search in other forms and pull out what can still fill this need to sublimate the feelings of impotency. In Brahminism you can see that the ideal man is a person who does not have strong muscles, does not have a low voice, does not run, never sweats, who is always very clean, very washed, a person who is never angry, who never has strong emotions. It is out of such images that things like Hatha Yoga grew.

So you have these three ways in which the basic feelings of impotency come out: first, through overt, boisterous aggression, which is often called in American psychology the penis complex, forms of exhibitionism—not sexual exhibitionism but personality exhibitionism, bragging, boisterous laughter, making jokes, being tough, showing off. The man who does that, who, to a large stratum of society, fits the picture of the "good male," is really behaving out of strong feelings of impotency. The second way is in the more mature, mental, intellectual interpretation of the need. You may know that it is ridiculous to drink at the pub, or to be a big champion; you may know that it does not get you anywhere, so you try to become a company director, investment broker, famous lawyer; you try for a strong professionalism, which is definitely attached to wealth, power and fame. In people who have a great deal of power, and very often in political leaders, you find the undertone of this impotency to be the basic driving force behind the person. Thirdly there is sublimation through effeminization. You want to be acceptable to women so you go not towards real womanhood, but the artificial role that womanhood is supposed to have, and you try to express yourself in that way. A typical example of that, which is beginning to be broken, is the case of shaving. (Since I have had both a beard and no beard and felt comfortable in both cases, I have the right to make some comment about it.) When a goat grows up and becomes a billy goat, he grows a beard; when a cub grows up and becomes a male lion, he grows a beard. When a man grows up, in exactly the same way, he grows a beard. It is exactly the same as pubic hair—every man who has a beard knows this, it is not the same as the hair on the head or the hair on the body, it is pubic hair—so it is a threat. You cannot show that you have become sexually competent, you must continue to have a baby face, soft and touchable, so you shave it off. I do not mean that every man who shaves his beard does not want to show his sexual possibilities, but I think it shows a socio-cultural development that we are just coming out of: an emphasis on effeminizing one's malehood.

The feelings of impotency in these three directions have all sorts of sub-forms; you can see very clearly why a man wants to be a hunter, why certain kinds of people perform certain sports. One would not expect a macho athlete to be homosexual, for instance, yet research indicates that they could have a tendency in that direction—if not in actuality, then at least in mental set-up. Schools used to separate boys into one class and girls into another, and sports used to be separate. Now schools have begun to see that sports develop a much better situation when they are mixed.

Without going too deeply into many of these things, we can now see side by side the sorts of suffering humanity goes through, a maturing process which builds the neurosis in, more and more strongly, and builds it in a very neat way, because the stronger it builds in, the more it finds in the other gender cultural patterns and signs to strengthen the divergence. In every male there is female, and in every female there is male—but maybe we should say that in both male and female there is always a positive and a negative (though these words may have connotations which confuse us). Every quality, every potential that we have consists of a very subtly balanced-out dominance between expressive and receptive forces, and every balance of every potential affects every balance of every other potential, so that the total comes up either positive or negative.

More and more you also find "role-switching" in society. Why?—basically because we feel most comfortable when we are complete. Man is a half-body, woman is a half-body; together they are one. The practice of wearing ties is now slowly dying out; most of us think of ties as something that men wear, but not many generations ago no man ever wore a tie and all women did. Most men today would not dream of wearing skirts—women wear skirts, men wear pants. Suddenly both wear pants, soon both may wear skirts. What we wear is always a cultural expression that symbolizes what part of ourselves we are comfortable in showing on the outside. If you look at previous fashions you will see that women wore pants and men wore skirts; and if you go even further back you will probably find that these things were switching continually, as also with the length of hair.

These feelings of inferiority, whether male or female, must be understood by yourself, inside yourself. If you are a man, you know you are basically not so terribly strong, not so incredibly dominant; basically you are soft and warm and vulnerable, probably far weaker than a woman. If you are a man you are also lonely; ever since you lost your mother you have been lonely, and even when you had her you were lonely. All the ways in which you are trying to resolve this need in yourself are, to me, abnormal; they are illnesses unless and until you complete them first in the natural way, the divine way. If anyone says that the union of man and woman is not divine, then I shake my head, and inside I feel pity for him, because that is the thing he longs for the most, the thing he is the furthest away from. The weakness you have if you are a male, that loneliness—it is like being a painter without a canvas to paint on; you cannot express yourself. You can paint on the water, on the clouds, on the trees, on the floor, anywhere: but the real thing you need in order to express yourself, the thing divinely ordained, that you should do first. You will find within yourself far greater strength through surrender than through dominance. You will find within yourself far greater respect through opening, through expressing that you are not all that strong, not all that sure, than through keeping it closed, because the way in which the feminine psyche is built up is precisely in these things; in some magical way which cannot be described, she responds and fulfills and completes.

In whatever culture we think of, whether Christian, Buddhist, Islamic, Hindu, western, eastern, the subject of man and woman is the most intriguing and the most feared, the most veiled and mysterious and often the most hyped-up. The subject of man and woman is not exclusively about going to bed and making love, neither is it exclusively about some platonic, ambivalent partnership or relationship. It is about fulfilling the divine plan of creation in the first and most elementary, natural way. If you are a male and you want to worship god, what you really want to do is to worship female; if you are female and you want to worship god, what you really want to do is to worship male. But somehow the worship of god is there—it is perfect, it is untouchable, it is unfathomable because no personality is involved. Maybe god knows all about you and that comforts you, and yet he is not there to threaten you by that knowledge in your immediate consciousness. Yet when you open to one another, what is the one thing which shows up immediately that threatens you? Your feelings of inadequacy, your feelings of impotency. If you are a woman then the man will know that you are not so hot or so great, and if you are a man, the woman will know the same thing . . . so you have organized culture. You are a man so you must become a scientist, you must get a diploma, you must go to school, you must become a good man, you must earn a lot of money. Or you say, "I will reject that trip because it is a false hypocritical thing. I shall be interested in deeper things like spirituality, yoga or eastern religions." Or you say, "I cannot really become rich because I am a poor worker, but I can boister my feelings away." Before any real deepening can happen, deepening in the real mystical life—not the runaway mystical life, whether it was the monks in the Middle Ages or the young men of today who turn to Zen Buddhism or any of these spiritual trips—before any of these things can really be deepened, you must complete, fulfill and mature your personality, your human needs. No man can be a man without a woman and no woman can be a woman without a man. I think that god will listen to you much more when you are one than when you are half. I think that your prayers will be understood much better when they are finished sentences than when they are unfinished thoughts and desires.

Out of this there comes another problem, and that is that man also has to be a father and a woman also has to be a mother. Somehow a woman is better equipped by nature—I do not really know why, but it seems logical and understandable that she is the mother, she will carry the child. That is another threat to male identity: we men will never carry a child, give birth to a child, breastfeed a child. Maybe, because woman can do that and realizes that she can, she deals with her problems much better and understands that she is built to become a mother. But one of the worst problems of the feelings of impotency is the knowledge that someday you will have to be a father.

What is it to be a father? What is it to be a husband? Being a husband is quite different from being a lover—you all know that. To be a father you have a child, or several children, you have responsibility, which means that you have to compete, not only for yourself—which you are not sure that you can do; not only for this woman—which is even more of a problem; but you have to compete also for the child. It means that not only do you have to compete, but that somehow you have to be something for that child, you have to deal with it. You cannot be closed to it, you have to be warm towards it, you have to love it; deep inside yourself you really want to, and yet you do not know how to deal with that at all. That gives you an even stronger feeling of impotency, you realize your immaturity, you realize your difficulty in expressing yourself, so what do you do? You say, "A child is the responsibility of the woman. She made it inside herself, she brought it out, she washes it, she cleans it, it is hers. I shall go out and earn the bread and she can do that." Yet always gnawing inside yourself is that knowledge that you are not a father at all.

With the first realization at about twelve or thirteen years old that you can perform the sexual act comes the thought that you could be a father. It is an incredible threat, this thing which will happen, which will drag on you, will hang onto you, this thing which you have to take care of and deal with. I know several people who became impotent during the pregnancies of their wives—why? Because suddenly comes this shocking thought: you are no longer just a man trying to be a man, you have to be an ideal man, a Jesus, a Joseph, you have to be a father and fulfill that—be a leader, a comforter, a provider, a supporter, a protector, all these incredible things, and all because of that one act. Impotency becomes even stronger: not only is it impotency because you are in competition with the malehood of the world, with your father trying to reach your mother, with your own feelings, but suddenly you also have to be a father. That in itself is very often enough to make you reject your essential malehood, because if you reject fatherhood, then you are impotent—you are the drone who did not make it. Your name will not survive, your seed will not survive, your genetic line will not survive, your creative power will not survive, no matter what value you have in whichever society, you feel completely impotent. So you shove the problem onto the woman, and the contact is pulled further apart. You go back to the old values which in some way you feel you can meet, and you run away from the new ones.

In Hinduism they say that the first guru is the mother, and the second guru is the father; and it makes a lot of sense. The first guru prepares for the second guru. Then the third guru is the child. All the things that you have grown up to be, man, provider, hunter, all the moral examples you are supposed to fulfill, the ideal you are supposed to live up to, the values of the society that are imprinted on you which you are supposed to maintain—all these things suddenly focus into one. You know that you are not there, so you avoid it away because you cannot meet it; yet there is not a single man anywhere in the world who will ever really be a man unless he can be a father. It is interesting that a lot of fathers who have no contact with their own children are liked by children who are not related to them, because the children are not their product—it is not you, a piece of you, a development of you which shows clearly but something else; you can be detached from that.

Inadequacy in woman was not called impotency because although it corresponds very closely to the whole sexual part of the female gender, it does not have exactly the same symmetrical correspondence as in the male; whereas impotency in its most crucial point does relate to the inability to deal with the result in material manifestation of sexual potential. I have tried to portray these two things, female inadequacy and male impotency; they refer to every woman, every man walking on the face of this earth, in every society, culture or value system. It is true that I have not seen the inhabitants of the Hawaiian islands, and I have not seen the aborigines in Australia or the Amazon Indians, but as a simple citizen I have seen a lot of the world, and to the degree that it was possible I have tried to live successfully in many different cultures. From the point of view of any one culture, the other cultures are supposed to be completely different, but my conclusion is that they are not different at all. They are all about the same problem, about being a man or a woman. All the little trips that are developed—structures, social norms, customs, traditions, moral rules, laws—are in some way superstructures which rise from that basic problem. Who am I and why am I here? Where am I from? Where am I going?

But the most important of these is the first, who am I? And this is why, in the teachings of Sufism we always insist, first of all, that the first answer to who you are refers to your gender. You cannot walk the face of this earth in any form without belonging to a gender, it is part of your basic identity. So we developed a phrase "basic insecurity pattern," which refers to a person who has not yet accepted the first answer to that question, who am I? A man, a woman . . .

May 6, 1974

RELATIONSHIPS

We now come to the subject of relationships. We have all seen many relationships between people formed and unformed, and over the years you can see patterns; in my own life experience I can also see many different lessons. To introduce this subject I would say first that the relationships between men and women are changing and certainly we should look first at the historical development, what kinds of taboos there used to be, how they were formed. Maybe then we can see where we are now, what taboos exist now and how they are formed. I would think that as far back as one can go in the history of civilization there has been a conflict between the sexes—maybe we could call it warfare between the sexes. There is a book called *Sex and Power in History*, by Amaury de Riencourt, which talks about that. In a sense every individual relationship between a woman and a man is also an expression of the total relationship which is going on in the collective. It is therefore especially difficult to see one's own personal feelings, emotions, likes, doubts, love, as basically a droplet in a big swirl of cyclic evolution. It is difficult to see that the particular thoughts and feelings and values that we have or that others had previously at any one time are not very original, or very specific, or very private, and we are very much a reflection of the influences of the state of mind of the collective at that time.

I do not know if it is helpful to evaluate one's own relationship in terms of the collective of the time in which it is happening; maybe it gives distance, maybe it gives more peace. But in any case you can see that the strange sort of warfare of different times was a warfare about different things. At one time it was about dominance, at another time it would have been about forms of sexual contact, at still another time it would have been about the social structure of the units of the relationship. Again at another time it would have been a conflict about sincerity, purity. And it seems that as this warfare has developed before and now, you can see from the collective of what is happening that whatever the little warfare is about, there is a conflict in terms of sharing, there is a conflict in terms of what the one or the other is supposed to do or feel or give as an answer to what we do or give or feel; and there is always an attempt at defining an equality.

I know this last may seem strange in terms, for instance, of the Moslem marriage where the woman is kept in the background in a burqa and can never appear, but on the other hand I am sure that in her relationship, while she has given up a lot of things, there are also tremendous new prerogatives that she has gained. I would say that historically the warfare, the conflict of sharing and of equality of relating, is primarily a problem of the female seeking her space and not being given that space. Secondarily it is a problem of the male, a feeling of impotency; a feeling that if you give all you lose all. It is strange that not long ago there used to exist the concept of chivalry; courting or dancing to come closer was all about the problem of chivalry and how to show it. In a sense, there the male had found, for a while at least, the formula for giving, in actions, in deeds, in words, even including his life—but not really himself.

The conflict of the woman finding her space, her place, can also be seen in history in terms of religion. In the past, in whichever religion it was (they are all different, but they are all very much the same) the female found an abode of sanctity in which she was able to be pure and have room, be on terms of equality with the opposing force. You could also see that she would find in the religious life a feeling of value, of very deep and subtle feelings, sentiments, self-identity, which in the normal, real, life-to-life relationship is generally rejected by the male in the need for more robust or gross strength in the expression.

I would like to suggest that the whole society is about the two trying to find a way to resolve their war and also to continue to wage their war. Where the woman does not find her place she constructs a more religious, symbolic and also, in a sense, an impersonal relationship in which she has space, in which some of the deeper part of her nature, the more subtle, more interior, more refined, more style-conscious aspects can come out. The whole society, in terms of commerce and building, power, order and strength, is where the male goes to find a refuge from not being able to surrender, and also to exude his strength without losing himself. You can see that, at present, the design of goods for consumption by males goes more and more towards slickness; there is no contact, it's like water off a duck's back, there is no absorption of any kind. It is beautiful, it is functional, it is strong, it is inert; and yet the word *slickness* suggests something about moving in, through and out and never being touched.

In the collective mind of all the men who are engineers and designers in the world, advertising consultants, marketing consultants, there is a reflection of the warfare of the relationships with their women. I thought for a while that the grandiose buildings of the Roman period which seemed to repeat themselves in every further civilization had come to an end; very few supremely grandiose buildings were built after the First World War, except maybe some in America. Now you suddenly find that the making of a house is again an expression of this warfare. In the past I think that the making of the house was a male thing, but now it seems to be more of a female thing because in the house she finds a space for herself, a space for her existence.

Let us now come down to some specifics in terms of one's own self. Many people have at some time or other, openly or partially, asked of others or of me: Is he the right man, is she the right woman? Should I have an abortion? Do you think we'll make it together? Or, afterwards, all the problems of splitting, of not having found it, the self-doubt; and the big, long, eternal question that comes up, and the defeat that comes up because we move in and out of relationships and we cannot find the right person.

It is interesting, some of the older members of society, when they see that this goes on, they become very critical and say, "Oh, what a terrible thing, what an immoral thing! It's free sex, free love. Look, I've been married for eighty years with the same man and we're happy. Why can't you live like that?" I would say that the reason this cannot be is that the value of the relationship (of what you want to get out of it) has changed. Second, there is no social criterion holding you together; and third, there is not someone else choosing for you. Before, Mama or Papa went to talk to the other Mama or Papa, and they said OK; that was it, and if you left that man or that woman, you left your whole family, you left your caste, you just could not do it. So, frankly speaking, you would be happy and whatever you had you would be happy with because the alternatives did not exist, there was no real freedom in the sense that there is today; but there may have been freedoms, or at least certainties, which we do not have.

In this society of permal singular relationships we still find a bit of the moral structure, the moral stigma, moral taboo of the previous society and thus we have a concept of ourselves that we should find a kind of eternal permanent relationship right off the bat or as soon as possible, and it should really work. When it does not work there is a contradictory confusion, not with the realism of what we were actually doing, which was just trying out whether the glove fits the hand, but with the previous value system of another civilization. I think that the value system of the other civilization was, relatively speaking, right, because you cannot have a particular taboo without a whole conglomeration of very complicated inter-related social needs, conditions, laws—the possibilities of women going to work, the amount of free time, the situation of legal guarantees of individual freedom, the technological advances allowing longer life, less drudgery, the changes in health, the decrease in infant mortality, the increase in schools, in education—all these things have so drastically changed. The previous value system was probably right, probably the best way to solve the problems of that time, but in the situation in which we live now, the degree of excellence of sincerity, the amount of psychological self-insight, the possibility of examining oneself and others, one's inner feelings and thoughts are so much deeper that it is basically impossible to live in the same bed with someone with whom you do not share very close inner spiritual bonds. Of course, that bond might have been there in the previous culture also, but due to family and caste cohesiveness, it would have been built into the partnership selection system in another way.

In a sense, therefore, I would say that by the previous set of standards, the apparent freedom that we have now is not a freedom at all. Before, people were free enough to stay with each other even if it was not so good, because it did not matter, and because probably they were not intelligent or developed enough to know. Now there is much less freedom because, compared with the past, the amount of harmony, of being in tune necessary to make life valuable, to satisfy the over-sensitivity, is much higher—so much higher that you cannot stay with someone you cannot live with—you do not go to the ducks and milk the cows and take care of fifteen babies each nine months after the other. Also the greater family does not exist. You no longer live with your great-grandmother and your grandmother and their caskets and all the aunts and uncles; the whole thing has changed. Your home is much smaller, even your physical home is much smaller, and if you can share that space—which is so much more of yourself—with another person, the unity needs to be much deeper than the standards that existed before. I know that all the crying mothers and grandmothers say, "Oh, my daughter is terrible, she is sleeping with every man...." I think you should answer that their daughters are trying to find a spiritual relationship, a soul relationship, a relationship based upon a degree of proximity, of entunement that the mothers cannot conceive.

Now I would establish some sort of morality and say, if it is the spiritual relationship which is our goal, then the possibility of so-called free sex does not exist. There is a much higher moral rule, a much higher taboo, and that is that you would only engage with a person if you feel a spiritual echo, if you feel an inner bond and if and when you really do feel that, yes, then there is a base of love, and thus a basis to make love.

Before I talk about the process of selection, I should like to discuss the question of when to split. In a sense it takes great wisdom to find the right person to live with, to find the person you can develop and be developed by, but I think it takes far greater wisdom to know how to part, when to part, when it is necessary and, if it is necessary, how to do it. It is these splits which very often break and destroy a relationship which really was very good; just because there was not the wisdom of knowing how to loosen, you destroy all that happened, all that was beautiful. You have been together for a year, six months, eight months, why destroy that? Once you've been together, once you've shared your soul, you're always together. You can never really be enemies, you're permanently married in a sense, you just don't live together any more.

The freedom to transit and the wisdom to do it, to know how to do it, is very important. Before, when splitting was not possible, humanity never developed the wisdom of how to allow people to split; you had to go to a judge who separated you, you signed a piece of paper and you fought about money and children and sheets and paintings—you've lived together and loved together all your adult life and suddenly you decide to split and you can't just do it. Once you have a really permanent bond then you're not really splitting; that is a wrong concept.

Having talked about the concept of splitting for a moment I want to talk about the concept of selection. The most serious problem with selection is lack of experience, which opens up entirely the licentious role of free relationships. I do not mean to say that in contradiction to the concept that you should only make love when there is a spiritual bond. I think both these things must be taken together. It took me a long time to see that people basically choose wrongly and continue the same wrong pattern all the time in the beginning until they finally make a real switch. I do not know how it was in the past, but in the present it is the woman who chooses, not the man; it may very well be the man who splits, but it is the woman who chooses. I think it is more reasonable to call that honestly what it is because it changes this confusion of the burden of initiative. Many people cannot seem to get this together, just because the woman expects the man to say "Let's do it"—and he's scared or he doesn't know and she blocks it or something. . . . It is the woman who chooses today, that is how the culture is; man does not do it any more. I think this is interesting because it allows a much greater sense of planning, of foresight, of freedom, of dignity for the woman herself.

When a woman cannot find anyone it is generally because she has far too high a standard. You suggest to her ten men and she says they are all terrible. The second problem, though, is that she wants someone to come to her and say, "Would you marry me?"—and then she's swept off her feet. This is an old concept, it's like virginity; virginity is a very beautiful ideal, but it's of another culture and doesn't work any more.

If the woman has the right to choose and the burden of choice is with her then there are definitely some criteria which can be defined for her part. The first is whether you could have that man's children, whether you would want to. I have expressed this before and sometimes girls run to me and say, "Hey, I want so and so, I'd love to have his children." That is the first thing they say, they haven't even thought about it, but I do not mean it in this superficial way. When you mate with someone you set in motion a genetic process of life, it determines who these children will be, what kind of people they will be, what kind of personalities they will have, what kind of influence they will have upon the world. It determines a lot, and since you are after all an incubator I think you should decide much more deeply when that machine starts working. Therefore the whole sense of choosing the man becomes more meaningful because you are not choosing emotionally in terms of love or attraction exclusively, you are choosing in terms of much more permanent and long-term effects of life. As long as you have not had enough experience to evaluate a particular choice, the only thing that may be wrong with the choice is just this shyness. A very important part of the experience is not just to try out every different man, it is also to go and look at couples; look at them and look at the kind of children they have together, what these children look like, how they develop. Since we have birth control and we don't have to have twenty-six children per woman, or whatever it used to be in the fourteenth century, every single child is much more valuable. It is no longer muscle-power, it is the personality of the child, its intellect, its depth which forms something for the future; and that man with whom you really could have children, with that man you share destinal bonds, even if he is not the one you like the most, even if he is not the most adventurous or the most sexy. It is a different kind of man from one you would choose to have an affair with; that is the man with whom you want to recreate life. As you see, today procreation is not an economic factor, it is in a sense a religion; the making of a family has become very much the same as what I think religion used to be.

There is another criterion and that is the question of inspiration. If you can inspire that man, if that man can inspire you, not just in terms of a short-term love but in terms of mental development, maturing, discipline, then you are much more likely to be a good couple.

I would say that the third criterion is: if you can have a good fight together, if you can have a good conflict and come out of it well, then you have a good relationship. It is a much better proof of a good relationship if you have a hell of a fight and come out well than if you have no fight at all and come out of nothing. Relationships are much stronger now, they are much more eventful, much more passionate, there is much more happening. It is not just that you get together and you go to bed and you have a bunch of children—no, you come together and the whole explosion of existence gets involved in your life.

Now we come to the criteria of selection for the male— and I have thought about these for a long time. I think it comes right down, in the simplest way possible, to smell; and I'm quite serious and sincere in saying that. The right woman is the one who smells right and that is all there is to it. Now you will ask how you know when she smells right. I think that somehow these polymers or the products of smell that we make reflect who we are, the kind of personality that we have, the kinds of feelings, and they definitely reflect our moods and our whole being. I remember going through many discussions and this is the most clear indication of the right person. That sense of smell, you see, it's total; it's clear, it answers you subconsciously, in the deepest of your being.

People may ask why I do not say that it is also the sense of smell for the female. It is because the requirements for the female are much more mental, much more esoteric; the female's experience of her man is an experiential level that I would consider mental; although we consider a human woman as emotional, the emotional level of her experience is symbolic, is projected, is also very often assumed, whereas the emotional level of the experience of the male is much more direct and therefore more shallow and much less symbolic.

I also think—and this is horrifying to some of you—it is clear that in the relationship a woman chooses, a man leaves. Now there comes a very important question of whether this is right, when it should happen and why, what is the moral basis, what is the justification? Many women would think, Well, why can't I leave, why shouldn't I be the one that splits? Well, of course, a woman can also leave; I am not saying that only a man can leave, but you can see that it is the woman who chooses in this culture, you can see that it is the man who leaves. Why? Because a woman is more patient, more absorbing, more bearing, more sedate in a sense, more yielding. She is also demanding, but she's more loyal, more willing to wait, more deepened. While she may know all along that it's not good, something in her feminine idealism makes her stay. This is the reality of how it is today, this is the reality of how the culture exists.

Now the question comes, If the burden of selection is on the woman and the burden of staying or leaving is on the man, when should you leave? I feel very strongly that as soon as there is a doubt it should be the signal to leave. Why? First, because a woman is a human being who senses all your thoughts and feelings very deeply, and if there is a doubt in your heart, she is already destroyed; she has no more chance. Also, because we are living in a different life value, life period: we are living in a life period where the possibility of meeting and living together is free, and so the burden is to find the best possible relationship, not to stay if there is a doubt.

Some people, especially our grandfathers and grand- mothers, would say, Why isn't there, as they say in Dutch, *doorzettings vermogen*, stay with it, do your duty and keep it up? As long as there is no doubt, there is the duty to do everything in your power to make the relationship as good as possible. There is the requirement, which certainly many men shirk, to try to live on the deepest possible level. I know that as soon as it appears that a man and a woman are together—let us say that he is sure of his sexual repletion, he is sure that he can make love that night, he won't be looking around—he is so sure that the woman is with him that he doesn't have to woo her any more. As soon as that happens a man lets up; he assumes, "All right, she's with me now; there she is and now I can look on to other things I'm interested in." This process sometimes happens very fast, overnight, or it may happen slowly. All the affection comes out to woo and get this woman—but now she's mine, now she's nothing.

This thing that happens is very important; it must be changed. Most women would have accepted that in the past, but now they don't have to accept it any more and they shouldn't accept it. You could say that to be permanently together means to live at that level where you are permanent- ly engaging to try and stay a little longer together. You know the first periods of wooing and of loving, they are so wonder- ful; and then things slow down. Why? Because you assume that it's set now—but if you would assume that it's not set, then this whole high of wooing goes on and on and on. Or, you say, Let it go. It's like the example of walking or running; at every step you fall, you are always off-balance and by being off-balance you are able to move forward. If you are in balance, then you are steady.

Men very often ask me the question, When is there a doubt? There I also make it very clear: it is just as with the sense of smell, the right woman smells right and there is no doubt about it, that's it. It could be that there is more than one woman who smells right, but the right woman smells right. What does it mean then if she smells right and yet there is a doubt? I think that the sense of smell changes. In life I think that there is an evolution and it could very well be that a couple does not evolve together. The idea of a permanent relationship assumes that two people evolve permanently together, that they are always good to each other, but that is not necessarily true; it is an assumption that people made in the past.

Now comes the question, Do I have a doubt, should I stay with this woman or not? Many men have asked this question, many more men than women. Many men who are staying with women in relationships have asked that question while these relationships are still on. I tend to answer that the decision to leave a woman or not must not have anything to do with any other woman. If you are living with a woman because you engaged to live, because it was really meaningful to you, you moved in to live together and then you fall in love with another woman and therefore you're frustrated and you decide you're going to leave the first one—then your leaving is wrong, it's immoral and it's disloyal and unfaithful and wrong. And this new marriage won't work out very often. Your attractedness to one woman is no justification to bring any kind of doubt into a relationship that you have now. The doubt should stand on its own. It has nothing to do with another person; it has to do with these two people.

Second, what is the doubt really about? The doubt is whether this woman loves you; however you may think of it, that is really the doubt; to put it in the most subtle way, does this woman love me? That is your doubt. Does she really love me? And in a sense you see that when marriages begin to have troubles, they begin to test that. Much of the time a man's behavior is simply an unconscious test of whether the woman really loves him. Well, we are all men or women, and I tell you, the doubt whether a woman loves a man is a doubt that all men have—it goes so deep that they can never express it and they have a tremendous need for assurance. It is because of that doubt that they can never really surrender. As soon as a man begins to feel, Well yes, she wants me, she doesn't totally love me—it is finished. You can go on for a year, you can go on for ten years . . . but it's finished and it's time to split because all the problems have eroded—there's no more real base and there's something wrong in a sense with that doubt, and that is that once there is that doubt it can never be resolved. If you have a doubt whether you are really loved it probably can never be resolved, even if she really does love you.

I think that a deeper bond has much to do with the possibility for self-expression. You express yourself into the other, you absorb the other, the other expresses herself or himself into you. These forms of expression cause continual changes and regenerations into each other. If I marry the wall, I express something to the wall and the wall is changed, it expresses something back. I get changed and it goes back and forth, back and forth. There is always something more to express because the previous entwinement engendered something new in you. If that growth does not happen, it ends.

It is sometimes useful to compartmentalize, one can understand things better; it is also sometimes confusing. I will try to compartmentalize a relationship under certain limited concepts, but do not make the mistake of thinking that these are in fact really separable, because they are not; it is simply a way of dividing emphasis. Of course, the possibility of expression exists primarily through the sexual union. There is a lot of emphasis on the sexual union and it is obviously very clear that if there is not a good sexual union the relationship is most likely neurotic and should not be kept together. Then comes the question of what a good sexual union really means. Can you define it? At times in my life I would say certain things and at other times other things, but it would always be approximately in this vein: A good sexual union is one which is steady. It is a union in which the sexual heat is regenerated on a regular, frequent, stable basis as often as possible. When the sexual union is sometimes really hot and then nothing, then that is not a good sexual union, even though there are orgasms and all these other things and you say, "Oh, it's so fantastic when we make love." Those are the unions that break. They think it's fantastic and they break—why? Because the heat is not regenerated on a regular, healthy, stable basis. So I am not saying that a good sexual union is an expression of the fact that the woman has an orgasm all the time, or the man has constant erections, no, because these are very hyped-up concepts, artificialized. A continuously repeating, stable sexual relationship shows the sexual union is good—there are no problems with impotency, there is no problem with lack of heat; the woman and the man both reinfuse each other sexually all the time—that is a good union. If you do not have that, reconsider very seriously how you live.

There is another compartment, and that is the compartment that one should call faith. No one here, nor anyone in the world, however hard they would want to deny it, can say that they do not have faith. I am not saying faith in god, faith in this, faith in that; I'm just saying, faith. Faith is something of the secret language of receptivity towards that which is beyond perception. It makes one feel a contact like that of the navel with the placenta; it makes one feel justified in one's identity, it gives one contact to live on. Sometimes people have faith in terms of their survival; particularly men. I do not quite understand why they have that more strongly than women, but very often men say in difficult situations, "Well, I knew I was going to come out of it all along, I have a knack for that, I knew it." They have no intellectual basis for saying that, no statistical basis, it's all a lot of nonsense—they just have faith. I think that woman's faith, in terms of its esoteric value, is more complete than man's faith. But these two faiths need each other, like music and an instrument, like woman and man—they need each other.

You see many examples, especially among younger couples today, of good sexual contact but no faith contact. Just as with the previous, the sexual compartment, there is a definite criterion for saying when faith contact is good. Faith contact is good when there is a feeling that the bond is a reflection of a higher intelligence, that it was meant to be, that it was called for, and that in the bond the two coming together can focus, can bring forth something in the material world. In a sense this is the spiritual base of marriage. This is why I referred previously to saying that the right man is the man with whom you want to have children, in a deep sense of the whole result of having that man's children in the world and that man having children with you. If you feel that you are together and that it is a higher thing that has brought you together, that you have something to do—it's not very clear what and how—but if there is a higher sense of purpose in it, then you share faith. Just as the pleasure and expression of sexuality is exchange in making love, faith is also exchange and I find many marriages very shallow, people never exchange faith, they never come to that, especially men, they are very much afraid of that—women express it more in their being.

The problem is that now faith is no longer expressible in words; maybe it never was, but it is obvious that before, certain kinds of words had an esoteric value and one could . express one's faith in those words. The symbolic charge of language has changed, words have changed, so that you can no longer "make faith" together in words—you have to find a way to express the significance of faith in some other way. One of the most logical ways which fits today very well is in the unplanned experiences of conscious united creativity. For instance—and this puts also the whole basis of marriage quite clear—to make something together. When you write a book together or you have a family together, you create something together and in that creativity there is an expression, even through archetypal influence, of your subconscious and of your faiths and it is in these creative endeavors that you can exchange your faith and absorb faith from each other. Everything that a couple makes is, in a sense, a child, a procreation. I think that it is primarily the male who resists that, in this life, in this period of evolution.

Another compartment of life together is the ability to compete. I introduced this chapter by saying that there is war, and whether by some value judgment you do not like the idea, it doesn't make any difference; there is, even if you think that you and your mate never have any war, no, it's a bunch of baloney—you do have war. We need tension, we need aggression; if we do not find the way to have it positively, we'll have it negatively. It is clear that you are the fastest sperm, that we are the evolutionary result of the most reactive, most adaptive, most tense little bit of DNA, the most convulsive—and our sense of experience of reality has to do with contradiction and apperception. We need a sense of gratification with reality, and the gratification, like peace, comes through conflict.

Somehow the Holy Maria image has made of a woman a being who cannot play war fairly, but it's not right, a woman is a very intelligent human being, very smart, very powerful and can war very well—and also be hurt very much. But a successful relationship is one in which there is a successful satisfaction of this need to fight, of combat, of strife; and there I find that it is usually the female who resists this engagement. She resists the challenge of combat, of intellectual exchanges, of conceptual conflicts, very often of the whole philosophic time-space continuum. And so the man does not have a partner in life with whom he can play war; so he won't live with that person and they have only half a life together.

Society has created an all-male culture: it would be very interesting to have armies of women. I think that armies could consist of couples; they would fight very well. Single people cannot fight. But there are all-male societies, male games, male clubs—what is the reason for that? Why has the woman been relegated to being neurotic? Because she hasn't been allowed to engage in combat, she hasn't been allowed to be free to fight. Many men, when the woman really starts fighting, have such a shock that they just run off, they can't believe it. And this sense of competition, of intellectual or mental competition, to strive, in ambition, for conception— that is a compartment, as I said, which is mainly resisted by women. Exchange of faith is mostly resisted by men.

All three of these are levels in which an exchange of self is possible, in which it can find a mirror, continue to grow, and live permanently with another.

I should like to end by saying that what I have tried to express is definitely an explanation of what is already happening. To find a proper relationship is part of being alive, and if you cannot find a proper relationship, at least to gain enough wisdom and experience and knowledge to come to that, you are not living fully. Life is different now from what it was before and to have a proper relationship with a person is most important, you must do it, it is part of growing. It is like modern tantric yoga continuing; and sometimes people give up too soon; sometimes there are all sorts of feelings that splitting is bad and getting together with the wrong person isn't good enough. I hope that one could become in one sense much more idealistic, that we really want to have a proper relationship and it can only be a proper relationship if it is spiritual, if it's really deep, deeper than anything our parents or grandparents had as far as we could see. On the other hand we must also be pragmatic, not be attached to emotional values that belonged to a previous period, to taboos that were formed in the totality of a value system of a previous time. We should form a taboo now and say that we should not live with people we are not capable of growing with, and we shouldn't live without realizing that if we do not develop good relationships something is wrong with us and we need to see why and what; and that is a major object of the exercise of this life. Just because a relationship isn't good does not mean that all life is finished—no, it means that you've got to figure it out and pick up and go on and try again. I think that this is very much a part of the *de facto* teaching which all modern people bring and contribute to the culture today.

Many people have probably heard parts of this before and I think that the most important thing I've tried to say is that it is the woman who chooses the man in this time of society. Before, it was the mother; before that it was someone else. Today it is the woman herself. Be conscious of that choice—make it. I think you could be capable of making good choices. I have also tried to suggest that all of the discussions and conversations with so many men show this one thing so clearly, that they would be different men if they had this doubt resolved in themselves as to whether you really love them. And I leave it up to all of us to decide why and how this doubt exists.

MARRIAGE
& LOVEMAKING

The bond uniting people together in life is the most essential relationship of meaning, purpose and continuity of mankind. Naturally many words can be said about it and I suppose that most of them are in vain, for one can never really capture the alchemical setting behind this binding quality.

As we are living in an age where sexuality as an expression of human worth is surging to the foreground—a position which it probably was more than due—there seem to me certain other aspects of this relationship which may be pushed a little bit more into the background. Also, commensurate with the growing awareness of orgasm and the rôle of the female and her worth in the human society on an equal basis, an aspect of female depth is being overlooked which may in the longer run come back to a place of attention. Of course, I do not want at all to discredit the present surge as expressed in these changes because they are due to an imbalance in society which, though culturally based, was obviously at the root of much neurosis and therefore inadequacy in marriage and family life in general.

Nevertheless, the kind of alchemical qualities which are also required for a deep, let us say spiritual bond, marriage, I would like to identify with the words *mellowness* and *reflection*. Yes, of course, the central part of a marriage is the sexual bond, the sexual relationship. But the sexual is not necessarily exclusively an affair of libidinous content. There is an aspect of the silent joy and approval of each other's company, an aspect of the support and faith in each other's potential which is also, in a transcendent sense, sexual.

I do not mean by mellowness a mediocre presence or the inconsequentiality of the female or the male. In fact this absorbing reflexive quality is in character female. The marriage relationship is also a psychological home, for rest of the spirit and quietude of the psyche, for a pause and purification in which anxiety and frustration can be both released and absorbed—not through words or deeds but through the alchemical recipient solvent of the true partnership. This is why in a sense I always refer to sexual foreplay as unnecessary in the real relationship—because the afterplay in a marriage lasts forever and becomes the essential foreplay in which the sexual encounter is a high but in a sense not exclusively necessary.

Mellowness, as a female quality, yields, and the present assertion of equal rights for womanhood endangers woman's special difference. In terms of her absorbing yielding presence, she is not equal as an initiator of life energy, of the tension to focus, of assertion. No, in the difference of this aspect she is being, enveloping presence, silent and dominated, even possessed. And the "masculine" finds home in it, in her, and the rest to regenerate, to re-extend. Yes, of course that would seem to mean that I am putting the woman back into her silent rôle of the dependent watcher and inferior acceptor who cannot develop an identity of her own. While on the one hand I do not wish to put her down there, still I do not accept that it really is "down" there. A woman is only downgraded when she downgrades her own womanhood; and some aspects of the present equal-rights-for-womanhood ideas do that in a way, because when one attempts to over-strengthen the masculine self, the female self which is also there is perhaps suppressed. Womanhood is equal, but different, and her real dignity is only in terms of the different complementary rôle. That principle of complementation which makes a marriage and family is engendered therein. Often, when marriages do not work, it was to my mind this alchemical yielding which was missing. No matter how hard sexual techniques were used to improve the relationship, the improved orgasm could not strengthen the bond in the end. And if the bond was otherwise good, the slight lack of this sexual excellence did not decrease its total worth. Of course, someone will say that I am painting a picture in which the woman has to take all the man's problems, faults, et cetera, and not the other way round. In a way that objection is true. That quality of mellowness and softness, absorbing, silent complementation, which is effected in presence and not in deeds, is also necessary in manhood's character. And this quality in both, created in a sense by the bond, by each other, in each other, for each other, is the marriage. Then I would say that the hue, the ring, the silent sound of this mellow ovular is set by the woman, by her character, by the depth of her spiritual self-contact. I would even go further and say that here in a sense she forms him, that through this tone-setting she makes her man the priest of her shrine, the adorer of her soul. She metamorphoses him into her truth, which becomes his and he then re-expresses it into her. While apparently he is doing all, she is nourishing the whole. I simply cannot accept that this is, as some would say, a thankless task. Many marriages break because of the shallowness of the unsupportive male, but I often see also the lack of female inner nourishment. Of course the one causes the other and so blame is on neither or on both. But what I want to suggest here is that marriage is and can be a growing rewarding bond, that it can become true if it is not yet and that its depth or its wounds or its lasting are not resolved by the sexual alone and that this other quality, an alchemical operative, an almost religious aspect of the relationship, is much closer to the inner core of its success.

Since we live now in an age where procreation is not really necessary in an individual sense for survival, this kind of precondition ought to become the factor to determine whether to create in the marriage one further level of unity—children.

Sex has happily become such a "liberated" subject that most people can finally freely talk and think about it in the western world. Probably the result of this liberalization is also contributing to greater enjoyment of our sexual potential, greater gratification of the need and so forth. The most important aspect of this liberation of information probably won't have a real effect until one or two generations hence, but it seems to me that the public emphasis which is, of course, manufactured by a response to its own need is overly concentrating on the orgastic experience as a technique, on libido as a quasi-chemical happening. There is insufficient emphasis on the greater aspects, the "spiritual" aspects of the sexual relationship in which the two bodies meet but the two beings also unite; and I also think that a lot of insecurity about performance as a result of sexual overtness in the media destroys the simpler, deeper, mellower aspects of the joy, the nature of intercourse as an exchange of warmth, affection, love, which is not at all dependent solely upon the excellence of the physical performance. But please do not make the mistake, in reading this, of thinking that I am knocking good, heavy, erotic sex. I simply see so many other aspects that are forgotten a little. For instance, while of course it is true that basically anybody can make love with anyone, doing just that would be very destructive in the long run. I suppose that any normal man could do it with any woman and vice versa, but only with certain of these is the experience on a deeper level of unity lasting and fine. Certainly the new-gained freedom has allowed lots of unsatisfactory marriages to dissolve and so forth. But the new freedom has not yet come around to create a sense of willfulness which is about the freedom to stay in the prison, in the marriage, and make it good.

I think that the classic female psyche of purity, loyalty and inner supportiveness cannot be entirely discarded for a freedom to move on to, say, a new relationship if one does not work. The same for the classic male psyche of nobility, honor and perseverance. The total demand which the new freedom to make (give) love should arouse in a partnership is to challenge oneself to sufficient self-examination and generous self-reconstruction so that one is willing (if love is there) to break out of one's mediocrities and really make a marriage. I think that the criteria for sexual freedom should also include the burden to make love and in that sense the understanding that we renew ourselves with what we have, with the one we live with, and not primarily through the newness of a relationship. The sort of sexual criteria for that would have to be associated with frequency, with re-evaluation of the self and with a search in the sexual expression to touch the "spirit."

Reaching the spiritual spheres of the sexual union requires a deep understanding of the workings of polarity, of attraction and repulsion, of dominance, or exchange, of sexual initiative and rôle interplay. Of course the most difficult concept to express is love. Reaching that sphere requires love; the only real aphrodisiac, the only real engendering force is love—but what is love? Does it really exist? In a sense, no. We create it as an outwarding of our self-love. Don't get me wrong here and conclude that I have gone all sentimental. Love is not the sweet, soft eternal. It brings pain, truth, anger, competition, attraction, wonder, quietude, energy, selfishness, possessiveness, generosity, and everything else you wish. When two partners commit themselves to each other, with each independently and true in that independent self-giving, then there is a stage of love—and only on that stage, created by one or both, is sex all *eros* and all *deos*.

There will of course be the question, well, how do you characterize that sexual experience which is also spiritual? In general I would answer that there is really nothing obviously different about it—just two people making love in their life. The difference is how those two relate to each other, for what cause they remain together and to which level they are capable of growing in consciousness by being together. In fact, the lovemaking as such may very well be less good than what a sexual therapist would call excellent. The difference lies for the female in an experience of time reversal. What I mean by that is that somewhere, somehow, during the experience she re-experiences the events leading up to where she is now, as if what is happening in her now is recurring and leading back to that time now where she can exit from the sequence again. She has an experience in which the time is reversed and re-sequenced dual to the happening, and while the present is in a sense not yet happening. When the resequenced experience rejoins the happening, the time reversal stops and she exits back into the now. During the resequenced experience the happening sexually appears to her as a universal occurrence in which her companion is not that one but the overbeing, an idealized potential of him. For the male the difference is that he touches so deeply outward through his exhortative reach that the experience forward is no longer connected with himself and thus he is in a state of self-loss. One could interpret that negatively, but it is not meant like that at all. I mean rather that in this outward-going reach he touches an emptiness so far that in the touch he has dissolved. Only the touching remains.

The sexual connotation of lovemaking in this setting is in no way less physically wonderful. One is as aware of the touch, smell and the tremendous stimulation and urgency to come. The sexual enjoyment, as it were, carries the experience to such a level of intensity that you climax as an elemental being and reach a transparency in which your body is finally free and your whole being is also totally released. In the event, the female experiences being in a warp of time where his overbeing and her overbeing are sexually-cum-spiritually life/love making.

The concept of the overbeing is basically tied to the existence of a sexual relationship, possible at the present and future period of mankind's evolution, where the real companionship is the new form of marriage. The real companionship of a singular nature where, probably after some searching, two souls, two humans attempt to integrate a cohesion between each other which through all the struggles of being what one is and having to become something else, and through all the tests of the exquisiteness of each particular personality, over time, welds a free relationship where a form of loyalty and love emerges which is not the desperate clutching on or the powerful dominating, but—in here again there are of course no words—the real soft intertwinement, where each separate has become more so through the other, yet totally exists in its own integrity and also describes a harmonious unity where one recognizes not only one being, the male or the female, but five beings. One recognizes the female alone in herself, one recognizes the male alone in himself, one recognizes the female, though in the unity with the male, one recognizes the male, though in unity with the female, and one also recognizes the female and the male together as a separate, fifth body. The recognition of this body is no longer corporeal, but a mental emanation. In a sense I would call that being this dual consciousness united. The female alone shows all of the signs of the usefulness of the companionship. Those signs are expressed, relatively speaking, in all one would attempt to look at; they would be expressed in her hair, in her eyes, in her body, in her bearing, in her health, in her expression. All would show a strange subtle combination of exuberance and shyness. The exuberance is an expression of the saturation of all her physical needs and all of her emotional needs, the shyness is an expression of a very deep knowledge, secret, that she bears within her. It is the unique, untouchable saintliness of the union out of which and through which she finds her existence fulfilled. The male also expresses clearly these two aspects, maybe in slightly different ways, but still there. On the one hand one sees a clear, vital life-force which can be seen in the eyes, in the bearing, in the expression, and in the stable, steady continuity in which he sort of plows through life. On the other hand one can recognize that while his personality is totally open, there is a definite unreachability, invulnerability, somewhere hidden deep within, which shows itself in a side-stepping in certain issues confronted which would require the expression of the emphasis of power; power used to crush. The primary motive force of the male, of the man who has not yet found out how to bring out, express and exhort his deepest soul vitally into his woman, turns anguished, abusive, becomes instead of the expression of the existence of a real love the subsistence of the need of possession of any kind.

On a higher level one recognizes the female together, unified with the male, and here we find two aspects: first, a total responsiveness, receptivity, completely able to absorb and absorb and absorb and contain within her being the ever-expanding search of creativity, of love of the male which goes in cycles—first to an ever-increasing reach, and second to an ever-increasing release. Second, one sees in the woman very clearly an extremely meaningful sense of expressiveness which can be seen in her creativity, in her activity, in her continual presence which is ebullient and inspiring. One finds that it is in this expressiveness, this display, that the female has learned one of the most important parts of companionship and that is to dominate, to overwhelm, to re-express and imbibe in the male her own whole, total growing self-essential existence.

In the male body as a part of the union with his woman one recognizes on the one hand this very definite tone of forthrightness. He is able to establish his direction, his being, through her and to a greater degree find within her existence the entire universe of his searching self-expression. On the other hand we also find in this male as a part of the female the clearest proof of successful deepening and therefore more and more permanent companionableness which is his total yielding, absorbing acceptance in which she, the woman, is able to recreate his tone as her tone—but it is not any more his tone, it is her tone which she expresses in a symphony. In this yielding trend the male, not devoid of his dominance but devoid of his need to dominate, because he has given all, receives finally the greatest nourishment for his self-expression and love which, on her part, the woman may not be aware of.

The fifth body—of the male and female together as one, that mental body—what can one recognize and say about that? It is totally good. It is probably the only thing that one can really call good, while all other things, even the concept itself of good, is irrelevant and rather tedious and cannot be defined and is dependent upon the conditions of viewing it and the particular relationship in the present and in the past and certainly in the future out of which one could recognize some sort of good. In this body there is an independent light, in this consumption of a real companionship one finds an atmosphere, an environment, a vibration which is to every sensitive (and even to the insensitive) a clear testimony of the good.

Now, of course, the question comes: How and why is it

that, while certainly in this day and age of humankind's evolution this ideal and singular companionship is desired, it is so difficult to find or achieve? Why is it so difficult for all of us, for anyone, for you, for me, to develop this? I could give so many different answers, and depending upon the different value systems of those answers they could all be true. One could point to so many different causes why it is difficult to live together in an ideal companionship, but at the same time that there are so many reasons it could also be said that there is only one reason, or a few reasons which become primarily one. And I would say that this reason has to do with the fact that one has to re-evaluate and adjust completely, recreate one's own identity in oneself and through, out of and into the other, and it demands such a complete amount of willingness into the adventure of living together that, especially when one becomes closer and closer, as so often happens when the first main sexual attraction or infatuation diminishes, one turns to welding the unity together either through what we call marriage or through children. To give the all requires so many deaths and so many rebirths that we demand at least as much in return and give, up to a point, all that we can as long as we are one, now. If I were to look at this ideal companionship which could develop and which does not need to develop out of any binding force except the continual commitment of both partners to engage and re-engage and renew and rediscover, to break and remake, then I would first of all say that it requires real flexibility. Flexibility of course within a certain tolerance—to be able to accept all and develop all and respond to all, yield to all and continuously re-examine one's own identity-base and include an ever-wider variety of shared and unshared recreated versatility of existence. While of course this flexibility on every possible level implies up to a point that one is able and willing and capable both of stretching out as far and as wide in all or any direction where the other's particular needs of existence or identity may be, and at the same time of learning in that outflexed hold to devalue the volume with enough relaxation so that as soon as possible the outstretched flexion can regrow sufficient depth, not only to envelop but also then to absorb, contain and re-express, it is also important that the flexibility of the other partner is sufficiently sensitive so that while the outflexed bond is holding it will be able to acquire the necessary volume for the flexion to have depth. Naturally this body outstretched to its last molecule of existence is stretched to such a tension that it has become a sinewed extension which may be incapable, in that hold, to be engendered with the lactation of inward-containing expansion. Sometimes, of course, the flexibility may be most on one partner while at other times it may be completely on the other. But the maturation of flexibility would have to come to the point where eventually both engaged in sufficient flexible enwebment, so that neither was overstrained and both engender the lactation of the securing depth into the other. This is in a sense a security-forming mechanism. Or, while the one demands a toleration, it must also give a re-approving strength for the other's flexible adjustment in order to suade this extension to self-identifying volume. If through lack of sensitivity the lactation of the approving extension is not given, the result can only be that the flexible extension comes slowly under more and more strain which may absorb therefore less and less of the other's expression and eventually become primarily a tense cramp, a grasping tentacle rather than a ripening union.

The requirement of sensitivity for such a union is the flexibility of the self-identification in the self while unified with the other, and in the self as a result of having been unified with the other. The flexibility can only be within certain nameable tolerance levels. I don't mean that this level is very dense and exact, but that the understanding of the tolerance level within which the flexibility can function is clearly envisionable. It is also important that the parameter of this tolerance level must be to some degree changeable and expandable as a result of the growing bond. That is in a sense conveyed by saying that the union needs continuously to remake and therefore also to break, so that up to a certain point there is always a reunion of its union in universal terms. The tolerance level parameters can be brought to the following three concepts:

First, life styles. While it is always possible for partners in a companionship to come from the widest possible backgrounds and still intend to engage in the future in the widest possible differentiations of life style, it must be very clear that this period of life is the shared companionship, whether it is a minute or a day or three hundred and sixty-five days or a lifetime. That unified life style must be a shared and enriching life style where both partners, companions, have adjusted at least somewhat in their differences and found a common ground of existence in the comfort and security and fulfillment which are sufficiently supportive and creatively enhanced by each other, for each other, so that life style is meaningful to both. Of course in the beginning conditioning it may be that a lot more life-style surrender or sacrifice may be made by the one or by the other, but the agreed-upon developed life style must be one which is creatively meaningful to both as engagement in their life.

Second, the flexibility requires a clear base of trust. Both partners must know, have total confidence and complete trust in each other; trust that in the companionship there is a real loyalty of life with each other, for each other; and that loyalty infers not only a loyalty in terms of the depth of living together but also that this particular engagement will not be shared by anyone else or with anyone else. And it also requires a level of trust and confidence which we could call sexual loyalty, a loyalty of affection, a loyalty of display and a loyalty of ideas. Of course, in some situations it is extremely difficult because it may very well be that one of the partners or both of the partners had some prior commitment to another, either sexually or materially or in terms of previously acquired responsibility or previously shared life union with someone else which through all true morality may not be totally releasable, and so it must be very clear there that the extent or the degree of loyalty must be openly understood and accepted and trusted between both partners including that the deviation from it, however it may be defined, will immediately cause a demand for flexibility which is no longer absorbable.

Third, the parameter of the tolerance level which in all

flexibility is possible, is purposeful and functional. It is a flexibility which idealizes a future or an ambition shared with the other, so that the companionship in a sense brings them both, maybe to different degrees, a meaningful focus in their particularly conceived life's purpose, which then makes a yielding, conductive and returning creativity from either to the other. The purpose or ambition or ideal, while of course in a sense different for each in its expression or color, must have some unifying source which brings both of them closer and closer to their mental and spiritual development in life. These parameters may change, all of them, and they may not be precisely expressed, but they must certainly be understood and felt between the two companions—otherwise it is not possible to engage in what appears as meaningless flexion into the other's need without useful relaxing deepening voluminance—i.e., other adjusted self-actualizing identity.

In companionship what one really wishes to do is to respond, fulfill, complete, satisfy the need of the other. And here the requirement for sensitivity is of a special nature; it is a sensitivity I would describe as the approving acknowledgment which expresses strength and security and pleasure to the other's having been successful and appreciated in his or her attempt to understand, yield or respond to "my" needs of him or her. On the grounds of the stage of the unity one can assume that normal receptive sensitivity is already there to begin with from both sides or from either side, even if it is more on one than on the other. This special kind of sensitivity, this being able to recognize and express satisfaction with the other's attempt to be flexible for us, must be actively expressed and it is not usually associated with this sensitivity which we call receptivity for the other. It is a sensitivity which implies the ability to recognize the other's flexibility.

Another kind of requirement for the companionship to re-engender itself on a more permanent basis is a need for display. Display is an aspect of self-expression in terms of love, intercourse et cetera which I will try to explain. Display is very subtle because it is completely involved in the whole self-identity structure. What we feel is in a sense denuding.

When we display ourselves we feel vulnerable, but we can only find out what we are and who we are by self-display. The companion serves as a displaying surface. What and how we display is at least in part a learned behavior and it requires a level of maturity and growth so that while displaying the self we are sufficiently aware of what and who we are expressing and also feel sufficiently received by the companion so that we can more and more display truly and sincerely what we wish to discover of ourself. The possibility for display requires from us a certain freedom of existence which can release or create our deepest feelings. Display is an artistry of becoming which has also a special receptivity of its own, because the expression of something which is unreceived returns to us as spent energy, a feeling of being without use.

There are two aspects of display which seem somewhat contradictory but both need to be developed and understood and in the companionship bond both must find fruition in the receptive surface of the other partner. First of all there is an aspect of displayal which requires a capacity of dramatization or overstatement of oneself, of one's feeling. This is sometimes difficult to do because in a way the overstatement appears to be false and therefore the receptive companion may be rejecting its trueness and even we ourselves may be rejecting its validity. But it is an interesting subtlety that while the dramatized self-display may be false, it expresses the true feeling behind it which was the causal energy for the display. And so the overstatement, this dramatization, is an important part of the relationship, and the display as an overstatement must be strong enough to create a continual re-interest and stimulation in the receptive surface, the companion—otherwise it will lose its focal vitality and the display will be unreceived. This overstated display of self which is an expression of our love and our experience of having been loved, can always find its balanced fulfillment when it is followed up in lovemaking. The overstatement causes a stimulation in the receptive companion which creates the immediate possibility for lovemaking. If it does not, the dramatization was insufficiently staged, or the receptive surface, the other partner, was insufficiently opened to the real basic feeling of wonder and love behind the display. Through this dramatization of our deeper feelings we can develop the vitality and ebullience of the experience of being ourself with and into the other.

There is a second aspect of display which I call the understatement. While overstatement may be seen as a more positive or masculine aspect (but should be engaged in by both partners), understatement can be seen as a more negative, feminine aspect—which should also be engaged in by both partners. It is much more difficult to express, because while the overstatement can be clearly seen and therefore also rejected, the understatement is not clearly felt and therefore it is much more easy to misunderstand the feeling. The understatement is very often not received and mostly not understood by the interpreting faculty of the other. The understatement is a subtle, warm, humble, kind portrayal and when it has not been interpreted, one feels frustrated and incapable of self-expression and thus we may erroneously conclude that the understatement was not true because it did not work. Display into the other makes the potential of the self as a self-actualizing focus. Companionship as full relationship is a fruitful sexual unity in which the dual self-created being becomes a blossoming unity in which both create each other. Children as a natural result can come here—or any other sufficient creation. In the kind of cultural state of consciousness in which mankind is now, children should come in only when this state of successful companionship has been reached.

Of course, some will think that I have covered a lot of abstract concepts and said little about lovemaking, sexuality, erotic expression and so on, therefore it might be useful to end this chapter by having a look at that, at sex.

I think that sex should be free, that people should searchingly engage in it to find a real companionship, and that this engagement should be entirely sexual first, and not second. The important aspects about the sexual nature of marriage can never be understated. It is a mystery.

While the wide-ranging information on how to make love, how to learn to have an orgasm, how to masturbate together, how to strengthen the pubic musculature, how to stimulate the glans, et cetera is probably far better than I could express, I would also like to add a few "technical" ideas. One (and I have said this before) is that good sex is very frequent and regular. If the relationship involves highs and lows of activity it is a danger signal. Sex-appeal is created by beauty and also by tension, and sexual excitement is not caused only by peaceful coexistence. There should also be a competition between the partners and some amount of repulsion besides attraction—just enough to trigger want and to strengthen the will to overcome rejection. Also there are so many positions now acceptable and illustrations with which to copy them, but very little is said about the fast-thrusting penis in a position where the female and the male are both capable of moving easily without any encumbrance. This may be achieved if he stands, leaning forward with his shoulders, chest and knees supported. She lies on a raised platform at penis level, her back, neck and head supported so that she is in a semi-reclining position. Her legs are opened wide with the knees supported, her feet rest with the toes against a ridge and a little above the level of her vagina. Her body is totally supported and nowhere cramped or strained. There is no physical contact between the partners of any part of the body, except for the genital area. They can easily see each other's faces and may hold hands if they wish. His insertion includes, by the natural reclining angle, very good clitoral stimulation. He is able comfortably and fast to thrust in and out without becoming strained or cramped for a long time. I would suggest that orgasm may comfortably be reached in this way, and since all the sensitivity is concentrated in the vagina and the penis, that the very fast, strong, deep thrusting can stimulate a tremendous release.

But do not forget that love and romance are also part of this position, even though I cannot describe a method for that. All other things being said, if you can get all the equipment together, you may like to try it this way too.

DRUGS

People have asked me many times to give some opinion or guidance on the subject of drugs. I have more or less avoided making any overt statements in public, but there are one or two general ideas which I could express.

The first thing which is quite clear is that our society is totally geared towards the use of drugs; you could almost say it is built on drugs. We spend our time seeking excitement, tension—and when we find it we quickly take a tranquilizer so that we don't really have to feel it. We spend the day at work drinking coffee to speed us up, then we go home, flop in a chair and have a drink to relax, watch a bit of television to create a bit more tension and finally have to take a sleeping pill in order to get some rest. It is a continual swing between unreal excitement and incomplete relaxation until we are hermetically sealed against feeling.

For some people work itself is a drug—perhaps to deaden their mind against the fact that their marriage is dead. To others their marriage is a drug—it is no longer a real companionship between two people, it is a device against the pain of loneliness. There are many people who spend much of their time "entertaining friends" because they just cannot stand being alone together and perhaps going deeper into themselves and their relationship.

To me it is when drugs—any form of drugs—become an escape from life that they are an abuse. People speak of "drug abuse" but I prefer to think of it as self-abuse; continual use of drugs for escape is self-abuse, and that is the one thing which I would call immorality.

There are so many forms of escape. Religion provides the perfect escape from having to think about what we really see as right or wrong. It is an escape because you are no longer responsible—if you do wrong in god's eyes, he will punish you, and if you do right he will reward you—you no longer even have to wonder what you feel yourself. So many young people today jump on the spiritual bandwagon so that they can sit and meditate and not have to face the day-to-day business of living—they will be enlightened, so all these boring things like work and money and making something of life will not affect them. But what are most of these techniques and tricks of meditation if not kicks, highs to help you fly along without having to come down to earth?

Our lives are so directed towards comfort and painless existence, so full of drugs to protect us from living that we cannot see these things for what they are, we do not even know any more what "real life" is. Even the birth of a child, which should be one real experience left in life, is so much toned down by the use of drugs and anesthetics that you can almost have a baby without noticing, but it still could be a real experience for those who dare to approach it in that way. When you really look at it, the only thing remaining which people cannot totally anesthetize themselves against is the sudden death of a husband, wife or child—presuming that there was some love between them. Imagine the incredible hole left in life—suddenly all the things you used to do out of habit come into question, there is a stark awareness of anything you do: not two coffee cups, just one; you don't need to remember your anniversary . . . god, why didn't I take her out last week when she wanted it? What the hell does it matter now? . . . Suddenly there is all this questioning, doubt, pain, fear, and this most inevitable thing in life becomes the only real experience.

There are, of course, those who use drugs such as hashish or LSD to open the mind rather than close it off. To a certain extent it may be possible to break through some thought-barriers by using such things, but it may also close one off to other areas in the same way as meditation and so on. Perhaps you cannot say which world is the more real, but you can easily see in which world we have to work, to live, to function, to love, to give birth, to grow and to die. It may be that Carlos Castaneda learned many things through the use of drugs and broke through a lot of barriers; but it could also be that it was more the attention given to him by his teacher than the drugs he took which really allowed these changes to happen. All of us feel that we are somehow very important and that we do not usually get the attention we need, or feel we deserve; by using hashish or LSD we are totally in the universe of our own thought.

This is closely connected with our search for divinity or a spiritual state—it is a state of magic. In a drug-induced state we can experience a godlike condition, or at least a condition which approaches our conception of that in which god might exist. At last you can just sit back and watch, you don't have to think and analyze, the mind just flows on and on, now—not five minutes ago or three days ago—thoughts come and are gone and are often impossible to recall. There is just what is happening, and what is happening is just happening. The trouble is, of course, that you have to come down again. Maybe for a little while some feeling of euphoria will remain, but eventually you are back where you started. Perhaps you began to realize in that state something which gives you a taste for a search in a particular direction, but it did not take you there. There really is no shortcut, no hitch-hiking, no one who can do it for you. On that search you are alone. There are maps, signposts, all kinds of pointers, but again you have to see them for yourself, you have to make the decisions, you have to get yourself there.

There are those who become heavily involved in more dangerous drugs, and these seem to be the people with the greatest inner pain, inner emptiness. They try to fill the emptiness within themselves but are like a bucket with a hole in it; it runs out and they have to refill it over and over again until they destroy themselves. The strange thing is that these people, although they cannot bear their own emptiness, are also incredibly resistant to change. There are many experimental clinics to which people can come and live a relatively normal life in a communal situation so that they all have a certain responsibility to the rest of the group. There are regular group meetings using encounter techniques, music, massage—allowing the people to express their feelings about themselves and each other. The groups are fairly small so that everybody gets considerable attention and for a while everything is fine, the people get more healthy, seem to enjoy the contact with others, and yet probably 90% of them leave before the course is completed and of those who leave about 96% go back to drugs again.

These people are the greatest self-deceivers: they will forever continue to believe that they are not hooked, they will forever continue to believe that they are useless, no good, and whatever you try to do, however you try to convince them that they are useful, lovable human beings, although they seem to accept that for a little while, ultimately they will go down again and all the negative feelings will flow back. There is always someone who can think better, work better, play music better, cook better than they can, they simply cannot accept that they are really all right, that they are just as perfect or imperfect as everyone else in the world. Perhaps it is this point which is the hardest for them to take: that they are not extraordinary, not bad enough to be notorious, not good enough to be famous, so they dig themselves into a pit of self-destruction as a rebellion against a world in which they do not stand out. You could also look at it in another way and say that they feel somehow superior to the rest of the universe—they are too good, too perfect to be bothered with all this little living trip, and this can also manifest as an inferiority feeling.

Perhaps we should bring into society some kind of initiation ceremony such as those held in the tribes of Africa, Australia and other such peoples—some kind of real ordeal in which you have to face danger, face death and have to use your own strength and will to survive. Maybe that would help people to have a little more self-respect, a little more meaning in their lives.

There may be many different causes for taking drugs and there may be thousands of excuses to explain that behavior in terms of harsh society, bad parents, et cetera. But the more I come into contact with those that seek escape, attention, inspiration or release through alcohol, LSD, cocaine or other drugs, I find three main types. One, which we may dispense with, is simply the weak personality, weak self-identity, who does it in emulation of others and pretends to the subculture mentality, whether the bar or pub mentality or the rock or getting-high-on-grass mentality. For them it is often a phase in a continuously meaningless life.

But the other, the long-term hooked, is a human being ridden with guilt. The guilt complex is so deeply embedded in that person that he or she cannot accept being sober with so much guilt. Strangely, the guilt is somehow tied to a structural paralysis in their personality which on the surface appears like an outright refusal to take whatever corrective action to change the guilt. The person in this state seems to refuse to overcome the basic errors in him or herself and, as if in a sort of schizophrenic state, uses all his creative or mental energy to confirm his incapability to be free from guilt or to redeem himself. Thus he will re-enact and re-evaluate everything that happens or did happen to come back again to the point of agonizing paralysis where only the drug can relieve the guilt, especially because it causes the worst guilt—which is the failure to deal with taking drugs. The apparent paralysis though, when viewed carefully—which is often very difficult because of personal involvement of the observer— can sometimes be seen to be an active screen, a self-created diversion. Thus it may not be a paralysis at all but a deeply embedded self-delusion which is of course ritualistically confirmed by the symbolic aspects of the drug or alcohol intake. Exasperatingly, one sometimes comes to feel that this personality tries in fact to fail and that it experiences its achievement therein.

What may be the reason for this almost inacceptable situation—as if a demon or bad spirit drove the person to do it, in an inescapable tragedy? I have to admit that mostly I don't know. There may be some clues in his past, in her character structure, in their personality. Clearly those people are often deeply undermotivated, highly intelligent and quickly bored. Clearly those people are lonely and unable to accept pressure. Clearly they have a high level of anger/frustration with themselves. But the only clue that seems to point to a deeper root cause is that they experience the reality of what is happening so that the good, the love, the security and all such positive life-sustaining input hardly reach them, as if they can no longer identify themselves or are even willing to accept themselves in terms of being good, being loved, being accepted. They do feel the burden of all the life-threatening input and even start accepting that their identity exists in terms of that reality. In brief, it seems that they are locked into a personality pattern that must hurt what treasures them, destroy what loves them and disown what gives them worth. When life comes to this level of destruction the drug is not an escape but a confirmation.

These personalities are often in other ways the deepest and most sensitive and capable; they are intuitive and have deep religious experiences and are capable of tremendous emotional depth. It is as if they can't hold that, though, and suddenly move to abort their own depth.

Of course one asks: But what to do? Here I can only answer that love, firmness and a true, real understanding support can maybe slowly strengthen the other reality input so that over time they may learn to accept this positive part. But if a person loves only, of course he or she will destroy that with drugs. Firmness and understanding are also needed. Finally I feel that these self-destroyers can only be changed if they come to accept that they do love, really love someone else who also loves them. And maybe, if they can believe in or accept that they actually do love, the relieving sigh of belonging may slowly heave the poisonous self-destruction out. Pity cannot help this drug-taker, probably psychology is not yet capable and may never really be able to reach this mind. Only the incredible mystery of the self-engenderment of love proves able to reach here.

The third type—often someone who is blocked and has difficulty in feeling himself free and capable of self-expression and contact with others—takes drugs, searching for ways to find a better self. He often finds it through drugs, more often not. But generally, he or she moves on to higher modes such as gestalt or spiritual meditation or simply outgrows the causal need which generally was an oppressive home and authoritarian upbringing or a childhood without real parental attention.

What surprises me in so many conversations about drugs is that a large part of society vociferously condemns the use of hard drugs and sometimes even soft drugs without acknowledging the problems of alcoholism, kleptomania, gun-wielding terror and so many other diseases of society. In any such discussions the individual is viewed, judged and/or pitied, but the society and its cultural faults are not looked at. And if we take an honest look at our history, we cannot avoid the discovery that the individual's particular alcoholism or opium addiction, or the subgroup involved with cocaine or terrorism, reflects a consumption deeply rooted in society and history. In fact—since these problems have always been with us—those who seem inclined to view heredity as the cause may find untold clues to a mutant gene which brings degeneration of the spirit; and those who seem inclined to an environmental view may be able to point to the innumerable errors of society, family, education, religion and so on.

Of course, we must have a society which produces the best and therefore shall also regenerate the worst. Civilization develops the psyche to its highest level and so consequentially some will get derailed along its line to perfection. The derailments of alcoholism and psychopathic rape will, as so many others, always be with us and if some are resolved the civilization will push new forms of failure forward. This is the point which comes home to me more and more clearly: that drugs as well as nourishment, that anything can be a cause for failure; and that success necessitates a rate of failure through which some people will always become a victim in their part in civilization's destiny. Thus I see that when the possibility to succeed as a healthy individual is too much encumbered by the general form and structure of the specific social norm for success and meaning, that the imbalance will increase the failure rate, or shall we say the escape rate. A society may be able to produce a greater excellence in a few and greater failure in many or the other way round or whatever its goals as a collective really are. And so the western culture, just as the Chinese culture around the change of this century, produces by its own goals its own derailing momentum, its own good guys and its own junkies. We are all involved in that process, we who talk about it, we who condemn those junkies and even we who help them to get better, yes, even we and I who try to explain it all . . . for nothing.

Yes, to a point the addictive personality may be on to a good thing. It destroys the good, the worth, the joy of this illusion. It brings all down to the somber painful self-infliction that defiles the true and bends the flow to return. It brings to worthless all we "believe in" and denies that life alone is really possible to live.

It is a repudiation of your/my faith and brings the stars and expanses of meaning's wholeness to destruction. The negative, the terror of the invading alcohol, junk or whatever, produced also by the good its father, shackles the benign to watch its suffering consequence, its failed creation. Maybe that is why we disdain you, worthless failure: you betrayed my zeal, my soul, my self, my love . . . of you.

And so I must return to the final individual view to try to deal with him or her, forlorn and self-deceiving, lost.

There is maybe a way to threaten or righten the individual imbalance. I see it only, and this may sound cruel—in fact it is cruel—by hurting and punishing and training (taming) the drug-user and setting up a continuous counter-punishing system so that the pain of using drugs is always and immediately worse than that of not using them, and by rewarding and sustaining every experience which is realistic and creative. By viciously destroying, over-destroying and hurting so deep, so terribly deep, every unrealistic self-deceptive addictive pattern of thought, expression or motivation while at the same time so consistently allowing and nourishing the slightest self-actualizing realization, the old pattern is eventually broken. I would do this so thoroughly through every form of mental, physical and other kind of torment and with every sort of reward imaginable so that maybe slowly the personality that has learned this behavior, which found sense in the deceit, in the drug, is annihilated and a new personality is slowly acquired—maybe the same personality but in reverse. Beware, though, to keep this up forever and unto death, for one slip could bring a fall back to the old. The old can never be destroyed without creating the new, though, and all the while you must be so strong, you the destroyer and creator, that you do not crush yourself in it. You can only do it if you really really love that drug-addictive personality, love that person, love that soul so much that you can punish it (and in that, of course, yourself) totally and reward it totally. Only when those two things work together because you really want to be, live, create with that person, can it maybe succeed. I know no other way.

PART 3
THE FUTURE OF SOCIETY

THE BIRTH OF THE NEW ERA

In the progress of education, the knowledge of the soul's purpose, the only thing worthwhile in life, is overlooked. Education qualifies a man to become selfish to the best of his ability, and to get the better of another. Art has lost its freedom of grace and beauty, since its reward depends on the approval of the heartless and blind. Science has degenerated for the very reason that the scientist has limited his view to the objective world and denied the existence of the life which is beyond perception. In the absence of a higher ideal the constant striving after material inventions has led man to such devices as have set the world on fire. Those who are under the spell of destruction are unaware of all this; they cannot know it until the clouds of gloom have dispersed, their hearts are clear, and their minds have recovered from this intoxication which prevents them from thinking and understanding.

The races in the coming era will mix more and more every day, developing finally into a world-wide race. The nations will develop a democratic spirit, and will overthrow every element which embitters them against one another. There will be alliances of nations until there is a world alliance of nations, so that no nation may be oppressed by another, but all will work in harmony and freedom for common peace.

Science will probe the secrets of the life unseen, and art will follow nature closely. The people of all classes will be seen everywhere. The caste system will vanish and communities will lose their exclusiveness, all mingling together, and their followers will be tolerant towards one another. The followers of one religion will be able to pray by offering the prayers of another, until the essential truth will become the religion of the whole world and diversity of religions will be no more.

Education will culminate in the study of human life, and learning will develop on that basis. Trade will become more universal, and will be arranged on the basis of a common profit. Labour will stand side by side with capital on an equal footing.

Titles will have little importance. Signs of honour will become conspicuous. Bigotry in faiths and beliefs will become obsolete. Ritual and ceremony will be a play. Women will become freer every day in all aspects of life, and married women will be called by their own names. The sons and daughters will be called by the name of their town, city or nation, instead of by the family name. No work will be considered menial. No position in life will be humiliating. Everybody will mind his own business, and all will converse with one another without demanding introductions. The husband and wife will be like companions, independent and detached. The children will follow their own bent. Servant and master will be so only during working hours, and the feeling of superiority and inferiority among people will vanish. Medicine will take away the need for surgery, and healing will take the place of medicine. New ways of life will manifest themselves, hotel life predominating over home life. Grudges against relatives, complaints about servants, finding fault with neighbours will all cease to occur, and the world will continue to improve in all aspects of life until the day of Gayamat, when all vain talk will cease, and when everywhere will be heard the cry, "Peace, peace, peace!"

Hazrat Inayat Khan, *The Birth of the New Era*. Sufi Message, Vol. VIII, p. 216 ff.

I always enjoy reading that chapter because it reminds me time and time again that in Sufism the vision of the future of mankind, an essential part of its teaching, definitely does not include a social structure in the manner or form in which it exists today. It cannot be said that what we stand for on a spiritual level can be separated from what we stand for on a social level. In other words, the way life is lived in society is the all-encompassing judgment of the depth of that society, of the esoteric, of the inner worth of that society. You cannot separate people, as one does in Islam, by saying, "These people who pray more Rakats are better than those people who pray fewer Rakats." Life is a whole, a twenty-four hour job.

Often one wonders. In other chapters I discuss certain "wonders," such as where the problems of the world come from; I talk about mental disease and the feelings of inferiority. The inferiority complex in the world, where does it come from?—from the way the social structure is formed, the way we begin to grow up. I relate the inadequacy feelings with which girls become women and mothers and the impotency feelings with which boys become men and fathers, and show how these two perpetuate one another in continuous neurosis. I discuss the search for power which engages people in large business enterprises, political or material ambitions in life, the fact that so much of the world's leadership is caused by the drive to overcome the inferiority complex, and that very few people of real wisdom ever reach positions of leadership in the world.

What is the cause of this? What really should change? I do not have any real answer, but it seems that the cause must be related to the way in which the mind develops as it begins to take consciousness, identity, self-awareness in the world—and that is a result of the structure of society, whether it is socialistic, capitalistic, communistic or anything else. Throughout the history of Sufism it is evident that the deeper leadership of Sufism always tended to be revolutionizing the social norms. Many great Sufi leaders were people who ran away from governmental positions, kings or lords or warlords or leaders who became disgusted with the world and made a haven of deeper thinking about how their lives could make a meaningful contribution to mankind. This process continues and at present we find ourselves here; and we see a society strongly in schism between insatiable outer values, goals, needs, morals and rules, which continue in an ever-perplexing array of exhibitionism, and man's inner needs, of which he is unaware—Why do I really live? What can I find in life?

There are many aspects of the social structure, some of which will be covered in later chapters, but starting with the chapter of Inayat Khan's *Birth of the New Era,* I would say that the mechanism of production will have to be arranged on the basis of the common good. Some time ago, I read the statement of the chairman of the board of the Swiss Bank Corporation to its stockholders at its annual general shareholders' meeting. In his report he described the financial position of the bank, and also described the social problems in Switzerland. He talked of profit-sharing and the demands of employees and also the danger that through the restructuring of society the assets of the bank could be disseminated, and also of the duty that he and the directors had to anticipate, to understand and to accept, that the present structure of society was coming to an end. It is interesting that a bank like that would print that kind of report for the whole world to see, and that the major aspect of that kind of report is the recognition that in the end all profit must be shared for the common good of mankind. The only assets that are real are human beings, not material wealth.

This is a very important, an integral part of the future vision which Sufism asks that man develop. The only way to break the selfishness—which is really self-pity, impotency, inferiority and all sorts of other problems—the only way to spiritualize, to etherealize, to lighten the world is to accept that commercialism as it is now breeds egoism. The profit made by one man is the loss of another; there is no working towards the common good. The International Monetary Fund, the World Bank, funds for international development and so many others show this: we are arriving at the end, at the apogee of the possibility of using energy, raw materials, productivity for selfish needs. We have complicated society so much that we must begin to cooperate, or the world will drown in an economic and social debacle. In a way we bring on our own changes; man always does.

The second subject that has been a part of the teachings of Sufism through the centuries is the family structure. The family structure of man in the natural state was a tribal structure, both economically and in terms of the education and guardianship of children, of security patterns and sexual responsibility amongst other things. Somehow the tribal system was replaced by the four-wall family system, which is the symbol of the neurosis in which, over the centuries, people have grown up to be afraid to be free, to live, to love, to work, to share, to be open. It is evident now that the family system is beginning to degenerate. It is also evident in most advanced western cultures that forms of marriage and parental bonds are degenerating. The teaching that the Sufi Message brings is freedom and equality of male and female, independent real companionship: a completely new and different family system. In a way it is again a tribal system—not the tribal system of survival but a new tribal system. It is bound to come, it is coming everywhere; whether we advocate it or not makes no difference.

The whole educational system also definitely needs to be restructured. Why do we want to educate a child; what do we want to educate? Do we want the child to become a human being or a clerk? What is a human being? What is our human quality? Should education bring us to understand ourselves or should it bring us to understand a machine? We may know the molecular structure of water, which is most of the consistency and weight of our body; but do we know what we are? Education must be completely reorganized to bring man, woman, child education to self-realization, self-development, development of a child so that it can become an independent, integrated whole human being.

These three things, work for the common good, organization for the common good and sharing for the common good, involve structures. Although we believe in a way in a democratic spirit, we do not believe in democracy. Democracy can be and usually is the tyranny of mediocrity. We believe in hierarchy, which also has problems. We have to accept that the Constitution of the United States, which has greatly influenced man's thought, is no longer valid in its basic precept. Its basic precept is that all men and women are created equal—but this is not so, and never will be. There is equality beyond, but in this moment there is inequality; our attempt must be to reorganize to compensate for inequality. But the management systems, order systems, control systems in the future must attempt to enlighten all, to share all, to work for the common good and yet find a way to resolve the conflict in the fact that man is not equal. In a purely democratic system, the tyranny of democracy is sometimes worse than the tyranny of dictatorship.

Somehow there must come a cross, a horizontal line, a democratic line of equality and a vertical line of leadership, and these two have to meet somewhere and harmonize.

On the subject of family systems: What really is a marriage? When should one really have children? It is meaningless now to say that one should only have children when one is married. Birth control is here, other ways of living together are here, ways of communication are changing, the female is more and more able to live independently. Marriage should not be a prison; it is already broken open and breaking more all the time. How can one create a cradle of love, warmth and security for a little child to grow up in without four walls of fear, neurosis and prejudice, anger, selfishness and possessiveness, so that the soul may grow to real security and freedom? What does that mean? What are the sexual responsibilities that we have today compared with yesterday? Yesterday it was different because if two people went to bed together, first there was virginity and then there was pregnancy. Both of these have changed, overlapped, gone. Does that mean there is no more responsibility? Is there such a thing as free love? Can love ever be free? Can there be freedom without love?

Next there is the question of education. We say that god has created us in his own image. Have we created god in our own image? Maybe both statements are equal. Something resides in us that we believe distinguishes us from animals. We can recognize that we are an evolution of consciousness. We can see things in ourselves that we recognize in animals and plants; all things have evolved to us here. We say we are human, we are special—but what are we and how should we really be? Thousands of people in the world, whether they live in one culture or another, struggle in the end only to understand themselves. Who are we, why are we, what is the purpose of this life? Thousands and thousands of women and men have lived and died, and for every one of them, their little lives were so important ... and history comes like a sea, like an ocean that absorbs all, and all that seemed to be so important washes clean. What is it really for?

It is to that vision that we need to educate our children, it is of those values that we need to make them aware. Yet how can we make them aware without brainwashing them, structuring them, making a new religiosity instead of a vibrant religion of living? Education systems must take into consideration the fact that most education is on a subliminal level: reflection. Children reflect the people they are in contact with, reflect their minds in some way. How can we give a wide enough scope for a mind to reflect? How to allow every child to develop its own rhythm, at its own speed and let reflections come into it which it is ready for, which will not destroy that future potential woman or man?

Think of the last statement in the chapter from Inayat Khan, "All vain talk one day shall cease ..." What does that really mean? How much of the day do we spend in vain? How much of the day do we spend in vanity? How much energy do we really dissipate which we could use creatively for the expansion of the flower of our consciousness?

The vision of Sufism for the future, which in a way is the experiment, a "real reality" which we are attempting at the Khankah and in workcamps, is a new structure, a new social, intellectual and spiritual structure, overturning things of the past and yet leaving whole as the center, the most important, the value of the human being, trying to develop the human quality; and that is very difficult. (It has been going on for seven years in the Khankah. How many times for hours do I pore through my mind, trying to draw conclusions, trying to understand out of the Khankah experiment in which way leadership, my leadership and the leadership of others should allow, should lead that community, that tribe, to grow, that family to develop.) How much should you push and how much should you allow things to go by themselves? Can nature assert itself if you let it? I can make one definite conclusion, only one; and that is that the greatest enemy of mankind is that he searches continually to reduce everything to the lowest common denominator. In his interrelationships, in her interrelationships, in our interrelationships we try to find the lowest common level in our possibility of meeting, and we always tend to reduce everything to what we think is practical; and just at that level where it becomes practical, it has no more depth.

To escape from this downward-pulling gravitational force is a most difficult thing. In 1967 I wrote in my diary that the most difficult thing to do is continuously to inspire people. Many years later I still find that to be the most challenging thing to do: to keep minds in that trance, that dance, that level of inspiration where life is three-dimensional, has space, has width, has breadth, has brilliance, where we look through glasses which give us scope to exercise the ability to experience, to express. Sooner than one thinks, however inspired one is, the walls squash back, the space is crushed, things become flat, inspiration washes away. And man feels hollow and empty inside and replaces the depth by outer brilliance, which becomes the consumption, the ever-consuming society we have today.

The future of man is as near, the new era is as close as the level of inspiration towards which we can bring ourselves. That level, the attitude of the poet, the poetic dance, the steps of freedom, to rise—to what does not matter, even if it is to nothing. It is the movement between one emptiness and another emptiness which is real, the changing flux. Sometimes you go to some far-away country and you see some simple people who are just like children, and you wonder. You could say a lot of bad things about their life—it is simplistic, elementary—and yet have we, with all our complications, really got something better? It is difficult to say either yes or no. It just seems that we do not know really why we live. We push these questions out of our minds, we surround ourselves with things that fill up that void, veil it, and so we continue an outer structure of society which ever maintains the escape from the real crux of life. That is the thing we pursued in religion and that is the thing we pursue now that we have thrown away religion, in all the fantastic expansion of spiritual groups and communities and rites which we find. We want some way to fill up, some way to answer a real, yet uncomprehended need within us. We have structured it by thought-forms, by education, by social forms, by morality, by law, by religion; we have tried to structure out of our minds, yet we cannot.

This little movement, then, this little message is very revolutionary, but that does not mean that we should go out and start a physical revolution or burn down a city. In a way the cultural revolution in China, what little we know about it, may be a much truer revolution, because what really must revolt is something inner, within the consciousness of each separate person so that the whole social consciousness can change. But there is a large difference between the Maoist kind of cultural revolution and the revolution that the Sufi teachings envision, and that is that no revolution can be truly successful unless each and every mind makes it, for itself. It is no use to try to change the world. You cannot change it, but you can change yourself—no one else can change you but yourself. Some tricks are possible to give you experiences; encounter groups, all sorts of activities can widen your psychological scope, your emotional depth; but really only you can change yourself.

How can you? If you want to. How should you? However you can. Why should you? Because without change there is no meaning, there is only fear, cramp, holding back, loss of life, gravity, weight, death. . . . But in any case, if there is a change, if a person, a consciousness, a woman, a man, really has changed, that person cannot then continue to live the same life, the same structure, be enslaved in the same patterns of mediocrity. Change is inner and outer—you cannot separate the two. That is why these outer structures are definite guidelines, they are not dogmas, they are guidelines which can show you the real anchors of man's consciousness. They are the whole economic system, the family/sexual system and the educational system—the three anchors you must look at, you in yourself, for yourself, by yourself. You will see what is really natural, what is divine in it, what is really meant to be. Was the mind of man created to run away from self-knowledge? What is the basic curiosity drive in the little baby when it makes its first reaching move?

It is true that in knowing others you will know yourself.

But if in knowing others you avoid the possibility to know self, what is the use of knowing others?

What is the real natural call in your heart? I think that in every man, woman and child, in every consciousness, in every heart the call is the same. We want to have a level of peace that is meaningful. We want to be able to love and be loved. We want to have warmth, we want to belong, we want to be stimulated, we want to be accepted. None of these things can we buy in a shop, manufacture in a factory or learn in a textbook. These things we can only live, learn to live. If we were to pursue these things, few men or women would live the life that they are living today.

July 8, 1974

SOCIAL STRUCTURES

To introduce the subject of social structures, it would be worthwhile to look at the structures that we know, and maybe from that we can derive some comparative knowledge before going too far into projecting a form of social structure we cannot yet know anything about.

Probably the oldest structure that has existed and still exists is the patriarchal form, the matriarchal form being the alternative to it. In the patriarchal social structure the family unit, or a larger version, the family clan, was the basis, and the senior male, the father or grandfather, was in charge. Although patriarchal societies have always been fairly stable, their peoples have been resistant to freedom and equality. They have always been very hierarchical, the base of that hierarchy being the muscular strength that the male could muster to dominate. As different patriarchal societies and small sub-units united there grew tribal and inter-tribal units, and eventually states and empires.

The hierarchy in patriarchal societies was structured in such a way that there was often very little room for lateral and upward movement. The Inca civilization, for example, was a very well-established, highly hierarchical social order, where power, knowledge and leadership were concentrated in a strongly centralized unit. That was very efficient as long as there was the ability to plan, to order, to further the situation, but then along came Cortez and with fewer than three hundred men he was able to destroy a large well-established society. How did he destroy it?—simply by knocking off the top; and when he had knocked off the top there was no one left. Whoever was not at the top was left leaderless, powerless, and so the society disintegrated immediately.

Another social structure that interestingly enough compares with what we have now is the slave system of the Ottoman Empire and the Egyptian Mameluke kingdom. In those societies powerful, dominant people who were free and equal bought slaves who were inferior, not free. Eventually the slaves learned the skills, the trades, the methods of execution, the lines of communication of their masters and gained control over them, so that the free people were ruled by the slaves. These systems sustained themselves against both internal rebellion by the free people and rebellion by the slaves who were not so high up, and so expanded their influence, fostered culture and the development of thought quite well.

If you read the history of Mecca you will discover that the second largest caravan that ever went to Mecca—a caravan of nearly two hundred thousand camels, and so probably half a million people—was led by the slave ruler of Egypt. Here the psychology is very interesting—again it was the slaves who, though they were not free, though they could not give leadership, organize, structure or effect decisions, gained access to the means of execution in the society, and thus had the power. Another remarkable aspect about these structures is that it was the slaves themselves who maintained the system. One would think that when a slave who was sold into slavery as a child eventually reached the top, he would say, "No, wait a minute, I suffered so much, everybody is free now"—but the slaves never did; they supported the system and the opportunities for free people, so that the free people could keep the slaves.

We have developed a form of slave system today. The lesson of the Mameluke and Turkish Ottoman kingdoms, the Incas and the Byzantine Empire shows that the real structure of society is not necessarily maintained by the power of authority, meaning exclusively violent, coercive power; the real structure of society is maintained by the people who have the effective skills and the lines of communication. Other examples show that when there is not a development of skills, nor of communication, society cannot develop. What has happened in Borneo is a typical example: How could it be that the people who have lived in Borneo for as long as people have lived in western Europe, though they began on the same basis, did not develop skills, communication lines, could not raise their level of abstraction? There was never any slavery in Borneo; they were always free people. They fought with each other, like everywhere else in the world, but the development of specialties, of valuable skills on which an economy could be based and from which free time could come, never came about.

Another society which has endured over centuries and been very much talked about is that of the Hindu culture. The Hindu culture was based on the caste system, another form of slavery. Somehow or other that was maintained, almost like a brave new world, for three thousand years. How did they do that?—by the subtle principle that there was not one caste of people—free people, free thinkers—and slaves, but that there were different layers of free people and slaves, so no one group in the structure could ever gain exclusive control over a sufficient amount of the skills or lines of communication to gain control over the society; and so the Brahmins ruled.

The Brahmins were the theologians, the philosophers, the thinkers, the counsellors, the consolers, the free men, but they could not make war to establish their power, they could only sustain their power by developing their intelligence, and all their intellectual skills they kept for themselves. The people who thought they had the power, the Kshatriyas, were allowed to make war, to have palaces, to have outer, apparent power, but they could not read or write, they could not think or theorize; in order to have a treasurer they had to have a Brahmin to keep accounts. They could not bother to perform labors which involved sustenance, so they could never function effectively without having beneath them a base of people who would grow their food for them; they themselves could not grow food—it was not allowed, it was unacceptable.

Forms of society are always based upon things that you

are supposed to do and things that you are not supposed to do. Today we think that we are free from these strictures, just as much as those people thought they were free from previous patterns which they could see. But they could not see the prisons that they were living in, and we cannot see the prisons that we are living in.

Hindu society also had the phenomenon of the power of marriage. Marriage in ancient society was the uniting of one tribe with another, one fort with another fort, one patriarchal family with another, one army with another. The Kshatriya maharaja would have to consult the Brahmin astrologer because he could not marry off his daughter unless it were a favorable marriage. The Brahmin astrologer, without a sword, could choose the daughter of the maharaja whose astrologer was his friend—so in reality, without a sword but with a brain, he had the power.

Beneath the Kshatriya were the tradesmen, but the tradesmen were not allowed to produce, they were only allowed to trade. Today there are international economic monopolies; the supermarket, for instance, owns the farms, the trucking and transport company, the auction house, the manufacturing plant and the distribution—all that is in the hands of one power, one unit, and as a result they can afford to counter the power of labor, the power of other people, since they are not forced to buy freely in the market from anyone else. By altering the whole direction of distribution they can affect the line of manufacturing, the whole economic base of their business.

Hindu society was so subtly thought out that the tradesman could own the supermarket, but he could not own the manufacturing plant that canned the meat, so there were never the underlying superstructures of power that we have today. Eventually there was the Hindu worker who could work with his hands or, if he was smart, could have two or three workers working for him; but he was dirty, he was filthy, he was no good, he could not stand in the shop and sell because he was only a low-level worker. In all cases of moral questions, marriages, deaths, taxes, assessments, major decisions in life, and of thinking, abstractions, writing, reading, recordkeeping—the worker could not do for himself. There could be a low-level Shudra worker with a big factory who had to have a Brahmin be his accountant—that was possible; but the Brahmin could not own the factory because that would be below his dignity. Thus the Brahmins, without ever using coercive power, always maintained their superior position, and in doing so they continued to legislate the morals and standards which supported the levels of all the caste systems, they made sure that they remained as pure as they were, and as new economic things happened, as culture changed they would invent new gods, discard old ones, invent new theories, throw away old ones, invent new moral values . . . always to adjust, a completely self-regenerating society.

Then Gandhi came along and decided, based on his English training, that all men are created equal, and cancelled it all. Whatever anybody wants to say otherwise about it, the result is, in fact, a complete and total débâcle—not because Gandhi was wrong, but because a major structural change in a society that has lasted for three thousand years cannot be made suddenly. A coolie mentality cannot do accounting, a farmer mentality cannot do manufacturing, a manufacturing mentality cannot do selling; it just does not work, and the result is a débâcle.

Today the social structures of the western world are organized primarily around the law of economics. There is the Communist bloc (which is not communist at all), and there is the capitalist bloc; these blocs are artificial, generalized and therefore invalid ways to look at situations. But the social structures have, over the years, adjusted themselves to support a given economic base of power, and the base of power is now very much the access to the economic means to legislate one's power and protect that legislation. There are certain things in our economy-structured society that did not exist before because we have had to give vent to the possibility for both upward and horizontal mobility, to the possibility for the son of a cemetery worker to marry the daughter of someone in a completely different job and of another religion. She could be a Catholic, and he could be a Jew, and they could get married, and he could do a completely different job, and organize a completely different kind of family. We allow lateral mobility whereas in earlier societies this was not done.

We have also allowed the venting of pressures through upward mobility. The pressures of the social structure in western Europe were vented in the United States, and as the United States populated, with all its own pressures, the lower-class, suppressed people in the social structure who had no way up were vented outwards. Now we can have a person with no education at all who has upward mobility; that upward mobility is determined primarily by the economic base of his or her income and then by the friends he or she has; whether by election to some parliament, or the charisma of personality—many things influence this. In Hindu society John F. Kennedy could have had all the charisma that he might or might not have had and would have become nothing; because his father was a maker of whiskey, he would be a maker of whiskey, and only the makers of whiskey would be interested in him. He could have organized the makers of whiskey into making more equitable whiskey or less equitable whiskey, but he could never have touched the makers of leather or the makers of anything else.

There are disadvantages to upward mobility which can be clearly seen in India, where it had been suppressed for thousands of years: When upward mobility is allowed everyone wants up, but everyone cannot be up, so up is pulled down. That is what I mean by the tyranny of democracy. It is true that in the unequal distribution of power as, for instance, in the aristocratic days in England or Holland, Germany or France, many wrong things happened, yet it is not hard to see there the possibility for cultural or intellectual development; free time to delve into deeper thought was exercised much more than it is today, but by a smaller number of people. Today we have more free time but, as a conglomerate of human sheep in the world, we do fewer things with it. Because we have more free time it needs to be satisfied in the fastest, easiest way to dull us, so the way to satisfy that free time is determined at the lowest level so that the largest number of people will be interested in it—because it follows economic law.

If the aristocracy existed today and were in control of television, there would probably be one channel for the people lower down the scale of the social structure, to brainwash them so as to maintain their belief that they are what they ought to be and belong where they are and should continue to serve for ever and ever, and to make them happier in that, to satisfy them in it. There would be another television channel on which high-level cultural, intellectual and spiritual concepts would be evolved and promulgated (which nobody would be interested in now). As it is now there is a level of television programs, of moviemaking, of methods of communication which are not quite so much down as to keep all the slaves free and happy to be slaves, but not sufficiently up to give the people who are not slaves the consciousness that they are really free. This situation says to me that we have come to the end of the possibilities of human evolution within this structure. It was good to reach the order of right by might, of right by achievement, by economic power—free technology has created all sorts of possibilities for mankind—but it seems that as the upward mobility becomes too strong, the chances to go upward do not increase, so the ceiling must come down and a new tyranny arises, the tyranny of being free and equal—which is as tyrannous as the tyranny of being unfree and unequal.

In the study of civilizations and societies it becomes clear that over a longer period the real development, the real evolution always devolves upon those parts of the society which gain the skills and the tools which that society needs to maintain itself or its base of indoctrination. That is a very important point on which we have to build, because as we come to the society of the future, the same thing will again be true.

It is interesting that what you hear from contemporary Chinese society seems to be sensational, revolutionary, "left," wild leadership to free oneself, to make everybody work, to make everybody equal, to progress, to go forward. That thought was spurred on by the ideology of Mao Tse Tung; but why is there continually the struggle for power and ideological leadership in China, especially now, after Mao's death? It appears that those people who shout the loudest about how everything ought to be, who are the most wild, most intense, most reactionary in their willingness to destroy, cannot run the society because they are the unstable elements. Unstable elements are necessary. The real power base of the Chinese government, covered over by the more wild, revolutionary propagandist outer veil, are very careful, capable people who do moderate, conservative things, probably ex-capitalists—like Liu Shao-ch'i,—who have in their hands the lines of communication, the skills of effective command, of leadership, of planning, of control, of structural conceptualization. They maintain the status quo, they keep things running, and the big fight is and always will be between the unstable elements and the stable elements. Certainly sooner or later the stable elements always win, even though unstable elements are necessary because they throw the thing off balance, they allow progress.

Progress and change can only be worthwhile if there is a flow, a pattern, a dance; otherwise it is chaos and then the progress becomes completely destructive and degenerative for a while, until it stabilizes at a lower base of organization, to re-emerge into evolution.

This is a remarkably subtle, worthwhile situation in China, although anyone who would question my right to talk about China is right because I do not know anything about it, none of us really do, but there is this picture of the last ten years, that the real struggle for power in China stems from the people who have the ideology, the opinion, who are the leaders of charisma, the leaders of people, even who have the coercive power, the overt power, finding their influence slipping away because they are not the people who have the skills, who have control over the lines of communication, who have access to the continuity and maintenance of the structure. Those are the same people who have always run any society.

In his Sufi Message, Inayat Khan often talks about the

conservative spirit and the progressive spirit, and I am sure that in the societies to come, however they may be, there will have to come a balance between these two spirits—which exist in any case in every human mind. The spirit to conserve and to maintain, to integrate, is the spirit to reap the harvest and keep it for the period of hunger in the winter. The progressive spirit is to break new land, to sow seeds and open new possibilities, have trust and faith in what the future will bring. In other words there needs to be a centralized decentralization, or a decentralized centralization. There needs to be a conservative liberalism, there needs to be (and this comes back to the only human attitude which integrates these two) a social order based on the courage to live. The word "courage" to me unites the conservative and progressive spirits. We often associate courage with fighting or with violence, but when we analyze the war heroes to whom we give medals, awards for courage, it often turns out that whatever they did, they did out of incredible fear, or in cold-blooded psychopathic deviation. This is not the courage I am suggesting. The real courage, free from the attachment of the value of heroism, the courage to live, is the courage to sow the new and reap the old. It is the courage to live where you are and yet go forward in the unknown, discover who you are and as you discover who you are, destroy that so that you can become something else; to further the social structure by looking into the possibility of new forms of social intercourse and yet, at the same time, proceed only at that speed of change which integrates, in the change, the necessity for stability and security and calm, out of which the change can be enriching rather than frightening.

People often ask how the new societies should be, will they be patriarchal or matriarchal or neither? Where will the lines of authority come from? How will people group together? As things progress it seems that the patriarchal society is doomed to disappear; patriarchy provided a security base in an environment where protection through physical power was necessary, and any attempt to maintain it in its present form or any other form will fail. Now it is intellectual power, personality and other forms of influence that provide security; the necessity for protection from outer, overt danger has gone. The beginning of the life insurance companies was the end of the patriarchal society; I am sure of that.

Will the elimination of the patriarchal form of society mean that the matriarchal society will come to the fore? I think that there is no real future for matriarchal forms of society either, because they have to do with the family system. Families were always far larger in matriarchal than in patriarchal societies. As we have come to the birth control pill, to different forms of education, to bringing young children to independence by the time they are fifteen and sixteen rather than twenty-eight and thirty, to a society where one can, relatively, maintain oneself with a few skills, to a social structure where social good, medical services, food, clothes, all these things are provided, the mother's role over an extended period of time, the security that the mother can provide, disappears and the woman is finding that she herself is more independent. Many women find now that family life in the old manner, either in a patriarchal or a matriarchal form, is not satisfactory.

Why does the woman still have to be the secretary and the man the executive?—the woman is really the better executive, but because of the sublimation of her womanhood, the man will be the executive and she will be the secretary. Slowly as these things equalize, neither the patriarchal nor the matriarchal form will really survive; they belong to an old environment, they come out of the jungle, out of the tribe, out of other periods. This really means that the basic form of cultural indoctrination will not be the family unit; it will probably be the television, if it is not already.

I remember once in India, there was a man by a river tending ducks, one little man with a little stick, and about one hundred and twenty or two hundred little ducks. These ducks were imprinted with their mama, and when they woke into consciousness they saw their mama, who was the old man; and from then on he never had to make them tame, he never had to do anything to them, he could teach them anything he wanted, to eat, to quack, to lay eggs where he wanted them to, anything, because he was their mama. I began to think about how the new society will be and where the first imprint will come from. When the child wakes up, will it be in an incubator, will it be in a laboratory? Where will it find its security, its warmth, its love, its stability, its comfort? Wherever it finds those things, there will be the center of the new social structure.

This may sound very revolutionary and it may seem that I do not advocate motherhood and fatherhood, but I do; I do not think that mankind can ever be natural, in any social order, without these functions. Fatherhood and motherhood in a non-patriarchal or non-matriarchal society will obviously be quite different. It will always be true that in some ways you can have a better, more detached bond of wisdom with children who were not born of your own self; you can love people who are a little bit further removed from you, though some may say that it would be artificial love or not so true as the love of the real mother—but who is the real mother, who the real father? Probably what will happen is that a child will have several mothers and several fathers at different periods in his life: an adoption system.

In the future there will probably be groupings around what people consider valuable. When the societies we know today began, what originally brought people together, so that there could be interchange and enrichment, was a wall. Whether you believe it or not, that really was the first way— because inside the wall it was safe and outside the wall you were alone; inside the wall you could not be plundered so easily, outside the wall you could be plundered; inside the wall you were together, you could talk, you were not alone, you could trade, while outside the wall. . . . Now, of course there will be other spheres of influence, and these will probably be tribal structures, spheres of influence which people flock to, choose to live in due to a certain attraction. Because of the level of abstraction that we have today, leadership in these spheres of influence will be dynamic, will not be elected or appointed or gained through warfare, it will be gained through the dominance of the mind, through personal influence; it will be leadership that one chooses individually and personally rather than leadership that one chooses through form or structure.

This is the way in which the first universities in Greece

grew. Today a student going to university will meet teachers who were hired to teach him, and have no choice about it. In ancient Greece, academies would be founded by one man simply on the basis that people liked his company and accepted the superiority of his mind, his influence. In the Greek system it was primarily men; in the future it may be a man, it may be a woman, it may be a couple, it may be a continually changing situation—nobody knows.

In the same way as in that period of Greek evolution, people will decide to go and live in a certain sphere of influence, to follow a certain lifestyle, to make that lifestyle a reality because they want to; that is the form of leadership that will have to come. There will still be hierarchy, there will still be law, there will still be authority, but the basis of the authority will be one's wanting to submit to it. That will only come about when all other forms of coercive power become equalized. A little while ago if a king wanted to enforce his law he would appoint a policeman, who would appoint a soldier, and the soldier would carry the course of power to the people, and when they saw the soldier or the policeman, his expressed power was greater than theirs, so they would follow the law. The policeman now will not want to, because he will see the ridiculousness of enforcing a law which may not be at all worthwhile; or perhaps because it will not be interesting to be a policeman. In other words, the coercive arm of leadership will degenerate of itself.

What happened to President Nixon may be a similar situation; the coercive arm eats itself and the structure collapses by its own structural contradiction. In that situation people have to destroy what is right because they have to, although they do not want to. When the coercive power is equalized everywhere and loses its force of coercion, the only form of leadership left will be the dominance of the mind. The dominance of the mind will gain that form because it will be the mind that has sufficient access, either on an individual or a collective basis, to the tools and skills and means of communication to maintain a sphere of influence such as that on which future societies will be based.

To summarize: in the past all societies came to develop by

power, which was strength, because strength was needed and required in the environment in which they grew. Eventually when these societies became an integrated web-work, a structure of interrelationships, the control went from those who had the coercive power to those who were at the center of the web, those who used a subtle combination of mind and strength, their own minds and the strength of others. They were the ones who brought savage, rough, wild, uncivilized man to civilization—by which we mean a certain level of development of mind and of abstraction. Someone who can think abstractly definitely thinks differently from a person who cannot. This is very clear when you come into contact with tribes who attribute the quality of realism to everything they see, feel, hear, touch; they can never understand abstract interrelationships and energy groupings which rule this outer, overt world. We have lost their naturalness, become civilized and, by losing their naturalness, have become uncivilized in a sense.

The influences and structure of society will still be based on leadership, on hierarchical concepts—they have to be. They will be organized around the sphere of influence made in some way for the common good of all those human beings in it, and the structure will be neither a matriarchy nor a patriarchy. There will probably develop some elite group or aristrocracy based on mental dominance, and the structures will be very free, decentralized and differentiated. There will be many different structures; some will go towards secure structured forms, others will go to free forms; some will go to high technology, others will go completely away from it. There will be a period of transition, after which they will all become fairly similar.

July 22, 1974

EDUCATION

In discussing the future of society I am trying to give an idea not of what it will actually be, but a view of what it could be. I shall continue now by examining the educational system.

In whatever society one lives, visits or studies, one finds the educational system a very important part of the socializing, acculturating process that perpetuates, maintains and develops the society. All sorts of interesting conclusions can be drawn from today's different educational systems; I have been involved with primary and elementary school systems in France and Holland, and with high school and college in the United States, and I think that because I went—as a child, as a growing person—through these different systems, I can arrive at conclusions which are valid and can serve as a basis for looking deeper.

The system which was in force in Holland and France twenty years ago was very much geared to teaching facts; those facts were of primary importance. Success in my education was tested in terms of whether or not I knew these facts as they were written down or taught and could repeat them exactly and correctly. I can remember learning the multiplication tables; I still do them in Dutch, because that is the way I was trained to do them. Every week in the third grade we had to learn a new table, and the teacher simply put big figures on the board in front of us: $1 \times 2 = 2$, $2 \times 2 = 4$, et cetera. I learned the symbols 2×2, I learned the facts by heart, and after a week the teacher would point at someone in the class and say, "All right, you," and the person would

stand up and say, "1 × 2 = 2, 2 × 2 = 4 ..." "All right, you
know it, next one ..." Then you would get a mark for being a
good student. I remember clearly that I did not understand
what it was all about, and even today I do not understand
what it was all about; I still do not know. It is interesting and
weird, this power of numbers, this geometric progression
which suddenly explodes. It was not, in fact, until later on
with algebra, learning the power of numbers, 2^3 really meant
2 × 2 × 2, that it started to make sense and become not simply
a fact—this thing is red, or 2 × 2 = 4—but a notion which had
meaning.

The interesting thing about the American educational
system which I observed immediately and never forgot, was
that most people did not seem to know how to multiply very
well; many did not know the tables above 5 by heart, and
they certainly had a relatively small number of facts to learn
or recall. But they spent a lot of time in the class discussing
and arguing in what probably seemed to the teacher to be
very boring, immature conversations, repeating themselves
again and again. It seemed that factual knowledge was very
low, but the motivation and involvement in the educational
experience of being in a group which was trying to look at
something—this is red. Why is it red? Because someone dyed
it red. How did he dye it? Do I like it or not? How do I relate
to this fact?—these continual discussions were very enriching. So I find myself somewhat biased, in that the comparison
of one educational system to another shows that most inventions, most scientific growth, most innovations, most technological refinements, most patents are happening in America,
not in Holland. Of course, in America there are two hundred
million people and they have big research grants and so on,
but I am not so sure that these differences are not part of the
difference in the educational system. In the United States
these innovations are happening whereas, interestingly, they
are copied better, done more correctly by people in other
countries who assimilate the new facts and assemble them
accurately to work for ever and ever.

Later on after school I was involved with the production
of computers. A computer combines so much of the techno-

logical, scientific and intellectual parts of man's knowledge, of the inventory of his knowledge. At one point in the fast expansion of the computer company they could not find enough engineers, so they began a widespread hiring drive. They went to France, to Holland, to Germany, to England, to Italy (this was during the brain-drain after the war), and they hired fifty or sixty engineers, ten or twenty from each educational group of the other countries; they hired the best men they could find, and they paid them very well. And within six months you could easily see the incredible differences in these functional minds. The French engineers, for instance, were primarily good at finding out why something did not work, but not at finding out how it could be made to work. They were very analytical; they refused to look at a plan unless they had all the data, all the information down on paper so that they could see it. If one little tiny thing was missing they would say, "No, this is incomplete, I don't want to look at it, don't bother me." The Dutch engineers were primarily useful at inspection. If you set up parameters to test something, they were not able to make a compromise, say "Well, the girl on the assembly line is so sweet, she has nice blond hair and blue eyes, I'll pass it"—no, they were rock hard, good or bad, nothing in between, but they made very little innovative design. If a screw was loose or something was missing, they would not fix it, they would send it back. The English engineers were transferred to lower jobs or fired within a year—not one kept his original position. I do not mean to attack the British nation as a result of that, but they were impotent, they talked and talked and talked about design and ideas, and never actually wrote anything down, never got down to work. There were only four or five Italian engineers, they were the most cliquish, one group; they all worked together, they all sat together, they all moved offices together and they worked well as a team. They discussed everything in Italian, although they all spoke perfect English, and they always kept their identity; they could not lose it. There were a dozen or so German engineers and they "Americanized," socially speaking, the fastest. They spread out into all the different branches of the company the fastest, lost their identity so quickly that I can't now make any statement about what happened to them or how they worked—they were gone, they were gobbled up; it was very interesting.

There is certainly no scientific conclusion you can make from these observations, and any conclusion would have to be prejudiced in a way also, but I remember that somehow each group had a definite mind that you could recognize, though you could not say one box looked like this and another box looked like that. There was a national mind, and in some way that national mind was constructed, formed, developed by that society; and the major influence in the way society had constructed those minds was the educational system.

To return to the original example, there is a definite need for two things in any educational system. First you need to learn facts. Second, you need to learn the ability to relate and interrelate these facts, select them and relate yourself to them. There are other aspects of education which in some way overlap or partially fall into these two extremes, but it is valid to say that these are the two things, the left and right hands: learning facts, being able to hold them, recall them, know them by heart, and then constructing meaning out of them.

We all know that children have a tremendous curiosity. Everything they see they want to know what it is, how it works, and of course we have to frustrate them, because whatever they begin to look at they will destroy, or worse than that. But that curiosity drive, to learn language, to learn about how everything is, taste the earth, to pierce through the unknown, the un-understandable—you can see the level of abstraction of this educational drive gradually change and mature. A small child looking at an intricately-patterned rug would not see the rug, it would see one little dot, right here, very clearly, for a very short time. Then his attention will turn to that little dot over there. When the child is four, five or six, maybe it will begin to see the rug, and at ten it can begin to see the room and get more abstract concepts of interrelationships and understanding of colors and shapes on a larger scale. We all know that, and we can also see that the first hunger for knowledge is for practical knowledge. "Why does my mummy open a can, and why does she do it that way? Why does she tell me I will cut my fingers? How do they light a match?" All these practical things they want to know, and later on comes the question, "How does the match light up?" When that question arises it is the beginning of more abstract research, more abstract curiosity about principles which are not necessarily material. Somehow—and I do not know why—we have interfered with the natural mental maturing cycle, the growth possibility, and decided that at six years old suddenly a child is old enough to learn simple arithmetic, at eight geography . . . but we do not really know whether this is true.

The child who is a genius develops well and extremely fast, but seems to reach a peak at eighteen or twenty, and by the time he is thirty, if he is not dead, he has lost the mental life-drive and he no longer develops. Very few genial minds develop after that age if they developed early. Other genial minds—of course, Einstein is an example, and Schweitzer another—were very slow learners at school, and never excelled. Their learning energy was never overtapped and they continued their mental growth, their growth into abstraction, and they did not reach their peak until they were seventy or eighty.

I know from my own experience how concerned you are as a parent with the first child, because you are still trying to find out what it means to be a parent. You hope that you will be a good parent and follow all these ridiculous directions that you read in books and learned from your own parents, and you want to prove your own independence as a man or a woman. You want your child to behave well, you do not want anybody to see it scream or shout or fight or spit. You want it to use a potty as soon as possible so that it is advanced. At a few months old it begins to walk and you are inspired and you think it is wonderful, and your whole structure of expectation is geared towards seeing the child as an adult. You want it to grow, you want it to learn—already at three it can write and draw, "Look, how beautiful . . ."; the hand muscles are hardly developed and you force it to make a straight line on a piece of paper. This is the same drive that is behind the school's beginning to force abstract learning, to tap the ability for abstract learning in the early stages, at five, six, or seven, when the child has not yet developed emotional maturity commensurate with abstract thought. Another reason for this drive to force abstract learning is the life-expectation which has lengthened—in the past it was not sixty-seven for a man, it was more like forty-seven, for a woman it was not seventy-six, it was more like forty-five—and so you had to start to learn early, because you would not live long. Yet another reason behind it is that children were an economic necessity in the past. If you were a shoemaker or a carpenter you could only earn so much, but your children could help you to cut soles and learn your trade. The sooner they learned it the sooner they could begin to help you support the family.

At that time there was probably child labor at five or six years old, but then we discovered that you never really get ahead unless you are educated—which is also a lot of nonsense. It is your personality which determines whether you will get ahead or not. Education can always be acquired. Even so, we made laws, moral laws—which were probably also very immoral—against child labor, separating the beautiful unity of children and parents. Most days the child can be with his parents only early in the morning and late at night; it cannot work for its parents, it has to be put in a separate place and be made into a good citizen, get a diploma so that it will be richer, better and more successful than its parents.

Sending children to school is as bad as, if not worse, than any form of child labor that we try to prevent with anti-child labor laws. We put children on a bench with pencils in their hands and we force them to work. Some sentimental person comes along, she probably has no children of her own, or she is afraid to have a family or to make love, so to sublimate all her motherly feelings she goes to educate. We send too many people to educate who have no children, or who go into education for the wrong reasons. They start with sentimental ideas that you should be nice to children, children should enjoy everything, they should learn by playing, everything should be beautiful and soft; so the children have that kind of standard set for them, or on them, in school. But they are also expected to learn. Parents expect one thing, the teachers expect another thing, the social system expects a third thing. The children come out of school with one behavior pattern, and at home another pattern, another kind of communication is expected.

Parents are often away and involved in a different mentality, doing different things, and no matter what the child does, he can never really contribute to the effort they are making in life for him to eat, live and have a roof over his head, a car and a television and an education. There are two different worlds, far apart, and somehow they are dissociated and there are serious problems.

One could go on for hours saying all that is wrong with the educational system; but here it is important to repeat that first, education is useless unless you want to learn. Whatever you are going to learn, under any system of coercion— whether it is subtle psychological coercion, real coercion, or the straightforward coercion of "this is the way the system works," "this is what is expected of you"—you can only learn easily what you are interested in. When a little child runs to a dot on the carpet because it wants to see, it is going to run over the flowers, knock down the candle, break everything in its path because it really wants to see what is there. The child feels a tremendous driving force, it wants to know what is there; it has a beautiful way, a beautiful mind, a beautiful concentration to bring to this point.

That drive, that energy, that curiosity to discover the environment, which is part of feeling secure, having a home, having a territory, knowing where we are—that is what we should go back to, what we should pick up and what we should develop upon and guide. Instead of having an educational system that separates adults from children, we should have an educational system that brings adult life and child life into more harmony, so that we do not build up inferiority complexes: not, "You are no good, you can never do anything anyway because you are only a child, you cannot do any of the special things that your parents can do, or that the adult world can do"; but, "You can contribute up to your attention span, you can belong up to your level of abstraction, the level of your consciousness, the level of your curiosity and your interest." Gradually this process of encouraging maturity should encompass more and more discipline, more guidance, until the child is no longer a child. And here is a very important separation, which explains another thing that is wrong with the educational system: we say that a person is an adult at eighteen or at twenty-one, he is an adult before the law—but it is not true; to me it is not true at all. I can think of people of forty or eighty who are completely immature, and I can think of people of fifteen and fourteen who show a great maturity, great stability. It would seem to me that one is a child up to the period of puberty, and that is one whole unit, which means up to about nine or ten years old. That period of childhood should be wholesome, as close to the parents as possible, without any formal education, only answering and guiding the increased natural curiosity drive to expand to an ever higher level of abstraction. Then comes the so-called difficult period of puberty (it is only difficult because we make it so), in which you suddenly discover that you are no longer a child, that you are becoming a woman, or becoming a man. That three-, four-, five-year period is a very subtle period and it is then that you begin to have formative thoughts about your future, to face the fact that one day you will be away from your parents, one day you will have children and a job. You begin to face these interesting things, you begin to search for your identity.

During that period of puberty the educational system should allow people to be away from their parents, especially if during the whole nine- or ten-year period of childhood they were together. Puberty is a strange period of transition, self-search, self-identity, when one should experiment with oneself, begin to relate to life, to reality, as independently as possible. Independence is something every human being, every character, every personality needs. You can never be independent in the sense of being isolated or totally self-sufficient, but you need to be independent in the sense of being able to function in life without being the factual, economic and psychological slave of a system which you are without power to change, or relate or contribute to. The period from nine or ten to about fourteen, when puberty is past, is one in which children want to be independent. Lord Baden-Powell resolved this when he made boy and girl scouts, but the world has since changed a little bit. Children should be allowed to travel, to see the world, to see themselves. In this searching for who they are, they will find out what they want to become. Of course, at a later stage of education this may change completely, but that does not matter—at least they have a path to follow for a while.

The third period is that of formal education. I suppose that most children will already have learned the more basic parts of reading, writing and simple arithmetic by then, without tapping their abstract energy to learn, in a natural way, in an almost playful way. Most children will have acquired ideas of how the economic structure works. For instance, the fact that whatever system you have you will always have to pay for what you get, earn what you want, return for what you take—all these natural things which are part of society they will have learned. At this point a young woman or young man of fourteen, sixteen, eighteen, is ready to learn because he knows why he wants to learn, knows approximately what he wants to learn, and, I am sure, will learn much faster.

The way medical studies are now, you may have to study for sixteen years to become a psychiatrist, that means if you start at sixteen you will not qualify until you are thirty-two—what a terrible thing! But this is because the educational system starts too early, teaches you too many things you do not need to know, and taps too much of your growth energy, so that when you are really ready to learn, your learning ability is used up and progress is slow. If you began formal education out of self-discipline, out of your own desire, out of the continuity of the curiosity of the child who runs and knocks everything down to get there, you will run and knock everything down and jump to that abstract point of what you want to become. In formal education you should not only be allowed to learn what you want to learn, but also to learn from those teachers with whom you want to be—teachers who should not really be teachers but a more subtle combination of parent, guru and teacher. If you want to become, say, a doctor, they should not necessarily teach you surgery or some other part of it—you should be close enough with them for a period of your life so that you can absorb, just as a child does, subliminally, unconsciously, whole attitudes, information, emotional concepts of what is learned out of experience, which no one can ever quantify or put in books or theories. In a sense your teacher becomes your second parent and your first guru, but you cannot have that teacher unless you have learned independence, and you cannot have independence unless you have had sufficient dependence that you have built up a secure personality in your early childhood by real, total, warm contact with those people who made you, to whom you belong. Knowing who you are means knowing to whom you belong.

And so I see three kinds of school. One is an informal school in which parents and children learn how to be parents and children, where both the parents and the children go to school to be better parents and better children. It is very difficult to be a parent—all your anxieties, your whole life, your entire identity is brought into question. It is very easy to make a child, it is not so easy to make a human being. It would make a lot of sense to bring parents together in playschool situations or environments where they can watch other children and compare and see that most children are savage and that their own child is not unusual, and thereby feel more secure and free. That situation should continue until puberty.

The second school, for the duration of puberty, should be an educational system where the embryonic adults are allowed cultural and social expansion that they can earn in work, in travel, through referral systems or friends. A young boy of twelve wants to go on a boat, he wants to work his passage to India—let him go. He will make it, and come back. Learn independence, learn to prove yourself to yourself. Apply all the skills you have learned as a child, learn to work with your hands; you feel good if you know that you can do something with your hands. It is quite a different feeling from that of being alone in the jungle with a gun, but still it is the same kind of safety and security; you feel that if worse comes to worst, you can do it, you can make it.

The third school is for formal education, but free, in the sense that the teachers are chosen by the pupils and the pupils are chosen by the teachers, who are far more than teachers, who occupy a much more important temporary role in the forming of knowledge and the psychology in which that knowledge has meaning. That means that you cannot have teachers who specialize in teaching a single miniscule subject. If you want to become a pianist, you would choose a great pianist whose music you like, with whom you can live and study and practice; but he will not teach you only piano playing, he will teach you how to read Greek, how to orchestrate, all the things you need to know to become a human being functioning in society as a pianist. If you want to become a pianist and after studying for a year you have grown out of it and you feel that you would prefer to do something else, then you should be able to change. The contract between pupil and teacher should last as long as the two want each other, and the teacher also should continuously learn and become wiser as a result of the questioning attitude and the continual curiosity of the student.

Gradually the whole society would become involved in education on the widest possible base. You can see, for instance, that a great pianist becomes attached to a particular piano-maker, who becomes attached to a particular kind of wood which is grown in a particular forest where there is a particular forester ... and he likes a certain kind of string made in a certain factory in Germany by a certain process ... and all these things interrelate, so you too would learn all these things. By the same token, all the people in whom the pianist is interested, all his friends and the things in which they are interested, these also become your teachers.

Some people will raise all kinds of objections, especially concerning organization and whether the educational system would be successful. Most engineers are not good engineers, so what will happen if you choose a bad one? I believe that a teacher is as good as the pupil makes him, and I also feel that when you are charged in life with the duty to educate and transmit your knowledge, you will never become conservative. The social dilemmas of the generation gap and the search for different ideals and values would never arise because your mind keeps young and the young minds keep being affected by the balance, stability, experience and influence of the mature mind—they both affect each other. I do not believe that bad engineers would make bad engineers; what will happen is in a way already happening, that excellent students will choose more excellent teachers, and that system of sorting will continue.

A good mind attracts a good mind: that connects with my original statement that we make a mistake in wanting all men to be equal. It is not true, it has never been true and it will never be true that all men are equal. If you make on one machine a million gadgets of the same material, with the same mold and by the same process, they will not all be equal.

There will still be inequality, but I feel that the inequality will be less competitive in its result because, whereas now there are good students and bad students competing, in that situation good students with a certain quality, a certain quintessence of mind would tend to find good teachers, and lesser students with not quite that quintessence of mind would find teachers who suited them; the competition which would remain, which has to be, would be much more individualized. I suppose the real inequality that I am talking about will never end.

I see education as something that the entire strata of society should be involved in, something based not on formal subjects or defined disciplines as we have now, but more on vocations and directions of thought. I can see that specialization would happen much later, and that although that could slow down the rapid development of knowledge, it may also uplift the entire stratum of the human genius to a higher level, instead of perpetuating the present pyramidal structure, where very few people have any concept at all of the more abstract knowledge of universal laws and principles, techniques and logic, and where most people remain the television-gazers who do not know what to do with their untapped, unmotivated, pain-filled minds and hearts.

September 23, 1974

ENVIRONMENT

I want, in this chapter, to look at the general subject of how the world might organize itself into physical sub-units. What will houses look like? What will cities look like? How will things run? How will things work?

Everyone, somewhere in his or her self, longs to live a natural life. I often allude to our concept of nature as a beautiful park with a long stretch of lawn nicely cut, a few little birds that say "tweet-tweet," some roses, no weeds and a nice little bench to sit on. Real nature, the uncultivated, undominated nature, where nature itself is the boss, is completely different. There is a tremendous difference between what nature really is and what it is of nature we really want, really long for, and because of this it is man's destiny to cultivate nature; he cannot help it, and there is no going back. That is a very important thesis, because although the idea of living in the jungle in some kind of survival training center has a romantic, adventurous attraction, I feel confident that no person from the civilized world would find a satisfaction in his life's calling for meaning, purpose and knowledge in that environment. Of course there would be a temporary challenge, a temporary satisfaction, but as soon as we go back to nature we start to cultivate it. For instance, as soon as you go back to nature, insects start biting you; after you have been bitten by a few hundred mosquitoes at the same time, I guarantee that you will cultivate nature, build a shelter to stop mosquitoes or burn a fire, or whatever.

Our desire to go back to nature, to live a natural life will always be with us, but nature does not exist; it is an artificial concept, a concept of original earth-communication, unity with the planet. Nature is there to be cultivated and every effort to live within it implies its cultivation. This distinguishes us from our predecessors in the evolutionary scale; they can find permanent life-fulfillment in the natural environment, we cannot. This is a very important point which we really cannot talk about enough, because in our evaluation of what we want to do with our life, in the conflicts that we face between the artificiality, the estrangement of the natural, and the wanting to return to the natural—which does not exist and is unfindable and could never fulfill us—we are caught somewhere, so we create an artificial nature. In the future man will attempt to recreate that part of nature which he needs to feel a subliminal earth-contact, harmony, and at the same time man will be nature's master, developer, cultivator. What we see around us is the expression of that same struggle through history to become the master of nature, which has removed us from it permanently.

It seems as though the cycle has come halfway and the future will be a recreation not of nature, because it does not exist, but of the nature that we humans want and need. I imagine houses, structural units in which to live, shelters, cities, population centers, more or less like a park. We will want to live more in the fresh air, out of doors, but we will still need all of the amenities of the high technology we have achieved. The problem today is not that there is anything wrong with our high technology, but that it is not applied consequentially because the economic requirements of society do not harmonize with the technological potential of man.

Within a few years we will have pierced the problems of converting solar energy, energy from wind, from waves, to energy for our uses. Once we have done that our technology will be at the point where we can build, in any part of the world, a center of dwellings which are, apart from money, self-sufficient. Where the energy is produced the waste will be recycled; land cultivation, irrigation, these things will happen so automatically, be so finely developed technologically that with almost no effort we can grow our own food, generate or regenerate our own energy, dispose of our own wastes and live totally isolated from any outer resource to sustain ourselves.

Every human being has somewhere the desire to be self-sufficient, to be independent. This is the strong natural force that comes out in a young child who wants to leave papa and mama, break out, make his own way. All the things that we have done as a civilization can also be seen in the light of asserting ever greater independence, the Cain force to master, and there is no reason why this should suddenly change; it will simply develop to its logical consequence, which will be that we will come to harmonize technology, psychology and the physical needs for living a healthy life.

What will a house look like? No one really knows, but in the abstract I believe it will be built into the land, into the earth, into the forest, the park. We will build an environment in which one of the elements is a dwelling in the midst of the totality of that environment, and not something which stands out as A House. Dwellings will, of course, be group dwellings, because man first needs another human being—not only as a man needing a woman and a woman needing a man, but as each human being with another human being. We are herd animals, we need groups to give us unity, direction, purpose and insight. The eyes of another human being are a mirror for us, by which we can know ourselves. The size of the group is important. A large group will always break down into subunits, because you can only relate to so many other human beings at one time. What the optimum group is I do not know—there can be no exact law, but it would probably be about one hundred; maybe less. These people will be grouped together in a dwelling situation where there is earth, air, space; and all the things that everyone needs to do will be centralized.

And mankind will surrender more parts of his individuality. Kitchens, washing facilities, energy production, toolrooms, of all these kinds of things there will be only one. It is more efficient, it makes sense, it makes survival easier. Around this central core of all things that everyone needs, there will be small cells, grottoes, or holes, or spaces, where each individual can find his place. There is a very good reason for that; experiments made in Communist China and in Russia have shown that you cannot take away mankind's territorial needs altogether. Most of these needs are exaggerated and unnatural, for if you look in nature at a bird or a rhino, even a fish or an insect, all will stake out their territory—but no animal will ever stake out unreasonably more territory than it needs. Man does. As a result of this there is an unequal distribution of space to develop one's potential, and that has to be brought back down to a reasonable level: but it can never be taken away completely. You can never have a healthy society where human beings have no territory at all.

I am sure that there will not be permanent property rights. Dwellings will belong to the community. Occupation of a particular dwelling will imply possession, but if you abandon your stake, your presence, ownership will revert to the community to be reassigned to another; and so it will be, not only with property rights but hopefully with just about all things that human beings need. Ten years ago there was a group of people in Amsterdam called the Provos. One of their principles was that anyone could use another's bicycle, so to get around Amsterdam they would just pick up a bicycle. This seemed such a threat to those people who possessed MY bike and wanted no one else to use it that the police started arresting the Provos for using bicycles they did not own, and for parking bicycles which were not locked (you cannot park a bicycle in Amsterdam without locking it). The Provos decided that they would have to comply with the law, so they put combination locks on all their bicycles and painted the combinations in white ink on the side of the bike. They complied with the law, but still anyone could use the bike; it was a nice thing.

Though there may be cars, helicopters, airplanes, rockets, subterranean or time machines, things which people need but which do not need a particular identity, these will also be community property. Today there are so many different cars being manufactured and marketed with great effort and varying success in the world; imagine the unnecessary duplication in effort and design, the assertions and differences which increase the costs. Since the forms of economic units, capitalistic units of production and profit that we have now will not exist, this kind of competition and duplication will not exist. There may be cars and bicycles and airplanes, but all forms of transportation which we all need will be the best that technology has available, the most useful, and they will cost very little. This will also create certain problems that are inherent in having the right to use something that you do not own. Whenever someone uses something that he does not own, he does not maintain it as well, he is not as careful about keeping it clean, in good order, or whatever. There will have to be some kind of community enforcement, so that if you had a car and the engine blew up because you did not put any oil in it you knew that you would have to wait two years to get another one. These kinds of laws or traditions will grow up.

In this environment, what will people do with themselves? What will they do with each other? In such an ideal environment if you want a car you go and get one, if you want a telephone you go and get one, everything you need, you have, you do not have to fight for it, struggle for it, long for it, see television advertisements to make your mouth water for it, it will be there—what will you do with your time? There will be much more time to spend acquiring knowledge, something I have alluded to before, and there will be much more time to spend on using that knowledge to a creative end. Usually when we think about being creative, we imagine sitting down in front of a canvas to make an oil painting or embroidering something beautiful. Many of these arts are useful, they are creative, but I think of them more as psychological therapies, meditations, forms of relaxation than as creative acts. Real creative acts will be using one's knowledge, one's energy, one's ability, one's concentration to further the inventory of knowledge for the betterment of the whole. In other words, we will all, instead of working for ourselves, be working for each other. Much later in life there will come specializations in one's creative line of endeavor, just as there are now; but those specializations will grow like a pyramid out of a broader base, life experience, knowledge, purpose and fulfillment, not out of the fear that it is too much to learn one whole field or subject; specializations will grow out of the creative forging ahead, bringing all one's abilities to best advantage, into focus.

The dwelling place itself should have space in which to communicate with one another, space to interchange, space to play the social game. There is a book called *Games People Play*, by Eric Berne—a nice book to read. We have a gaming mind; maybe some very interesting games will be developed.

All the things that we now consider horrible, terrible, shocking, awful and unnatural—should they exist in that environment, in that milieu? What things are they? Genetic control, birth control, brain transplants, heart transplants, personality inventory tests, computerized dating systems, futuristic things that scare us, these things will all come or are already here; we cannot stop them and if we think that we can, then we have already become conservative. Heart transplants, for instance: who are you? Are you your heart which goes plonk, plonk, plonk? Brain transplants: who are you? (What a terrible thing to be carrying someone else's brain. I would not want to do it; I am certainly conservative enough to say that I would not want to, but it is coming.) Genetic control, it will be a necessity. If you think of the problems of having to support a population greater than the planet would be able to support; if the goal is health, in some way you have to begin to select. These things will probably be ruled and controlled very much as they are now, except that the whole policy will move from comfort, lassitude and ease, to health. There will have to be more self-discipline, more self-enforcement. A person who is found to have the potential of genotypes which have problems will decide himself or herself not to perpetuate these problems in the race and make the choice of procreation accordingly.

Every dwelling will have a little computer station. Eventually computers will be built which you can carry with you, and they will have the same potential as the largest systems that we are building today. All knowledge, all data, all that you need to know for analysis and self-analysis will be available, right in front of you; and you will use it to choose for what appears, based on those values, to be the best.

How will society handle the problem of health? When health—mental health, physical health, spiritual health—becomes the most important thing, many of these problems will go away of themselves. The need for medical attention as it is now will decrease, but there will still be some. I can even foresee that the inability to recuperate will become a socially acceptable justification for suicide. We will begin to see that as those people, those minds, begin to apperceive that within that value system, a constructive life is not possible because the state of the art of healing has not yet reached the point of being able to resolve their particular malaise, they will find it fruitless to live.

There will, of course, be birth control. I am sure that the world will eventually come to zero population growth, not because I or anyone else is saying it but because it has to happen. In fact we are probably facing the prospect of serious mass deaths in the next hundred years. There are in the world probably two or three million minds growing up today which can never be sufficiently mentally healthy to function, even according to the norms of our present standards, due to malnutrition, to serious environmental problems and to severe emotional deficiencies caused by artificial insemination of one culture by another without natural growth. Unfortunately most of these people live in underdeveloped countries, and for some strange reason they always have to pay the most for the malaise of society.

The social structure will be based on one's own choice, almost an existential choice, to live. Where to live? I think that everyone will want to live everywhere, which means that when you no longer have a particular possession to protect from somebody else, and you no longer have particular walls to keep up, you are so free that you can move, go away, not only from the physical spaces, the physical prison but also from the psychological space, the psychological prison. There will, therefore, be much more travel. The history of civilization shows that its advance and development was caused by travel, and travel was always justified by one of two things: warfare or conquest, and pilgrimage. Through the need for either war and conquest or pilgrimage, people met people, learned from people, disseminated what they knew among people, and so things moved and the brew proceeded. (Then we started tourism and sped things up to the point that something went wrong. Even now when someone thinks of going to Italy or Spain, he thinks to stay somewhere with some nice folksy, friendly people on a little farm somewhere far away and really talk to them, have a nice time and learn something about how others live. But that ideal place does not exist except when it is built for tourists, with people walking in the right uniform. When they get there, what is waiting for them is a hotel or motel which has all the things they need.) In a way travel in the future will mean that every place you live will be a temporary place, a hotel or a hostel; everywhere will be a home, nowhere will be a home. That causes problems because we need a territory, a geographical territory in matter, but we also need a psychological territory, a home, a niche of safety and security where we can lay our heads and die. I would hope that society will discourage that in the future because as soon as you have decided unconsciously, "That is where I want to die," the inflexible, conservative attitude takes hold, because as it is now it is perfect, and we want to maintain it because this is where we want to die. You are afraid of death, but maybe it will be acceptable in this place. The conservative spirit sets in when we want our home to be somewhere instead of everywhere.

I hope that the dervish spirit can gain ascendancy for a while, feeling that every child belongs to god, every soul belongs to the universe, every mind belongs to the future which it can bring to the present. Life belongs to that moment of liberation when it can transcend this illusion into another. I would hope that the purpose of the environment and the social structure, the economic system, the educational system and the psychological power that people feel behind them is not to create a milieu where one wishes to die, but an environment where one can live.

These challenges which lie ahead, they are ideals, they are ideas; they will probably not happen, but with these ideas, these concepts in mind we can investigate our own life and how we live. Do we live in the basement of our potential, or are we ready to begin to climb the stairs so that eventually we are high enough to jump into everything? So often we say we are afraid of the plastic world with the nylon rugs, the powdered milk, the computerized letters, the printed forms; these things will not disappear, they will become better, more organized. I think that the problem is the plastic feeling, the sharp thought-forms, taut value systems; the base of insecurity out of which we cannot rise to live and love freely is self-alienation.

Maybe someday in that society to come man will belong to the eternal moment of life. What does "life" mean? I think the answer can be found only by pursuing life itself. There are different ways of doing that; pursuing life as it is, or pursuing life as it could be, and bringing that about by going towards that already, coming out of where we are now.

Someday there could be a value structure in society such that when health in the total sense is not possible on earth, man will end his life. Frankly, though maybe in a symbolic way, I think that is already a fact. We may be building coffins or crematoriums that do not carry those labels on them, but we are there and that is what we have to get out of. Health means being alive, being real, and there where there is no reality, where all illusion that one tries to understand ebbs away into meaninglessness, one of the few realities that we can create is our own commitment to finding it. I think that the new religion will not necessarily be to have faith in god and worship god, but to have faith in an eventual reality through our own act, through our own affirmation, through our own worship of it, though we will never know what it is, we will never find it, we will always find its illusionary cover.

In the future society where things will be decentralized, where we will be divested of most of the things which now encumber our life, where life will be based on health and freedom, the whole environment, physical, psychological, mental, intellectual, technological, will be to pursue, to worship, to affirm reality. I think it can only be found when "I" no longer exists.

September 30, 1974

PART 4
DEVOTION & MYSTICISM

THE WORSHIPPER
& THE WARRIOR

There are definite very clearly marked directions in what I call the spiritual search. One is the devotional. People search for something inspiring to believe in and receive support from as a result of their support of it; in his book *The Perennial Philosophy* Aldous Huxley wrote about that; "the middle way." There is another direction I generally characterize as mystical. Aldous Huxley also refers to a third, which he calls "philosophical," but the philosophical approach is necessary in either the devotional method or the mystical method; otherwise either one of these methods is devoid of real conceptual content, and if devoid of this content, it is not a meaningful way of spiritualization, but an effortless idealization without the thing behind it which requires growth. It is true, of course, that the philosophy completely devoid of either the mystical approach or the devotional approach also has value, because it can definitely interrogate all the known, and search and emulate the unknown. But regardless of that, I feel that there are these two ways: the devotional approach and the mystical approach; and both have to include philosophy and effort and—because of this philosophical content— some intellectualization or conceptualization of what one is in the process of doing or searching for is required; otherwise it is meaningless.

Things which require no conceptualization are things

which feed the body, which are at the instinctual level of existence. You do not need any philosophical justification to eat, to sleep or to die, because they just happen, they are the organic functions or biological constituents of life. As long as the spiritual search does not have philosophical content, it is simple and organic, an instinctual thing that does not bring one to any consciousness expansion.

The devotional approach and the mystical approach are distinguished periodically. In certain periods of one's expansion of consciousness during the devotional approach, one can suddenly clearly distinguish it from a mystical approach; at other periods, one cannot clearly distinguish it. It works the other way round, too—in the mystical approach the distinguishing of its methodology from the devotional approach is also periodic. If I were now to comment upon where you are, who you are, what you are doing, and what your level of conception is, I would say that the difference between the devotional approach and the mystical approach is "this," and if I were to draw an artificial line in the present moment, it would be inaccurate because it would not correspond to any periodicity, and it would certainly be unfair at least to the potential of conception of any one mind. Therefore, in a sense the difference between devotional and mystical is partially the function of the individual. Where there is light there is dark, wherever there is good (which of course there is not) there is bad, and wherever there is real there is false; so, wherever there is a valid devotional approach there must also be an invalid devotional approach, and wherever there is a valid mystical approach there will be an invalid mystical approach.

As I grew up on the laps and in the houses of people totally involved in seeking spirituality, I often experienced shocking revelations of both of these approaches, which helped me later in life to see more clearly the distinction between valid and invalid devotional approaches, valid and invalid mystical approaches. If the devotional approach in its primary effect relieves an individual on that particular path of the necessity for human love and the individualization of the expression of love and the personalization of our deeper self, then it is invalid. Whenever a devotional approach focuses devotion in such a way that the people in that focus no longer need to love, as normal natural human beings, each other, as normal natural human beings, no longer need to express themselves as individuals who need to be loved and understood, respected and cared for, that devotional approach, although very useful for a while, I find basically invalid. In order to illustrate this point I must oversimplify: the devotional approach of the Christian nun or the Buddhist monk, in which she or he in a way marries the deity and therefore deflects the normal human need to love and marry another human being, while very valuable, I call invalid, because *a priori,* any spiritualization should correspond to life, to normalcy, to health, to humanity.

To be spiritual is not to be some sort of soul that is lost somewhere; it has never been defined as that except by those who search in the spiritual to escape life's demands and confrontations.

In the same way, the mystical approach which serves primarily to mystify, to infer all sorts of hidden powers, magical charms, simulations of occult or other special understanding, influence of one particular mind which is superhuman over another, insights into the past and future—all these aspects of the mystical approach, while they again bear some relation to the truth, are false. Why? Because they do the same sort of thing, they deflect the primary justification for any spiritual search whatever, which is to be a better human being, a total human being, not some special or magical creature. Both of these approaches, deflecting human love to impersonalization, or deflecting human communication to some sort of level of magic, as they do, are clearly a kind of role-playing. It may be difficult for you to distinguish between what is role-playing and what is sincere—and of course there can be both sincere role-playing and sincerity without role-playing. I did not want at this point to distinguish clearly between the devotional approach and the mystical approach, but I did want to call attention to invalid devotionality which dehumanizes our natural existence and our normal conceptual power.

Any approach, therefore, which estranges one, alienates one from the goodness of what is in every human being, I emphatically deny as useful in the long run; though of course there are spiritual trips which may be useful for a while, and help people to concentrate better, or at least encourage them to believe in something while they cannot yet believe in themselves, or to love something while they cannot yet love themselves or others.

If you were to try to characterize, not to distinguish, but to emphasize more clearly the difference between the devotional and the mystical approach in their valid forms, I would say that the devotional approach is that of a worshipper, and the mystical approach is that of a warrior.

The worshipper does not know who or what he is worshipping. And here you ought to realize that as soon as you know what you worship, you can no longer worship it. Knowledge in a sense is devastation. So there is already an overlap between the two approaches: there is something mystical in the devotional approach in that the worshipper does not know what he is worshipping. There is pain in the devotional approach too, for as the worshipper is in the process of finding out what he is worshipping, there is a moment when the worshipped falls from its platform, and that is very painful. Probably because that moment is painful one tends to block the discovery—and therefore the major obstruction to the devotional approach is this inherent resistance to discovery of verity. If one is worshipping the candle—"Oh, it's magic . . ." —and then finds that there is no magic about it, another level of understanding immediately arises that sees the candle as simply a symbol representing in its consumption a higher principle. In the devotional approach when a particular symbol falls off its platform one can, by not resisting, immediately see what is behind it, and then worship that until it comes too close, then toss that away, and so on—until one finally worships, presumably, the real, which, by definition, cannot be deposed.

In the mystical approach the warrior is a quixotic figure who is in the process of warring with things which need to be

conquered or defrayed or deranged or dethroned, and therefore he also has that same painful moment when he discovers
that his battle was with a projected, unrealistic enemy, and
that the real suffocation he should have been battling has
escaped his energy and attention.

Interestingly, the mystical and devotional approaches
often aid each other in development, because the mystic
warrior may slash the worshipper's symbol into bits, while
the devoted worshipper may clearly see beyond the intense
density of the battling warrior, that he or she is missing what
really needs to be fought. The two in a way aid and abet each
other: because if the worshipper sees and views his worship
wrongly, he can derive continual self-righteous justification
from it out of not understanding, or resisting to understand
the battle of the warrior—therefore causing the symbol of his
worshipful attention to be static. At the same time the warrior
can find in the blank, almost ineffectual contact of the
worshipper's devotion a self-rationalizing justification of his
war which does not necessarily help in discovering that the
battle was engaged with a false or nonexistent enemy. Worshipper and warrior can help each other and both can abet
each other.

Both can be found in one human mind; I think the
mentality or cloak of that learned expectation of what we are
tends to prevent us from being free to become what we are.
While many come across the platform of the mystical warrior,
I find—and this is not a challenging accusation so much as a
characterization—that most spirituality-seekers are involved
with the devotional approach and have not yet lost or puri-
fied this self-identification with the worshipped. While I
mentioned periodicity, and therefore inferred that a worshipper cannot worship all at the same time, slowly by slowly,
through worshipping in a gradually more encompassing
scope, he comes to worship all eventually.

The warrior also needs to select what he should battle
with. In a sense you can fight all, but if you fight all you may
as well stop fighting, because your approach supports nothing
and therefore nothing is left to support you in the battle

against everything. The warrior's selective process must be different from the selective process of the worshipper because though you can suggest that you worship the same thing you fight, there are different distributions in periodicity as to when you can worship something and when you can battle with the same thing. And while we select what we worship, there is a very natural hierarchical order of selection which makes us begin with the most familiar, that nearest to our level of conceptualization where the border between the unknown and the known lies. If the known is here and the unknown is beyond here, the warrior is engaged somewhere in between. We can worship something just past this delineation, something which is still, though unresolved, partially influenced in shape, color, form, tone and effect by what we know, though unknown. As our ceiling of knowledge expands, the object of worship selectively changes. At the same time, the warrior is fighting a battle against what holds the level of knowledge down, what prevents sight expanding further into the yet-unknown, which can be known. The warrior is battling what is just below the level of knowledge, still clearly in the known, but therefore the false presence preventing the sight of the unknown.

The warrior is battling the person standing in the doorway, and the worshipper is worshipping the person standing behind the doorway. These are very subtle images of the same thing, though different.

There is a very clear resistance when we try to talk about this imaginary ceiling between the known and the unknown because whatever we can say about either the known or the unknown, the further out it goes, the more its character, its quality, is abstract. Sometimes we find there is a valuable backlash where, because the unbelievable mental, intellectual, conceptualizing effort requires more than we are willing to give in commitment—which is the same problem as in alienation from living—people in both the mystical and the devotional approach have a backlash to the particular thing they are either worshipping or warring with. In this way, I find the Jehovah's Witness in today's world is a backlash to the mystical approach, because the Witness advocates the battle in divisive conceptions, whereas the level of abstractness of that with which they are battling is far below that which they are capable of, as a result of their education and their envisionment potential. In the same way there is a falling-down, a backlash of the devotional approach, for instance in the Hare Krishna movement or some Buddhist movement, which brings the level of worship to a much more concrete form than the worshipper would actually be capable of worshipping. The reason for this is that we are no longer demanding the commitment of energy to keep up, to expand against the gravitational forces of the known which fall in upon us. This is the same as the general alienation of any human being to living itself, and psychology will bear this out. If you were to make a standard personality test on the people in these backlash devotional and mystical groups, you would find very strong statistical evidence of personal alienation in society and culture.

The mystical warrior is trying to reduce the obstruction in the doorway, and the worshipper is attempting to reach the construction behind the doorway, almost out of sight. There is a gap between these two, which is what I call the vague band between the known and the unknown. In that band rapture is possible, in that band ecstasy is possible, in that band the strange Alice in Wonderland-type un-understanding experience is possible. If that band becomes rather wide, the devotional approach has been developed too far in the totality of that particular culture, and the mystical approach has been insufficiently developed; therefore they no longer affect or interchange with each other, aid each other, abet each other—and both then become sterile. If the band is too narrow, this possibility of a peak experience, of rapture, is almost impossible; therefore the hardness of life, the obliterating, piercing, cornered, squaredness of life becomes so strong that the escape mechanisms of the culture are the most developed—and so it becomes more and more materialistic and less balanced philosophically and spiritually.

It is also possible in the devotional approach—and this is in a way the problem of communication between people— that the object of devotion corresponds to a conceptual level still in the known, placed where the mystical warrior is trying to battle; this is, I think, the situation developing at present. First, there is a very strong backlash everywhere because there is an out-of-balance situation; and second, the devotional approach tends to distintegrate, and when it disintegrates one of the two approaches which keeps both in harmony and at bay is rendered so ineffective that the other also loses something of its tension, something of its meaning in contradiction to the other.

I think therefore, while there is a mystical approach and a devotional approach—and I have also suggested that these two should be united as different mentalities in one consciousness—that when a particular individual loses the possibility of worshipping or of warring, he is subject to a development of mind which will turn back on him and come to nothing. Both ways need to be in some sort of balance. You also find that since the duality, the schizophrenia is not there in what the person is searching for, it finds expression in other things, in ways that tend to make even more obvious and strong divisions in the personality—because if the personality is not necessarily divided in what it is in the process of idealizing or searching for, then it becomes more divided in what it is now.

The less you are divided in the future, the more you are divided in the present; then you find that one side of yourself denies the other, and you live in a dissatisfied world where all hopes are stillborn.

DISCIPLESHIP

The subject of discipleship is, to the logical mind, a paradox. Why is it such a paradox? I think because there are two main thoughts or ideas about it which go in different directions or contradict each other—so that, in the end, when you can resolve that paradox there may be true discipleship.

One side of the paradox is the thought that you must do it for yourself. I'll come back to that, but I certainly would emphasize, before confusing you with anything else, that I completely agree with that. The way to a kind of expansion of consciousness and improvement, realization of your real self, how you should live and so on—that is something you must do yourself. Therefore a teacher, or the person, idea, ideology, method, or teaching you follow, takes away this point, this responsibility to yourself; and it also probably takes away the opportunity for self-leadership.

The other side, which is equally strong and important, is that on that road to self-improvement (whatever you may want to call it) you must find a teacher, you must find a guide—mind you, I am using the word "must" on purpose—you must have a guide; without a guide your attitude is not right and in the end you cannot come further because you need to learn discipleship. Through discipleship you can come further. Real discipleship in the deepest sense of the word does not just mean pupilship in an intellectual sense, it means the deep devotion, trust, receptivity of your being in the sense of being a disciple.

There is the essential paradox. You can see that paradox

very clearly in the history of development of esoteric training-schools, you can see the same conflict everywhere. Of course, when we think of the word or the concept of discipleship we usually associate it primarily with spiritual development. When we think of the terms "guru," "chela," "mureed," "murshid," we think essentially of spiritual development, but—and this may be helpful to the understanding of the paradox—the kind of relationship in which discipleship has brought people to realize great aspects of themselves exists far and wide outside that field of spiritual development. To give an example, between Jung and Freud you can see an aspect of discipleship which was not in the field of spirituality—although you might say that it was. In certain similar fields like medicine, violin-building, wine-growing, watch-making, I think that there are aspects of discipleship existing in the relationship of teacher and pupil which continue to this day and will continue forever in the future.

I remember quite clearly the conflict, the tension, the illogical situation that I came into myself when I was much younger and worked in a production planning department. I learned how certain things ought to be done, and I learned them very well, performed them all right; and then I was transferred to work for a completely different boss to learn systems analysis. One of my assignments was to design a system with the help of a computer which would do the job that all the production planners were doing manually—which I had been doing manually and very well. The man I was working for did not know that work at all, had never done it—yet he was my boss and he was a great systems analyst. I remember the interesting conflict of being his disciple, his pupil and having him teach me how to design a system for something that he knew nothing about, but he knew, he had a style, a *savoir faire*, an intuitive approach to order and organization which I did not have. I think therefore that I can say with complete conviction that the person who cannot be a disciple also cannot be a teacher, that the person who cannot, who will not accept leadership also cannot give leadership. I would go even further and say that the person who cannot accept authority cannot rule himself either.

Now we must go further into this paradox: there are problems which result from the idea of doing it yourself and there are problems which result from the idea of having a teacher. To create concepts which are generally valid for the whole class of problems that these two approaches create, I would like to use the words *dependence* and *independence*. We could say that the idea of doing it yourself is the idea of independence, and that the idea of being a disciple is an idea of dependence. You can see that in an extreme situation independence cannot logically exist; it is not possible for more than one thing in the entire universe to exist independently. That independent thing which, for whatever reasons in the internal make-up of its existential, cannot accept as part of its identity dependence—that thing does not exist, it has no existence in the universe. Let us assume that there is a star in the universe which is wholly and totally independent of all else in the universe—you can readily see that its existence, if it had any, would be beyond and outside of anything else—therefore it could not be. You can also see, as a less extreme example, that a thing which is struggling too hard to maintain its independence—whether a star or a human being—is, in a sense, in flight from relationship, continuously in flight; it does not want to accept a certain amount of dependence in order to be. Yet when the requirement for less dependence, or more independence, is beyond a certain level of balance or tolerance, its independence is its isolation, its lack of contact, its lack of influence, its lack of knowledge, its lack of control, its lack of belonging. If there was a star in the cosmos which could only come so close to another star that it would never feel any gravitational influence, it would be a lonely, lonely star. It would have to be the only star in so much void; its matter could never create, commingle its energy and its atoms with any other star, and it could never therefore have a consequential influence in the totality. If you change the word "star" for the word "human," then you can also see that the do-it-aloner is not necessarily wrong or right, that it is in the extreme of the argument that you find an error; doing it alone in the pure sense of the word, to become a better human being, means that it is impossible to become a better human being, because you cannot come close enough to any other human being to become better in relationship to it.

When we look at the other side of the paradox and talk about dependence, it is even more clear that dependent relationships which become too dependent dissolve so much of the self-identity structure that the particular thing has no identity of itself and therefore also is not. If a star, in order to keep together as a mass, required the gravitational strength of another star, would it really exist? Change the word "star" for the word "human" and you can easily see that if a disciple relationship creates a dependency which is so strong that the person is no longer himself, that he has no more moral judgment, no more absorption of independent thought, no more choice, no more self, no more will, then he is not really human anymore except in flesh and blood: he is basically an android or a machine. So that in independence there is an extreme in which existence is gone, and in dependence there is an extreme in which existence is gone. So, to recap a little, in attempting to travel the road of self-development alone there is beyond a certain level of reasonableness an extreme in which it is a senseless argument. In the same way on the road of discipleship where the discipleship relationship is beyond a certain reasonable level of dependence, you can see that the relationship destroys the very essence of what it is supposed to create.

As long as that paradox remains clear, then you can see that existence is found at the point of greatest tension. Existence is found at the point of greatest independence, balanced with greatest possible dependence. At the point where there is enough independence that there is a real self, and enough dependence that there is a real other, there I think is true discipleship. We could call this the point of "creative interdependence."

To leave the paradox aside for a while, it is also important to talk about what discipleship is, how it works, why you do it, how you relate. (I don't want to go too deeply into the escapes that are often the reasons people are looking to become disciples, and I don't want to look at all into the problems of teachership, although these are both problems which exist.) It is also very interesting to look at why there are teachers, why they need to be. Maybe the only thing to say on that subject is that disciples make teachers, not the other way round. Yes, the chelas make the guru, and the greater the chela the truer the guru. If you read the *Sufi Message* you will see that my grandfather always put the burden of discipleship on the sense of truest friendship: the guide is the real friend, not a friend who helps you the way you want to be helped, the friend whom you can trust in terms of evading your problems, but the friend who is loyal to the deepest of your self, the friend who supports that part of you in which you have no trust. I think that is the healthiest way to characterize the guru-chela, murshid-mureed relationship—friendship. Friendship is a form of relationship which transgresses all other human boundaries, all other human definitions, all other human limitations; it includes all other and it excludes none. In friendship can be found, subordinate to that, enmity, love. In friendship can be found, subordinate to that, dominance, support. In friendship can be found, but subordinate to that, every other sentiment of true human feeling. A friend, a real friend may betray you, may abandon you in terms of betraying and abandoning your expectations, in terms of betraying and abandoning your prison. But the friend will never abandon the true disciple, never. Why? Because the true disciple continuously recreates, regenerates, readjusts the loyalty bond.

There is a story I have told many times which I think is quite valuable. Once upon a time there was a grave in Afghanistan, and that grave had become a shrine of pilgrimage—some wonderful saint was buried there. After the saint died, his servant, his chela, his disciple built a little grave, prayed there, made a beautiful little garden and soon enough, through the saint's fame and through the loyalty of his disciple, people started coming there to seek solace, warmth, understanding, comfort, and quietude—and so, over forty or fifty years it became a place of pilgrimage. Now—and there is great symbology in this—the disciple who took care of the shrine married and had children and at a certain time his eldest son became of age and quite wisely the father, the disciple, said to the son: Now is your time to go into the world. There comes a time for every father, for every relationship in a sense, for every leader to be able to say to every follower: Go. That does not break the relationship. There comes a time for every dependent relationship to be ripe enough so that the dominant factor in it can guide the disciple to independence. Every disciple relationship must reach that point of independence, otherwise the dependence is useless. So, in the same way, the father was very wise and thought that the son was ripe and the son was very wise and didn't revolt, he didn't need to, he didn't run away. And the father gave his son a donkey and some food and a bit of money and sent him out into the world. The son went out to meet the world and, as you can imagine, it was difficult—there were robbers and the desert and not enough food. He met many difficult and dangerous things and realized that he wasn't yet so capable and didn't know so much and was not much respected being alone. But his father had told him to travel far away, so he went on and on. After a while his money ran out and then the last thing he had, his donkey, died (of course, it was probably an ass, but I prefer to think of it as a donkey, it is more subtle). He buried his donkey and cried and felt very lonely and, since he had no money and nowhere to go, he just stayed where he had buried his donkey. After a while some people came and saw him there and helped him. Maybe ten or fifteen years later, an eternity later, stories started coming through to his old, wise father that somewhere else was a new shrine growing up—and now fewer people came to his shrine and more went to the new one. The father decided that he would like to know what this was all about and who lived there, so he went to visit the new place of pilgrimage. And, there he met his son, who was now much more mature. The son told him of his travels and how terrible it had all been and that eventually the donkey had died and he had buried it and had just been sitting there crying his eyes out and people had come and he had called the donkey by its name and the people had thought that it was a holy man who was buried there. So the people helped him to build a grave, and then a hut, and he looked after the grave—well, he knew how to do that from his father. And people came back, and left again, and said what a wonderful meditation they had had there, and the son realized what a wonderful thing his father had taught him. He asked his father not to tell anyone because no one knew that it was only a donkey buried there. The father looked at the son and after a while he said: The same thing happened to me, son. There is a lot of symbology in that story.

I could speak out against the tricksters, the treachery, the commercialism, the ego-trips of the swami-guru nonsense trip that is sweeping the world. I could fulminate about all this total nonsense that is going on, and I do, but the subject is discipleship and I would say that the benefit of discipleship comes from the truth of the disciple first. It comes from the purity of heart, the receptivity of heart, the real inner dedication of the disciple—that is the first and the foremost, and undoubtedly from that comes benefit. Undoubtedly that benefit comes because of the psychological setting in which the disciple puts himself. You can say that your teacher has a wonderful atmosphere of peace, calm and quietude, but it is the attitude of the disciple, the receptivity of the disciple that creates or recreates it. The true teacher is created by the true disciple—you can read that in the *Sufi Message* of Inayat Khan. There is no denying that discipleship has a place in life, and that to become a good surgeon you simply need to go to medical school and to be taught surgery properly; but to be a great surgeon you need to have walked on the road of discipleship of another surgeon. To be a good, average, mediocre person, "normal," you can simply live life as well as you can, dealing with it and dying; but to bring out of yourself the greatest aspects that are within you, that are possible, you need to go through the bond of discipleship.

Discipleship, then, is a self-tuning state, a feminine state, a yin state, a state of receptivity, of humbleness, of loyalty, truth, sincerity. I think that that is what it creates in the end: sincerity. If you can reach that depth of discipleship that you are totally sincere in the discipleship then you have found the deepest sincerity in yourself.

To leave this aspect aside for a while: there is another aspect of discipleship which is much more mystical. There have existed from very ancient times esoteric traditions, schools of influence—the African medicine men, for instance, who passed on something of their tradition, their occult, mystical, spiritual influence. How interesting it is that Africans were taken out of Africa as slaves; millions of them died, many were brought to North and South America, yet while they were totally cut off from their culture, denatured almost, their esoteric traditions continued in the new world. In a sense you could say that there are esoteric traditions which further themselves through generations of humanity out of a mystical occult-like mandalic seatedness in consciousness, in the pool of consciousness. These traditions continue—some die away over generations, some change names, some reappear and some entirely new ones come. Just as you could write the history of human civilization by following the science of mathematics or the refinement of music, you could also write the story of human evolution in consciousness by following the history of the esoteric initiatic traditions which exist. Here I would want to define *a priori* that the genuineness of the initiatic tradition is, derives its energy from and is embedded in particular groupings of persons or single individuals, but is independent of them. That is very important. Imagine that we make a candle, light it, put out all the lights in the room and give this lighted candle to a man. For that moment he carried the light. Now he passes it to another man and the other man carries the light. He passes it on to a woman and she carries the light. While one of the men or the woman carries the light, he or she can be seen and the rest of us are in darkness—and while he or she can be seen, some part of his or her consciousness and influence is dominant and radiates with the light over the earth, or over us. But the light is the light and not this man or that man or that woman, and when the light is passed on it is passed on. That is the concept of the initiatic traditions, that a self-promulgating radiance of a particular wavelength in

consciousness, embedded at particular times in the consciousness, continues over hundreds of thousands of years in
human evolution. You could almost say that just as much as
the first man chose the light to carry, that the light chose the
man—it is very difficult to say what is really cause and what
is really effect. A candle does not seem to have its own flow
of choice possibility, but an energy radiance of consciousness
does. Those people whose consciousness is tapped as part of
the energy-flow field of the Sufi Order appear in, of and by
themselves to have chosen to come to it—which is right,
which is the experience they should have—but from a more
destinal point of view, they were chosen by it.

If you question in yourself whether, although you are a
disciple, you are following the right person, whether the
person is true or not, and all those things, first, you could say
that all humans are true and false, all humans are at some
time more true and at some time more false, and yet all
humans are valuable and all humans are perfect. I think that
you can only judge whether you are on the right path—not
necessarily because you follow the right teacher, but also if,
not fanatically but intuitively, you feel that you are at home in
that tradition, in that force-field of consciousness. It's a bit
like this: a computer can choose a date for you and probably a
better date than you can choose; but the inner feeling that
there is a marriage is another feeling, and that feeling of
being home, of being really a part of that other person, as if
you have always been there—that is right. You may be
intellectually, educationally, culturally, physically, morally,
religiously against what is being taught, you may be continuously in doubt in yourself. In fact doubt is a guiding principle
of spiritual growth; without doubt there is no growth; there
has to be doubt. Learning to doubt the right thing is more
important than learning not to doubt. The only person who
can trust is the person who can doubt. But it is another feeling
which a discipleship period in life eventually touches—a real
discipleship period—and that is the feeling that you are at
home, that the light has chosen you, that you were born to
bathe in, to be the wax of, to be the battery of that light; that
you belong.

There are many esoteric traditions in the world and I think that it is important to resolve a little bit the problem of the bewilderment that people feel when faced by these different traditions. They are all very similar and they are all very different. Sometimes they are in competition with one another and sometimes they contradict each other, sometimes they oppose each other and sometimes they are in the process of destroying each other—yet they are both traditions and that is a problem. They are both spiritual and one says the other is wrong, and that makes more problems. Well, it is this mystical integrity, which is not a thought-teaching, a thought-form teaching, that is the definition of its genuineness. Not because what it teaches at any particular time is right or wrong, but because it is an answer to the cultural need of that time, the capacity to respond at that time, and the psychological state of consciousness of the minds who are expressing the teaching at that time. The mystical genuineness is not a thought-form, it is an integrity in consciousness beyond thought-form or understanding, beyond right and wrong, beyond all these things. It is simply a color-wave, a style, an influence, a numerological principle, a wavelength, a particular self-integrity. Discipleship then, in a sense, or in essence, above and beyond the human relationship, is a self-tuning being-tuned situation in which there is an instrument, there is a string on a violin or tanpura that is tuned to the pitch of that wavelength of the mystical integrity of that tradition.

One aspect of discipleship that is important—and I come back a little to the dependence-independence situation—is that discipleship assumes learning. If you want to become a good heart surgeon you have to learn that from another. And so (and here I do take exception very, very much with most of the things that happen today) if you are learning from a surgeon to become a surgeon, eventually you come to the point of practicing surgery with an attempt to reflect and absorb the whole intellectual and intuitive level and style of your teacher. Discipleship is a process of learning about yourself, which means also about life, about how to live, about who you are, about who, therefore, others are—it is not

about how to meditate, about what particular tricks to use. I
suppose that a lot of people who are looking for spiritual
development are looking for relationships of discipleship
where, as a disciple, they are told or given a particular
practice to meditate and a particular belief to accept, a
particular doctrine to follow. But that is not discipleship—or it
is only a very small portion of discipleship. Assuming that
spirituality is, as I have always tried to define it, living a total,
real, human life at the highest level of sincerity which you
can exude and reach in yourself, discipleship is about living.
As long as you are still learning a teaching, a method, a
practice, a belief, a doctrine, a trick, you will not in the
deepest sense be a disciple. When discipleship reaches that
level that you are involved in learning "aliving," then discipleship reaches its fullest. So to that degree that discipleship
is defined, guruship is also characterized because, referring
to what I said before, being against a lot of what is happening,
the guru who reaches guruship, the teacher, the guide, the
priest in the church who is in the process of teaching "things,"
something, is not a guide in life. Teaching should be through
being at it. Surgery, teaching surgery is through the practice
of surgery, teaching about life is through being at it. At what?
At life!—with all of the realities, tensions, conflicts, goods,
bads, successes, failures, with all the real, practical realness
of being alive, of living. I remember my grandfather talking
with great disappointment about all the people with all their
questions—like whether the Dalai Lama would be exiled
from Tibet, whether a particular way of thinking would
produce Nirvana, so many things . . . if I do it like that, will
this happen? And nobody wanted to *live*. Then he said a very
interesting, almost shocking thing which I think is very characteristic—which, some day, those who are interested will
find, with all the things he said, all the things the people
wanted to know. The *Sufi Message* is so carefully edited that
it all comes through as a teaching, and much of the actual
happening—that he said certain things to reach certain people who were there at the time—is lost. But there, suddenly,
his real feelings just came straight out of the paper—the
feelings that people were his disciples, that they wanted

something interesting, they wanted food for the mind, they wanted a teaching about how to live right as a methodology, about how to think right, in such terms as how you learn that $2 + 2 = 4$, a way of thinking that learns calculus. But life as a style, as an engagement with self and other, as an interdependent, creative relationship—people are not looking for that. Maybe because the Christian ethos, which still very much rules the world, establishes that the right can be achieved to the exclusion of the wrong by a particular methodological approach.

It would be good to end therefore by expressing that the character, the color, the tonality of the tradition which is this tradition, Sufism, does not separate right from wrong; in fact it deludes both of them in recognition of their mediocrity; it is characterized by greater tension, greater intensity, greater focus, greater involvement—in both! Deeper contact with the whole centrality of aliving.

THE CONCEPT
OF AVOIDANCE

While the mind, as a tremendous relativation potential, in its conceptualizing matrix searches to behold the real, the highest level of its focused power generally corresponds to the most absolute self-integrated image that can be conceived therein.

Of course, the fewer coordinates, prerequisites with prior information, that any particular conception has within the matricial resolution while compensating into conceptual recognizability, all the more unconditioned and therefore more real emphasis or self-identifiable expression this particular concept must have of itself.

When a concept would in fact require no coordinates at all and is therefore totally self-evident, self-contained and self-maintained, it projects the greatest and purest entitic power which the mind is capable of distinguishing.

There could be some validity to the definition that such a concept is as nearly identifiable as possible with the idealized induced supposition of the existential real, the taoistic ground of being, which the mind searches for.

Any concept examined for total self-integrity and no conceptual coordinateness usually fails this test of absolute entitic induction. The only concept at the present level of foreseeable abstraction which fulfills this requirement, the only such concept is the concept of avoidance.

The resultant comparative parallelism between on the one hand the mind's seeking of the existential—which is in a sense the basic reason for its continuous conceptual focus and upheavals, searching to find an absolute that is—and on the other hand the concept it finds of avoidance—which fulfills this existential requirement yet produces nothing, resolves nothing, suggests nothing that can be resolved—is really a fantastic and incredible completion of the focal apparatus.

It may be difficult to envision what is meant by avoidance, because one would tend to link it in the matrix with a coordinate to see how it works, since it is not a familiar concept; for example: Avoidance of.... However, clearly avoidance can stand on its own as a concept denoting an effect which, in a sense, has not happened. Avoidance even connotes its own avoiding and therefore does not only image a cause but also an effect; yet both do not exist. At the same time the concept stands on its own and does not require either the cause or the effect for conceptual resolution, and expresses emphatically something that is totally understandable while being entirely meaningless. The awesome power of this force is that, while it is incongruous, it demands total reckoning and deludes any other projection the mind can induce or deduce from it.

Avoidance stands on its own as a principle of absence and, when once conceived, is such a forceful presence that it seems to aberrate the linear tangential and curvial fields of the matrix of conceptual resolution. Of course it becomes almost unimaginable then even to resolve the question of why the mind can conceive of it at all. The answer may be that while it might be characterized as a conception, it could probably be better identified as the non-conceived. Whether the recognition of undistinguishable non-conceived is a conception, remains again in avoidance of a reply. Avoidance suggests nothing, digests everything and ingests to the focal apperception a self-vilification.

The reason this avoidance is entirely existential is that the mind's ever-fluctuating process of focus and upheaval cannot dislodge it or find it. In the attempt to pejorate avoidance with qualifiable or quantifiable or classifiable annotation, it emerges from the acidic test not only unscathed but also, as it were, as gluttonous involuate which has even absorbed the queric source. In fact, one would wonder whether the concept of avoidance has ever been conceived at all.

With this question begins the dubious process of ascertaining whether what has apparently been conceived was not a delusionary mental avoidance of the principle to begin with, by some sort of deflective mechanism, resulting from the basic survival instinct which, when faced, even on this abstract level, with implicit immediate annihilation of all thought processes, deceives the attempted conceptual resolution of the actual concept. In other words, we may be imagining an avoidable avoidance while avoidance itself is absolutely unavoidable.

Could it be that the devotional process and corresponding beautifying consolidations which the collective genius has historically engaged in simultaneously with its search for reality, i.e., the existential, has been a self-preserving residualizing of the search itself? Or the obviously not-understood perpetuation of illusion as a reaction and recompensation to an ecclesiastic momentary realization of the all-annihilating appearance of that very existential itself, during the search for its seizure?

The conception of avoidance even brings to investigation whether the concept itself is not actually causal of conceptive avoidance, and that therefore what is avoiding may not only be the power of that character that is conceptualized, but in addition also an avoiding exclusion of the cogniscient activity of our own mind.

Does the concept of avoidance condition its attempted conceptualization with avoidance of its resolution? A hypothetical supposition and therefore of course valuable invalidity of thought could propose an unavoiding conceptual state where the concept of avoidance would thus be permissible. In this apostolic vision all occurring interaction shall be conclusively subjugated to this primordial real of the concept of avoidance.

As far as it is possible potentially to suppose without loss

of succinctness to the defined centrality, all other distin-
guishables from this entitic omni-absence would then be
avoiding patterns in which the avoidance, through the continual quality of its existence, expresses itself. The presence that
such a hypothetical sight would then view will be a self-
evident absence, through which the laws of avoidance function. What is happening in such a state would then be the
unavoidable patterns of avoidance, in which its systematic
continuity is maintained.

Referring back to the norm of the non-hypothetical state,
it could be reasoned by deduction from the hypothetical
vision that all the normally conceived may actually be the
perpetuation of the unconceived real avoidance.

Of course, there is an obvious ambivalence between the
logic of the conceived and the aberration of the avoided. To
reduce this duel may be the final war, the victory of which is
an unrecognizable defeat, not of possible or impossible, not of
presence or absence, but of reduction of their jagging separation to total interchangeability, where the omnivalence is a
sway towards a way while remaining in the play.

This warring call gnaws at the limitations of consciousness and the warrior embattled by self-decay needs a special-
ized weapon called constriction forceps, with which his
engendered wounds can be vortexed through birth to their
eventual death, in order to overcome his acquiescent enve-
loper. When this birth brings the unavoidable avoidant step-
wise nearer, the battle with the real slowly abates and the
warrior engages more and more in peaceful absence from the
strangulation of the enveloping patterns of presence. With
these forceps of constriction eventually comes to birth the
eternal volition of arrayance. Herewith warrior's mystic mind
heuretically* discovers construction of the reincarnating
tomb in which commencement overcomes its end. In this
tomb the avoiding entity is stillborn.

An idealized search for the existential brings rapture
then for a while with what is, and then for longer with what is
not, and then for longer still with what might be, while what
has been overflows from the beholder's absorbing vial into

* Heretically + heuristically = heuretically

the what-could-have-been. Let us battle thereafter for what-is-to-come, and when that outcome is decided for what-should-not-come, to rest eventually in what-could-not-be, thereby enlivening its fleeting reality, without poisoning this immaculate with the degeneration of being.

The concept of avoidance is a phallic sword, a vulvic shield, an escaping reach and a dead-aiming sight, with which the shambles of manifestation can be hewn into pyrrhic eliminators of the desultory conception. While of course such thoughts are at first complicated, too abstract and therefore rejected for lack of meaning, they are the menial study of the free-thinking.

To avoid their consummation can only reconcile the concept of avoidance with its enigmatic vitality and thus reduce the deserter once again to the prison of dissatisfaction, which will necessitate the continuation of petite and decoration of the encompassing bars of random's mean with that entropic picturesque or coward's imbibement with hedonic spew through the unsevered umbilical lean.

Is madness not, after all, a false consignment to the chaotic ventriloquation of apperception's distinctions with truth?

The truthful arrayance must obviously disorder chaos into unavoidable interceptions.

At those points there must be verification of existence!

The linear approach towards any one of these nodes is a pathway for the unleashed perseverance to escape in forwarding momentum which avoids the teeming hold of mind's conceptive activity, abounding in furtive resolution which pre-empts conception of its treasured by idealization. To conceive of an avoidant reign is the mystic warrior's battling station. It is not for life or death, that fighting, but for the real freedom of unconditioned emission of the existential.

While possibly the power of avoidance does not yet really exist, it rules surreptitiously and without fission.

The warrior's freedom marks conveyance of avoidance's sway.

September 27, 1975